HUMAN, ALL TOO HUMAN

FRIEDRICH NIETZSCHE

SIRIUS

SIRIUS
This edition published in 2025 by Sirius Publishing,
a division of Arcturus Publishing Limited,
26/27 Bickels Yard, 151–153 Bermondsey Street,
London SE1 3HA

ISBN: 978-1-3988-5150-4
AD007696UK

Printed in China

CONTENTS

INTRODUCTION

Nietzsche's essay, *Richard Wagner in Bayreuth*, appeared in 1876, and his next publication was his present work, which was issued in 1878. A comparison of the books will show that the two years of meditation intervening had brought about a great change in Nietzsche's views, his style of expressing them, and the form in which they were cast. The Dionysian, overflowing with life, gives way to an Apollonian thinker with a touch of pessimism. The long essay form is abandoned, and instead we have a series of aphorisms, some tinged with melancholy, others with satire, several, especially towards the end, with Nietzschian wit at its best, and a few at the beginning so very abstruse as to require careful study.

Since the Bayreuth festivals of 1876, Nietzsche had gradually come to see Wagner as he really was. The ideal musician that Nietzsche had pictured in his own mind turned out to be nothing more than a rather dilettante philosopher, an opportunistic decadent with a suspicious tendency towards Christianity. The young philosopher thereupon proceeded to shake off the influence which the musician had exercised upon him. He was successful in doing so, but not without a struggle. Hence he writes in his autobiography:[1] '*Human, all-too-Human*, is the monument of a crisis. It is entitled: "A book for *free* spirits," and almost every line in it represents a victory – in its pages I freed myself from everything foreign to my real nature. Idealism is foreign to me: the title says, "Where *you* see ideal things, I see things which are only – human alas! all-too-human!" I know man *better* – the term "free spirit" must here be understood in no other sense than this: a freed man, who has once more taken possession of himself.'

The form of this book will be better understood when it is remembered that at this period Nietzsche was beginning to suffer from stomach trouble and headaches. As a cure for his complaints, he spent his time in travel when he could get a few weeks' respite from his duties at Basel University; and it was in the course of his solitary walks and hill-climbing tours that the majority of these thoughts

1 *Ecce Homo*, p. 75

occurred to him and were jotted down there and then. A few of them, however, date further back, as he tells us in the preface to the second part of this work. Many of them, he says, occupied his mind even before he published his first book, *The Birth of Tragedy*.

It must be clearly understood, however, that Nietzsche's disease must not be looked upon in the same way as that of an ordinary man. People are inclined to regard a sick man as rancorous; but any one who fights with and conquers his disease, and even exploits it, as Nietzsche did, benefits thereby to an extraordinary degree. In the first place, he has passed through several stages of human psychology with which a healthy man is entirely unacquainted; e.g. he has learnt by introspection the spiteful and revengeful spirit of the sick man and his religion. Secondly, in his moments of freedom from pain and gloom his thoughts will be all the more brilliant.

Thus neither the form of this book – so startling at first to those who have been brought up in the traditions of our own school – nor the fact that the writer was in poor health should deter us from perusing it as carefully as we can. We may be sure of an adequate reward; for here no abstract philosopher is discoursing, no harmless dealer in 'isms' and 'ologies' – but a man of the world, who had previously come into contact with some of the best men and women of his time and who had travelled a great deal. From Greece, Nietzsche brought back his standard measure, his infallible scales, and religions were weighed by him, found wanting, and severely censured.

The aphorisms in this book are essentially for an order of minds which can afford *otium*; but *sine dignitate* if possible – for the British 'dignity' is another obstacle in the path leading to a complete understanding of our author. Indeed, these aphorisms would be much out of place, and might be quite false, if applied in other directions. Take, for example, No. 434, containing the now celebrated dictum that women always intrigue in secret against the higher souls of their husbands. While this statement is correct as applied to artists, it is obviously not intended for business-men, whose wives in many instances spur them on – not to philosophy or art, but to money, comfort, and worldly success.

But statesmen and politicians, who, no matter what may be thought to the contrary, require new ideas occasionally, will find much to interest them here. They seem to have a certain difficulty nowadays in meeting the argument of Socialism. In aphorism 451, Nietzsche gives them a hint. The governing classes, says he, can, if they choose, treat all men as equals, and proclaim the establishment of equal rights: so far a socialistic mode of thought which is based on *justice* is possible; but, as has been said, only within the ranks of the governing classes, which in this case *practises* justice with sacrifices and abnegations. On the other hand, to *demand* equality of rights, as do the Socialists of the subject caste, is by no means the outcome of justice, but of covetousness.

Theologians on the other hand, as may be expected, will find no such ready help in their difficulties from Nietzsche. They must, on the contrary, be on their guard against so alert an adversary – a duty which they are apparently not going to shirk; for theologians are amongst the most ardent students of Nietzsche in this country. Their attention may therefore be drawn to aphorism 630 of this book, dealing with convictions and their origin, which will no doubt be successfully refuted by the defenders of the true faith. In fact, there is not a single paragraph in the book that does not deserve careful study by all serious thinkers.

On the whole, however, this is a calm book, and those who are accustomed to Nietzsche the outspoken Immoralist, may be somewhat astonished at the calm tone of the present volume. The explanation is that Nietzsche was now just beginning to walk on his own philosophical path. His lifelong aim, the uplifting of the type man, was still in view, but the way leading towards it was once more uncertain. Hence the peculiarly calm, even melancholic, and what Nietzsche himself would call Apollonian, tinge of many of these aphorisms, so different from the style of his earlier and later writings. For this very reason, however, the book may appeal all the more to English readers, who are of course more Apollonian than Dionysian. Nietzsche is feeling his way, and these aphorisms represent his first steps. As such – besides having a high intrinsic value of themselves – they are enormous aids to the study of his character and temperament.

J. M. KENNEDY.

PREFACE

1.

I HAVE been told frequently, and always with great surprise, that there is something common and distinctive in all my writings, from the *Birth of Tragedy* to the latest published *Prelude to a Philosophy of the Future*. They all contain, I have been told, snares and nets for unwary birds, and an almost perpetual unconscious demand for the inversion of customary valuations and valued customs. What? *Everything* only – human – all-too-human? People lay down my writings with this sigh, not without a certain dread and distrust of morality itself, indeed almost tempted and encouraged to become advocates of the *worst* things: as being perhaps only the *best* disparaged? My writings have been called a school of suspicion and especially of disdain, more happily, also, a school of courage and even of audacity. Indeed, I myself do not think that any one has ever looked at the world with such a profound suspicion; and not only as occasional Devil's Advocate, but equally also, to speak theologically, as enemy and impeacher of God; and he who realises something of the consequences involved, in every profound suspicion, something of the chills and anxieties of loneliness to which every uncompromising *difference of outlook* condemns him who is affected therewith, will also understand how often I sought shelter in some kind of reverence or hostility, or scientificality or levity or stupidity, in order to recover from myself, and, as it were, to obtain temporary self-forgetfulness; also why, when I did not find what I *needed*, I was obliged to manufacture it, to counterfeit and to imagine it in a suitable manner (and what else have poets ever done? And for what purpose has all the art in the world existed?). What I always required most, however, for my cure and self-recovery, was the belief that I was *not* isolated in such circumstances, that I did not *see* in an isolated manner – a magic suspicion of relationship and similarity to others in outlook and desire, a repose in the confidence of friendship, a blindness in both parties without suspicion or note of interrogation, an enjoyment of foregrounds, and surfaces of the near and the nearest, of all that has colour, epidermis, and outside appearance. Perhaps I might be reproached in this respect for much 'art' and fine false coinage; for instance, for voluntarily and knowingly shutting my eyes to Schopenhauer's blind will to morality at a time when I had become sufficiently clear-sighted about morality; also for deceiving myself about Richard Wagner's incurable romanticism, as if it were a beginning and not an end; also about the Greeks, also about the Germans and their future – and there would still probably be quite a long list of such alsos? Supposing however, that this were all true and that I were reproached with good reason, what do *you* know, what could you know as to how much artifice of self-preservation, how much rationality and higher protection there is in such self-deception – and how much falseness I still *require* in order to allow myself again and again the luxury of *my* sincerity? ... In short, I still live; and life, in spite of ourselves, is not devised by morality; it *demands* illusion, it *lives* by illusion . . . but – There! I am already beginning again and doing what I have always done, old immoralist and bird-catcher that I am – I am talking un-morally, ultra-morally, 'beyond good and evil'? . . .

2.

Thus then, when I found it necessary, I *invented* once on a time the 'free spirits', to whom this discouragingly encouraging book with the title *Human, all-too-Human*, is dedicated. There are no such 'free spirits' nor have there been such, but, as already said, I then required them for company to keep me cheerful in the midst of evils (sickness, loneliness, foreignness – *acedia*, inactivity) as brave companions and ghosts with whom I could laugh and gossip when so inclined and send to the devil when they became bores – as compensation for the lack of friends. That such free spirits *will be possible* some day, that our Europe will have such bold and cheerful wights amongst her sons of tomorrow and the day after tomorrow, actually and bodily, and not merely, as in my case, as the shadows of a hermit's phantasmagoria – *I* should be the last to doubt thereof. Already I see them *coming*, slowly, slowly; and perhaps I am doing something to hasten their coming when I describe in advance under what auspices I *see* them originate, and upon what paths I *see* them come.

3.

One may suppose that a spirit in which the type 'free spirit' is to become fully mature and sweet, has had its decisive event in a *great emancipation*, and that it was all the more fettered previously and apparently bound for ever to its corner and pillar. What is it that binds most strongly? What cords are almost unrendable? In men of a lofty and select type it will be their duties; the reverence which is suitable to youth, respect and tenderness for all that is time-honoured and worthy, gratitude to the land which bore them, to the hand which led them, to the sanctuary where they learnt to adore – their most exalted moments themselves will bind them most effectively, will lay upon them the most enduring obligations. For those who are thus bound the great emancipation comes suddenly, like an earthquake; the young soul is all at once convulsed, unloosened and extricated – it does not itself know what is happening. An impulsion and compulsion sway and over-master it like a command; a will and a wish awaken, to go forth on their course, anywhere, at any cost; a violent, dangerous curiosity about an undiscovered world flames and flares in every sense. 'Better to die than live *here*' – says the imperious voice and seduction, and this 'here', this 'at home' is all that the soul has hitherto loved! A sudden fear and suspicion of that which it loved, a flash of disdain for what was called its 'duty', a rebellious, arbitrary, volcanically throbbing longing for travel, foreignness, estrangement, coldness, disenchantment, glaciation, a hatred of love, perhaps a sacrilegious clutch and look *backwards*, to where it hitherto adored and loved, perhaps a glow of shame at what it was just doing, and at the same time a rejoicing *that* it was doing it, an intoxicated, internal, exulting thrill which betrays a triumph – a triumph? Over what? Over whom? An enigmatical, questionable, doubtful triumph, but the *first* triumph nevertheless; such evil and painful incidents belong to the history of the great emancipation. It is, at the same time, a disease which may destroy the man, this first outbreak of power and will to self-decision, self-valuation, this will to *free* will; and how much disease is manifested in the wild attempts and eccentricities by which the liberated and emancipated one now seeks to demonstrate his mastery over things! He roves about raging with unsatisfied longing; whatever he captures has to suffer for the dangerous tension of his pride; he tears to pieces whatever attracts him. With a malicious laugh he twirls round whatever he finds veiled or guarded by a sense of shame; he tries how these things look when turned upside down. It is a matter of arbitrariness with him, and pleasure in arbitrariness, if he now perhaps bestow his favour on what had hitherto a bad repute – if he inquisitively and temptingly haunt what is specially forbidden. In the background of his activities and wanderings – for he is restless and aimless in his course as in a desert – stands the note of interrogation of an increasingly dangerous curiosity. 'Cannot *all* valuations be reversed? And is good perhaps evil? And God only an invention and artifice of the devil? Is everything, perhaps, radically false? And if we are the deceived, are we not thereby also deceivers? *Must* we not also be deceivers?' – Such thoughts lead and mislead him more and more, onward and away. Solitude encircles and engirdles him, always more threatening, more throttling, more heart-oppressing, that terrible goddess and *mater saeva cupidinum* – but who knows nowadays what *solitude* is? ...

4.

From this morbid solitariness, from the desert of such years of experiment, it is still a long way to the copious, overflowing safety and soundness which does not care to dispense with disease itself as an instrument and angling-hook of knowledge; to that *mature* freedom of spirit which is equally self-control and discipline of the heart, and gives access to many and opposed modes of thought; to that inward comprehensiveness and daintiness of superabundance, which excludes any danger of the spirit's becoming enamoured and lost in its own paths, and lying intoxicated in some corner or other; to that excess of plastic, healing, formative, and restorative powers, which is exactly the sign of *splendid* health, that excess which gives the free spirit the dangerous prerogative of being entitled to live by experiments and offer itself to adventure; the free spirit's prerogative of mastership! Long years of convalescence may lie in between, years full of many-coloured, painfully-enchanting magical transformations, curbed and led by a tough *will to health*, which often dares to dress and disguise itself as actual health. There is a middle condition therein, which a man of such a fate never calls to mind later on without emotion; a pale, delicate light and a sunshine-happiness are peculiar to him, a feeling of bird-like freedom, prospect, and haughtiness, a *tertium quid* in which curiosity and gentle disdain are combined. A 'free spirit' – this cool expression does good in every condition, it almost warms. One no longer lives, in the fetters of love and hatred, without Yea, without Nay, voluntarily near, voluntarily distant, preferring to escape, to turn aside, to flutter forth, to fly up and away; one is fastidious like every one who has once seen an immense variety *beneath* him – and one has become the opposite of those who trouble themselves about things which do not concern them. In fact, it is nothing but things which now concern the free spirit – and how many things! – which no longer *trouble* him!

5.

A step further towards recovery, and the free spirit again draws near to life; slowly, it is true, and almost stubbornly, almost distrustfully. Again it grows warmer around him, and, as it were, yellower; feeling and sympathy gain depth, thawing winds of every kind pass lightly over him. He almost feels as if his eyes were now first opened to what is *near*. He marvels and is still; where has he been? The near and nearest things, how changed they appear to him! What a bloom and magic they have acquired meanwhile! He looks back gratefully – grateful to his wandering, his austerity and self-estrangement, his far-sightedness and his bird-like flights in cold heights. What a good thing that he did not always stay 'at home', 'by himself', like a sensitive, stupid tenderling. He has been *beside himself*, there is no doubt. He now sees himself for the first time – and what surprises he feels thereby! What thrills unexperienced hitherto! What joy even in the weariness, in the old illness, in the relapses of the convalescent! How he likes to sit still and suffer, to practise patience, to lie in the sun! Who is as familiar as he with the joy of winter, with the patch of sunshine upon the wall! They are the most grateful animals in the world, and also the most unassuming, these lizards of convalescents with their faces half-turned towards life once more: there are those amongst them who never let a day pass without hanging a little hymn of praise on its trailing fringe. And, speaking seriously, it is a radical *cure* for all pessimism (the well-known disease of old idealists and falsehood-mongers) to become ill after the manner of these free spirits, to remain ill a good while, and then grow well (I mean 'better') for a still longer period. It is wisdom, practical wisdom, to prescribe even health for one's self for a long time only in small doses.

6.

About this time it may at last happen, under the sudden illuminations of still disturbed and changing health, that the enigma of that great emancipation begins to reveal itself to the free, and ever freer, spirit – that enigma which had hitherto lain obscure, questionable, and almost intangible, in his memory. If for a long time he scarcely dared to ask himself, 'Why so apart? So alone? denying everything that I revered? denying reverence itself? Why this hatred, this suspicion, this severity towards my own virtues?' – he now dares and asks the questions aloud, and already hears something like an answer to them – 'Thou shouldst become master over thyself and master also of thine own virtues. Formerly *they* were thy masters; but they are only entitled to be thy tools amongst other tools. Thou shouldst obtain power over thy pro and contra, and learn how to put them forth and withdraw them again in accordance with thy higher purpose. Thou shouldst learn how to take the proper perspective of every valuation – the shifting, distortion, and apparent teleology of the horizons and everything that belongs to perspective; also the amount of stupidity which opposite values involve, and all the intellectual loss with which every pro and every contra has to be paid for. Thou shouldst learn how much *necessary* injustice there is in every for and against, injustice as inseparable from life, and life itself as *conditioned* by the perspective and its injustice. Above all thou shouldst see clearly where the injustice is always greatest: namely, where life has developed most punily, restrictedly, necessitously, and incipiently, and yet cannot help regarding *itself* as the purpose and standard of things, and for the sake of self-preservation, secretly, basely, and continuously wasting away and calling in question the higher, greater, and richer – thou shouldst see clearly the problem of gradation of rank, and how power and right and amplitude of perspective grow up together. Thou shouldst—' But enough; the free spirit knows henceforth which 'thou shalt' he has obeyed, and also what he *can* now *do*, what he only now – *may do*....

7.

Thus doth the free spirit answer himself with regard to the riddle of emancipation, and ends therewith, while he generalises his case, in order thus to decide with regard to his experience. 'As it has happened to *me*,' he says to himself, 'so must it happen to every one in whom a *mission* seeks to embody itself and to "come into the world". The secret power and necessity of this mission will operate in and upon the destined individuals like an unconscious pregnancy – long before they have had the mission itself in view and have known its name. Our destiny rules over us, even when we are not yet aware of it; it is the future that makes laws for our today. Granted that it is *the problem of the gradations of rank*, of which we may say that it is *our* problem, we free spirits; now only in the midday of our life do we first understand what preparations, detours, tests, experiments, and disguises the problem needed, before it was *permitted* to rise before us, and how we had first to experience the most manifold and opposing conditions of distress and happiness in soul and body, as adventurers and circumnavigators of the inner world called 'man', as surveyors of all the 'higher' and the 'one-above-another', also called 'man' – penetrating everywhere, almost without fear, rejecting nothing, losing nothing, tasting everything, cleansing everything from all that is accidental, and, as it were, sifting it out – until at last we could say, we free spirits, 'Here – a *new* problem! Here a long ladder, the rungs of which we ourselves have sat upon and mounted – which we ourselves at some time have *been*! Here a higher place, a lower place, an under-us, an immeasurably long order, a hierarchy which we *see* here – *our* problem!'

8.

No psychologist or augur will be in doubt for a moment as to what stage of the development just described the following book belongs (or is assigned to). But where are these psychologists nowadays? In France, certainly; perhaps in Russia; assuredly not in Germany. Reasons are not lacking why the present-day Germans could still even count this as an honour to them – bad enough, surely, for one who in this respect is un-German in disposition and constitution! This *German* book, which has been able to find readers in a wide circle of countries and nations – it has been about ten years going its rounds – and must understand some sort of music and piping art, by means of which even coy foreign ears are seduced into listening – it is precisely in Germany that this book has been most negligently read, and worst *listened to*; what is the reason? 'It demands too much,' I have been told, 'it appeals to men free from the pressure of coarse duties, it wants refined and fastidious senses, it needs superfluity – superfluity of time, of clearness of sky and heart, of *otium* in the boldest sense of the term: purely good things, which we Germans of today do not possess and therefore cannot give.' After such a polite answer my philosophy advises me to be silent and not to question further; besides, in certain cases, as the proverb points out, one only *remains* a philosopher by being – silent.[2]

Nice, Spring 1886.

2 An allusion to the medieval Latin distich:

O si tacuisses,

Philosophus mansisses. – J. M. K.

FIRST DIVISION.
FIRST AND LAST THINGS.

1.

Chemistry of Ideas and Sensations. – Philosophical problems adopt in almost all matters the same form of question as they did two thousand years ago; how can anything spring from its opposite? For instance, reason out of unreason, the sentient out of the dead, logic out of unlogic, disinterested contemplation out of covetous willing, life for others out of egoism, truth out of error? Metaphysical philosophy has helped itself over those difficulties hitherto by denying the origin of one thing in another, and assuming a miraculous origin for more highly valued things, immediately out of the kernel and essence of the 'thing in itself'. Historical philosophy, on the contrary, which is no longer to be thought of as separate from physical science, the youngest of all philosophical methods, has ascertained in single cases (and presumably this will happen in everything) that there are no opposites except in the usual exaggeration of the popular or metaphysical point of view, and that an error of reason lies at the bottom of the opposition: according to this explanation, strictly understood, there is neither an unegoistical action nor an entirely disinterested point of view, they are both only sublimations in which the fundamental element appears almost evaporated, and is only to be discovered by the closest observation. All that we require, and which can only be given us by the present advance of the single sciences, is a *chemistry* of the moral, religious, aesthetic ideas and sentiments, as also of those emotions which we experience in ourselves both in the great and in the small phases of social and intellectual intercourse, and even in solitude; but what if this chemistry should result in the fact that also in this case the most beautiful colours have been obtained from base, even despised materials? Would many be inclined to pursue such examinations? Humanity likes to put all questions as to origin and beginning out of its mind; must one not be almost dehumanised to feel a contrary tendency in one's self?

2.

Inherited Faults of Philosophers. – All philosophers have the common fault that they start from man in his present state and hope to attain their end by an analysis of him. Unconsciously they look upon man as an *aeterna veritas*, as a thing unchangeable in all commotion, as a sure standard of things. But everything that the philosopher says about man is really nothing more than testimony about the man of a *very limited* space of time. A lack of the historical sense is the hereditary fault of all philosophers; many, indeed, unconsciously mistake the very latest variety of man, such as has arisen under the influence of certain religions, certain political events, for the permanent form from which one must set out. They will not learn that man has developed, that his faculty of knowledge has developed also; whilst for some of them the entire world is spun out of this faculty of knowledge. Now everything *essential* in human development happened in pre-historic times, long before those four thousand years which we know something of; man may not have changed much during this time. But the philosopher sees 'instincts' in the present man and takes it for granted that this is one of the unalterable facts of mankind, and, consequently, can furnish a key to the understanding of the world; the entire teleology is so constructed that man of the last four thousand years is spoken of as an *eternal* being, towards which all things in the world have from the beginning a natural direction. But everything has evolved; there are *no eternal facts*, as there are likewise no absolute truths. Therefore, *historical philosophising* is henceforth necessary, and with it the virtue of diffidence.

3.

Appreciation of Unpretentious Truths. – It is a mark of a higher culture to value the little unpretentious truths, which have been found by means of strict method, more highly than the joy-diffusing and dazzling errors which spring from metaphysical and artistic times and peoples. First of all one has scorn on the lips for the former, as if here nothing could have equal privileges with anything else, so unassuming, simple, bashful, apparently discouraging are they, so beautiful, stately, intoxicating, perhaps even animating, are the others. But the hardly attained, the certain, the lasting, and therefore of great consequence for all wider knowledge, is still the higher; to keep one's self to that is manly and shows bravery, simplicity, and forbearance. Gradually not only single individuals but the whole of mankind will be raised to this manliness, when it has at last accustomed itself to the higher appreciation of durable, lasting knowledge, and has lost all belief in inspiration and the miraculous communication of truths. Respecters of *forms*, certainly, with their standard of the beautiful and noble, will first of all have good reasons for mockery, as soon as the appreciation of unpretentious truths, and the scientific spirit, begin to obtain the mastery; but only because their eye has either not yet recognised the charm of the *simplest* form, or because men educated in that spirit are not yet completely and inwardly saturated by it, so that they still thoughtlessly imitate old forms (and badly enough, as one does who no longer cares much about the matter). Formerly the spirit was not occupied with strict thought, its earnestness then lay in the spinning out of symbols and forms. This is changed; that earnestness in the symbolical has become the mark of a lower culture. As our arts themselves grow evermore intellectual, our senses more spiritual, and as, for instance, people now judge concerning what sounds well to the senses quite differently from how they did a hundred years ago, so the forms of our life grow ever more *spiritual*, to the eye of older ages perhaps *uglier*, but only because it is incapable of perceiving how the kingdom of the inward, spiritual beauty constantly grows deeper and wider, and to what extent the inner intellectual look may be of more importance to us all than the most beautiful bodily frame and the noblest architectural structure.

4.

Astrology and the Like. – It is probable that the objects of religious, moral, aesthetic and logical sentiment likewise belong only to the surface of things, while man willingly believes that here, at least, he has touched the heart of the world; he deceives himself, because those things enrapture him so profoundly, and make him so profoundly unhappy, and he therefore shows the same pride here as in astrology. For astrology believes that the firmament moves round the destiny of man; the moral man, however, takes it for granted that what he has essentially at heart must also be the essence and heart of things.

5.

Misunderstanding of Dreams. – In the ages of a rude and primitive civilisation man believed that in dreams he became acquainted with a *second actual world*; herein lies the origin of all metaphysics. Without dreams there could have been found no reason for a division of the world. The distinction, too, between soul and body is connected with the most ancient comprehension of dreams, also the supposition of an imaginary soul-body, therefore the origin of all belief in spirits, and probably also the belief in gods. 'The dead continues to live, for he appears to the living in a dream': thus men reasoned of old for thousands and thousands of years.

6.

The Scientific Spirit partially but not WHOLLY Powerful. – The *smallest* subdivisions of science taken separately are dealt with purely in relation to themselves; the general, great sciences, on the contrary, regarded as a whole, call up the question – certainly a very non-objective one – 'Wherefore? To what end?' It is this utilitarian consideration which causes them to be dealt with less impersonally when taken as a whole than when considered in their various parts. In philosophy, above all, as the apex of the entire pyramid of science, the question as to the utility of knowledge is involuntarily brought forward, and every philosophy has the unconscious intention of ascribing to it the *greatest* usefulness. For this reason there is so much high-flying metaphysics in all philosophies and such a shyness of the apparently unimportant solutions of physics; for the importance of knowledge for life *must* appear as great as possible. Here is the antagonism between the separate provinces of science and philosophy. The latter desires, what art does, to give the greatest possible depth and meaning to life and actions; in the former one seeks knowledge and nothing further, whatever may emerge thereby. So far there has been no philosopher in whose hands philosophy has not grown into an apology for knowledge; on this point, at least, every one is an optimist, that the greatest usefulness must be ascribed to knowledge. They are all tyrannised over by logic, and this is optimism – in its essence.

7.

The Kill-joy in Science. – Philosophy separated from science when it asked the question, 'Which is the knowledge of the world and of life which enables man to live most happily?' This happened in the Socratic schools; the veins of scientific investigation were bound up by the point of view of happiness – and are so still.

8.

Pneumatic Explanation of Nature. – Metaphysics explains the writing of Nature, so to speak, *pneumatically*, as the Church and her learned men formerly did with the Bible. A great deal of understanding is required to apply to Nature the same method of strict interpretation as the philologists have now established for all books with the intention of clearly understanding what the text means, but not suspecting a double sense or even taking it for granted. Just, however, as with regard to books, the bad art of interpretation is by no means overcome, and in the most cultivated society one still constantly comes across the remains of allegorical and mystic interpretation, so it is also with regard to Nature, indeed it is even much worse.

9.

The Metaphysical World. – It is true that there *might* be a metaphysical world; the absolute possibility of it is hardly to be disputed. We look at everything through the human head and cannot cut this head off; while the question remains, What would be left of the world if it had been cut off? This is a purely scientific problem, and one not very likely to trouble mankind; but everything which has hitherto made metaphysical suppositions *valuable, terrible, delightful* for man, what has produced them, is passion, error, and self-deception; the very worst methods of knowledge, not the best, have taught belief therein. When these methods have been discovered as the foundation of all existing religions and metaphysics, they have been refuted. Then there still always remains that possibility; but there is nothing to be done with it, much less is it possible to let happiness, salvation, and life depend on the spider-thread of such a possibility. For nothing could be said of the metaphysical world but that it would be a different condition, a condition inaccessible and incomprehensible to us; it would be a thing of negative qualities. Were the existence of such a world ever so well proved, the fact would nevertheless remain that it would be precisely the most irrelevant of all forms of knowledge: more irrelevant than the knowledge of the chemical analysis of water to the sailor in danger in a storm.

10.

The Harmlessness of Metaphysics in the Future. – Directly the origins of religion, art, and morals have been so described that one can perfectly explain them without having recourse to metaphysical concepts at the beginning and in the course of the path, the strongest interest in the purely theoretical problem of the 'thing-in-itself' and the 'phenomenon' ceases. For however it may be here, with religion, art, and morals we do not touch the 'essence of the world in itself'; we are in the domain of representation, no 'intuition' can carry us further. With the greatest calmness we shall leave the question as to how our own conception of the world can differ so widely from the revealed essence of the world, to physiology and the history of the evolution of organisms and ideas.

11.

Language as a Presumptive Science. – The importance of language for the development of culture lies in the fact that in language man has placed a world of his own beside the other, a position which he deemed so fixed that he might therefrom lift the rest of the world off its hinges, and make himself master of it. Inasmuch as man has believed in the ideas and names of things as *aeternae veritates* for a great length of time, he has acquired that pride by which he has raised himself above the animal; he really thought that in language he possessed the knowledge of the world. The maker of language was not modest enough to think that he only gave designations to things, he believed rather that with his words he expressed the widest knowledge of the things; in reality language is the first step in the endeavour after science. Here also it is belief in ascertained truth, from which the mightiest sources of strength have flowed. Much later – only now – it is dawning upon men that they have propagated a tremendous error in their belief in language. Fortunately it is now too late to reverse the development of reason, which is founded upon that belief. *Logic*, also, is founded upon suppositions to which nothing in the actual world corresponds – for instance, on the supposition of the equality of things, and the identity of the same thing at different points of time – but that particular science arose out of the contrary belief (that such things really existed in the actual world). It is the same with mathematics, which would certainly not have arisen if it had been known from the beginning that in Nature there are no exactly straight lines, no real circle, no absolute standard of size.

12.

Dream and Culture. – The function of the brain which is most influenced by sleep is the memory; not that it entirely ceases; but it is brought back to a condition of imperfection, such as everyone may have experienced in pre-historic times, whether asleep or awake. Arbitrary and confused as it is, it constantly confounds things on the ground of the most fleeting resemblances; but with the same arbitrariness and confusion the ancients invented their mythologies, and even at the present day travellers are accustomed to remark how prone the savage is to forgetfulness, how, after a short tension of memory, his mind begins to sway here and there from sheer weariness and gives forth lies and nonsense. But in dreams we all resemble the savage; bad recognition and erroneous comparisons are the reasons of the bad conclusions, of which we are guilty in dreams: so that, when we clearly recollect what we have dreamt, we are alarmed at ourselves at harbouring so much foolishness within us. The perfect distinctness of all dream-representations, which pre-suppose absolute faith in their reality, recall the conditions that appertain to primitive man, in whom hallucination was extraordinarily frequent, and sometimes simultaneously seized entire communities, entire nations. Therefore, in sleep and in dreams we once more carry out the task of early humanity.

13.

The Logic of Dreams. – In sleep our nervous system is perpetually excited by numerous inner occurrences; nearly all the organs are disjointed and in a state of activity, the blood runs its turbulent course, the position of the sleeper causes pressure on certain limbs, his coverings influence his sensations in various ways, the stomach digests and by its movements it disturbs other organs, the intestines writhe, the position of the head occasions unaccustomed play of muscles, the feet, unshod, not pressing upon the floor with the soles, occasion the feeling of the unaccustomed just as does the different clothing of the whole body: all this, according to its daily change and extent, excites by its extraordinariness the entire system to the very functions of the brain, and thus there are a hundred occasions for the spirit to be surprised and to seek for the *reasons* of this excitation; the dream, however, is *the seeking and representing of the causes* of those excited sensations – that is, of the supposed causes. A person who, for instance, binds his feet with two straps will perhaps dream that two serpents are coiling round his feet; this is first hypothesis, then a belief, with an accompanying *mental* picture and interpretation – 'These serpents must be the *causa* of those sensations which I, the sleeper, experience' – so decides the mind of the sleeper. The immediate past, so disclosed, becomes to him the present through his excited imagination. Thus every one knows from experience how quickly the dreamer weaves into his dream a loud sound that he hears, such as the ringing of bells or the firing of cannon, that is to say, explains it from *afterwards* so that he first *thinks* he experiences the producing circumstances and then that sound. But how does it happen that the mind of the dreamer is always so mistaken, while the same mind when awake is accustomed to be so temperate, careful, and sceptical with regard to its hypotheses? So that the first random hypothesis for the explanation of a feeling suffices for him to believe immediately in its truth? (For in dreaming we believe in the dream as if it were a reality, i.e. we think our hypothesis completely proved.) I hold, that as man now still reasons in dreams, so men reasoned also *when awake* through thousands of years; the first *causa* which occurred to the mind to explain anything that required an explanation, was sufficient and stood for truth. (Thus, according to travellers' tales, savages still do to this very day.) This ancient element in human nature still manifests itself in our dreams, for it is the foundation upon which the higher reason has developed and still develops in every individual; the dream carries us back into remote conditions of human culture, and provides a ready means of understanding them better. Dream-thinking is now so easy to us because during immense periods of human development we have been so well drilled in this form of fantastic and cheap explanation, by means of the first agreeable notions. In so far, dreaming is a recreation for the brain, which by day has to satisfy the stern demands of thought, as they are laid down by the higher culture. We can at once discern an allied process even in our awakened state, as the door and ante-room of the dream. If we shut our eyes, the brain produces a number of impressions of light and colour, probably as a kind of after-play and echo of all those effects of light which crowd in upon it by day. Now, however, the understanding, together with the imagination, instantly works up this play of colour, shapeless in itself, into definite figures, forms, landscapes, and animated groups. The actual accompanying process thereby is again a kind of conclusion from the effect to the cause: since the mind asks, 'Whence come these impressions of light and colour?' it supposes those figures and forms as causes; it takes them for the origin of those colours and lights, because in the daytime, with open eyes, it is accustomed to find a producing cause for every colour, every effect of light. Here, therefore, the imagination constantly places pictures before the mind, since it supports itself on the visual impressions of the day in their production, and the dream-imagination does just the same thing – that is, the supposed cause is deduced from the effect and represented after the effect; all this happens with extraordinary rapidity, so that here, as with the conjuror, a confusion of judgement may arise and a sequence may look like something simultaneous, or even like a reversed sequence. From these circumstances we may gather *how lately* the more acute logical thinking, the strict discrimination of cause and effect has been developed, when our reasoning and understanding faculties *still* involuntarily hark back to those primitive forms of deduction, and when we pass about half our life in this condition. The poet, too, and the artist assign causes for their moods and conditions which are by no means the true ones; in this they recall an older humanity and can assist us to the understanding of it.

14.

Co-echoing. – All *stronger* moods bring with them a co-echoing of kindred sensations and moods, they grub up the memory, so to speak. Along with them something within us remembers and becomes conscious of similar conditions and their origin. Thus there are formed quick habitual connections of feelings and thoughts, which eventually, when they follow each other with lightning speed, are no longer felt as complexes but as *unities*. In this sense one speaks of the moral feeling, of the religious feeling, as if they were absolute unities: in reality they are streams with a hundred sources and tributaries. Here also, as so often happens, the unity of the word is no security for the unity of the thing.

15.

No Internal and External in the World. – As Democritus transferred the concepts 'above' and 'below' to endless space where they have no sense, so philosophers in general have transferred the concepts 'Internal' and 'External' to the essence and appearance of the world; they think that with deep feelings one can penetrate deeply into the internal and approach the heart of Nature. But these feelings are only deep in so far as along with them, barely noticeable, certain complicated groups of thoughts, which we call deep, are regularly excited; a feeling is deep because we think that the accompanying thought is deep. But the 'deep' thought can nevertheless be very far from the truth, as, for instance, every metaphysical one; if one takes away from the deep feeling the commingled elements of thought, then the strong feeling remains, and this guarantees nothing for knowledge but itself, just as strong faith proves only its strength and not the truth of what is believed in.

16.

Phenomenon and Thing-in-itself. – Philosophers are in the habit of setting themselves before life and experience – before that which they call the world of appearance – as before a picture that is once for all unrolled and exhibits unchangeably fixed the same process – this process, they think, must be rightly interpreted in order to come to a conclusion about the being that produced the picture: about the thing-in-itself, therefore, which is always accustomed to be regarded as sufficient ground for the world of phenomenon. On the other hand, since one always makes the idea of the metaphysical stand definitely as that of the unconditioned, *consequently* also unconditioning, one must directly disown all connection between the unconditioned (the metaphysical world) and the world which is known to us; so that the thing-in-itself should most certainly not appear in the phenomenon, and every conclusion from the former as regards the latter is to be rejected. Both sides overlook the fact that that picture – that which we now call human life and experience – has gradually evolved – nay, is still in the full process of evolving – and therefore should not be regarded as a fixed magnitude from which a conclusion about its originator might be deduced (the sufficing cause) or even merely neglected. It is because for thousands of years we have looked into the world with moral, aesthetic, and religious pretensions, with blind inclination, passion, or fear, and have surfeited ourselves in the vices of illogical thought, that this world has gradually *become* so marvellously motley, terrible, full of meaning and of soul, it has acquired colour – but we were the colourists; the human intellect, on the basis of human needs, of human emotions, has caused this 'phenomenon' to appear and has carried its erroneous fundamental conceptions into things. Late, very late, it takes to thinking, and now the world of experience and the thing-in-itself seem to it so extraordinarily different and separated, that it gives up drawing conclusions from the former to the latter – or in a terribly mysterious manner demands the renunciation of our intellect, of our personal will, in order *thereby* to reach the essential, that one may *become essential*. Again, others have collected all the characteristic features of our world of phenomenon – that is, the idea of the world spun out of intellectual errors and inherited by us – and *instead of accusing the intellect* as the offenders, they have laid the blame on the nature of things as being the cause of the hard fact of this very sinister character of the world, and have preached the deliverance from Being. With all these conceptions the constant and laborious process of science (which at last celebrates its greatest triumph in a *history of the origin of thought*) becomes completed in various ways, the result of which might perhaps run as follows: 'That which we now call the world is the result of a mass of errors and fantasies which arose gradually in the general development of organic being, which are inter-grown with each other, and are now inherited by us as the accumulated treasure of all the past – as a treasure, for the value of our humanity depends upon it. From this world of representation strict science is really only able to liberate us to a very slight extent – as it is also not at all desirable – inasmuch as it cannot essentially break the power of primitive habits of feeling; but it can gradually elucidate the history of the rise of that world as representation – and lift us, at least for moments, above and beyond the whole process. Perhaps we shall then recognise that the thing in itself is worth a Homeric laugh; that it *seemed* so much, indeed everything, and *is* really empty, namely, empty of meaning.'

17.

Metaphysical Explanations. – The young man values metaphysical explanations, because they show him something highly significant in things which he found unpleasant or despicable, and if he is dissatisfied with himself, the feeling becomes lighter when he recognises the innermost world-puzzle or world-misery in that which he so strongly disapproves of in himself. To feel himself less responsible and at the same time to find things more interesting – that seems to him a double benefit for which he has to thank metaphysics. Later on, certainly, he gets distrustful of the whole metaphysical method of explanation; then perhaps it grows clear to him that those results can be obtained equally well and more scientifically in another way: that physical and historical explanations produce the feeling of personal relief to at least the same extent, and that the interest in life and its problems is perhaps still more aroused thereby.

18.

Fundamental Questions of Metaphysics. – When the history of the rise of thought comes to be written, a new light will be thrown on the following statement of a distinguished logician: 'The primordial general law of the cognisant subject consists in the inner necessity of recognising every object in itself in its own nature, as a thing identical with itself, consequently self-existing and at bottom remaining ever the same and unchangeable: in short, in recognising everything as a substance.' Even this law, which is here called 'primordial', has evolved: it will some day be shown how gradually this tendency arises in the lower organisms, how the feeble mole-eyes of their organisations at first see only the same thing – how then, when the various awakenings of pleasure and displeasure become noticeable, various substances are gradually distinguished, but each with one attribute, i.e. one single relation to such an organism. The first step in logic is the judgement – the nature of which, according to the decision of the best logicians, consists in belief. At the bottom of all belief lies *the sensation of the pleasant or the painful* in relation to the *sentient subject*. A new third sensation as the result of two previous single sensations is the judgement in its simplest form. We organic beings have originally no interest in anything but its relation to us in connection with pleasure and pain. Between the moments (the states of feeling) when we become conscious of this connection, lie moments of rest, of non-feeling; the world and everything is then without interest for us, we notice no change in it (as even now a deeply interested person does not notice when any one passes him). To the plant, things are as a rule tranquil and eternal, everything like itself. From the period of the lower organisms man has inherited the belief that *similar things* exist (this theory is only contradicted by the matured experience of the most advanced science). The primordial belief of everything organic from the beginning is perhaps even this, that all the rest of the world is one and immovable. The point furthest removed from those early beginnings of logic is the idea of *Causality* – indeed we still really think that all sensations and activities are acts of the free will; when the sentient individual contemplates himself, he regards every sensation, every alteration as something *isolated*, that is to say, unconditioned and disconnected – it rises up in us without connection with anything foregoing or following. We are hungry, but do not originally think that the organism must be nourished; the feeling seems to make itself felt *without cause and purpose*, it isolates itself and regards itself as arbitrary. Therefore, belief in the freedom of the will is an original error of everything organic, as old as the existence of the awakenings of logic in it; the belief in unconditioned substances and similar things is equally a primordial as well as an old error of everything organic. But inasmuch as all metaphysics has concerned itself chiefly with substance and the freedom of will, it may be designated as the science which treats of the fundamental errors of mankind, but treats of them as if they were fundamental truths.

19.

Number. – The discovery of the laws of numbers is made upon the ground of the original, already prevailing error, that there are many similar things (but in reality there is nothing similar), at least, that there are things (but there is no 'thing'). The supposition of plurality always presumes that there is something which appears frequently – but here already error reigns, already we imagine beings, unities, which do not exist. Our sensations of space and time are false, for they lead – examined in sequence – to logical contradictions. In all scientific determinations we always reckon inevitably with certain false quantities, but as these quantities are at least constant, as, for instance, our sensation of time and space, the conclusions of science have still perfect accuracy and certainty in their connection with one another; one may continue to build upon them – until that final limit where the erroneous original suppositions, those constant faults, come into conflict with the conclusions, for instance in the doctrine of atoms. There still we always feel ourselves compelled to the acceptance of a 'thing' or material 'substratum' that is moved, whilst the whole scientific procedure has pursued the very task of resolving everything substantial (material) into motion; here, too, we still separate with our sensation the mover and the moved and cannot get out of this circle, because the belief in things has from immemorial times been bound up with our being. When Kant says, 'The understanding does not derive its laws from Nature, but dictates them to her,' it is perfectly true with regard to the idea of Nature which we are compelled to associate with her (Nature = World as representation, that is to say as error), but which is the summing up of a number of errors of the understanding. The laws of numbers are entirely inapplicable to a world which is not our representation – these laws obtain only in the human world.

20.

A Few Steps Back. – A degree of culture, and assuredly a very high one, is attained when man rises above superstitious and religious notions and fears, and, for instance, no longer believes in guardian angels or in original sin, and has also ceased to talk of the salvation of his soul – if he has attained to this degree of freedom, he has still also to overcome metaphysics with the greatest exertion of his intelligence. Then, however, a *retrogressive movement* is necessary; he must understand the historical justification as well as the psychological in such representations, he must recognise how the greatest advancement of humanity has come therefrom, and how, without such a retrocursive movement, we should have been robbed of the best products of hitherto existing mankind. With regard to philosophical metaphysics, I always see increasing numbers who have attained to the negative goal (that all positive metaphysics is error), but as yet few who climb a few rungs backwards; one ought to look out, perhaps, over the last steps of the ladder, but not try to stand upon them. The most enlightened only succeed so far as to free themselves from metaphysics and look back upon it with superiority, while it is necessary here, too, as in the hippodrome, to turn round the end of the course.

21.

Conjectural Victory of Scepticism. – For once let the sceptical starting-point be accepted – granted that there were no other metaphysical world, and all explanations drawn from metaphysics about the only world we know were useless to us, in what light should we then look upon men and things? We can think this out for ourselves, it is useful, even though the question whether anything metaphysical has been scientifically proved by Kant and Schopenhauer were altogether set aside. For it is quite possible, according to historical probability, that some time or other man, as a general rule, may grow *sceptical*; the question will then be this: What form will human society take under the influence of such a mode of thought? Perhaps the *scientific proof* of some metaphysical world or other is already so *difficult* that mankind will never get rid of a certain distrust of it. And when there is distrust of metaphysics, there are on the whole the same results as if it had been directly refuted and could no longer be believed in. The historical question with regard to an unmetaphysical frame of mind in mankind remains the same in both cases.

22.

Unbelief in the '*Monumentum aere perennius.*' – An actual drawback which accompanies the cessation of metaphysical views lies in the fact that the individual looks upon his short span of life too exclusively and receives no stronger incentives to build durable institutions intended to last for centuries – he himself wishes to pluck the fruit from the tree which he plants, and therefore he no longer plants those trees which require regular care for centuries, and which are destined to afford shade to a long series of generations. For metaphysical views furnish the belief that in them the last conclusive foundation has been given, upon which henceforth all the future of mankind is compelled to settle down and establish itself; the individual furthers his salvation, when, for instance, he founds a church or convent, he thinks it will be reckoned to him and recompensed to him in the eternal life of the soul, it is work for the soul's eternal salvation. Can science also arouse such faith in its results? As a matter of fact, it needs doubt and distrust as its most faithful auxiliaries; nevertheless in the course of time, the sum of inviolable truths – those, namely, which have weathered all the storms of scepticism, and all destructive analysis – may have become so great (in the regimen of health, for instance), that one may determine to found thereupon 'eternal' works. For the present the *contrast* between our excited ephemeral existence and the long-winded repose of metaphysical ages still operates too strongly, because the two ages still stand too closely together; the individual man himself now goes through too many inward and outward developments for him to venture to arrange his own lifetime permanently, and once and for all. An entirely modern man, for instance, who is going to build himself a house, has a feeling as if he were going to immure himself alive in a mausoleum.

23.

The Age of Comparison. – The less men are fettered by tradition, the greater becomes the inward activity of their motives; the greater, again, in proportion thereto, the outward restlessness, the confused flux of mankind, the polyphony of strivings. For whom is there still an absolute compulsion to bind himself and his descendants to one place? For whom is there still anything strictly compulsory? As all styles of arts are imitated simultaneously, so also are all grades and kinds of morality, of customs, of cultures. Such an age obtains its importance because in it the various views of the world, customs, and cultures can be compared and experienced simultaneously – which was formerly not possible with the always localised sway of every culture, corresponding to the rooting of all artistic styles in place and time. An increased aesthetic feeling will now at last decide amongst so many forms presenting themselves for comparison; it will allow the greater number, that is to say all those rejected by it, to die out. In the same way a selection amongst the forms and customs of the higher moralities is taking place, of which the aim can be nothing else than the downfall of the lower moralities. It is the age of comparison! That is its pride, but more justly also its grief. Let us not be afraid of this grief! Rather will we comprehend as adequately as possible the task our age sets us: posterity will bless us for doing so – a posterity which knows itself to be as much above the terminated original national cultures as above the culture of comparison, but which looks back with gratitude on both kinds of culture as upon antiquities worthy of veneration.

24.

The Possibility of Progress. – When a scholar of the ancient culture forswears the company of men who believe in progress, he does quite right. For the greatness and goodness of ancient culture lie behind it, and historical education compels one to admit that they can never be fresh again; an unbearable stupidity or an equally insufferable fanaticism would be necessary to deny this. But men can *consciously* resolve to develop themselves towards a new culture; whilst formerly they only developed unconsciously and by chance, they can now create better conditions for the rise of human beings, for their nourishment, education and instruction; they can administer the earth economically as a whole, and can generally weigh and restrain the powers of man. This new, conscious culture kills the old, which, regarded as a whole, has led an unconscious animal and plant life; it also kills distrust in progress – progress is *possible*. I must say that it is over-hasty and almost nonsensical to believe that progress must *necessarily* follow; but how could one deny that it is possible? On the other hand, progress in the sense and on the path of the old culture is not even thinkable. Even if romantic fantasy has also constantly used the word 'progress' to denote its aims (for instance, circumscribed primitive national cultures), it borrows the picture of it in any case from the past; its thoughts and ideas on this subject are entirely without originality.

25.

Private and Ecumenical Morality. – Since the belief has ceased that a God directs in general the fate of the world and, in spite of all apparent crookedness in the path of humanity, leads it on gloriously, men themselves must set themselves ecumenical aims embracing the whole earth. The older morality, especially that of Kant, required from the individual actions which were desired from all men – that was a delightfully naive thing, as if each one knew off-hand what course of action was beneficial to the whole of humanity, and consequently which actions in general were desirable; it is a theory like that of free trade, taking for granted that the general harmony *must* result of itself according to innate laws of amelioration. Perhaps a future contemplation of the needs of humanity will show that it is by no means desirable that all men should act alike; in the interest of ecumenical aims it might rather be that for whole sections of mankind, special, and perhaps under certain circumstances even evil, tasks would have to be set. In any case, if mankind is not to destroy itself by such a conscious universal rule, there must previously be found, as a scientific standard for ecumenical aims, a *knowledge of the conditions of culture* superior to what has hitherto been attained. Herein lies the enormous task of the great minds of the next century.

26.

Reaction as Progress. – Now and again there appear rugged, powerful, impetuous, but nevertheless backward-lagging minds which conjure up once more a past phase of mankind; they serve to prove that the new tendencies against which they are working are not yet sufficiently strong, that they still lack something, otherwise they would show better opposition to those exorcisers. Thus, for example, Luther's Reformation bears witness to the fact that in his century all the movements of the freedom of the spirit were still uncertain, tender, and youthful; science could not yet lift up its head. Indeed the whole Renaissance seems like an early spring which is almost snowed under again. But in this century also, Schopenhauer's Metaphysics showed that even now the scientific spirit is not yet strong enough; thus the whole mediaeval Christian view of the world and human feeling could celebrate its resurrection in Schopenhauer's doctrine, in spite of the long achieved destruction of all Christian dogmas. There is much science in his doctrine, but it does not dominate it: it is rather the old well known 'metaphysical requirement' that does so. It is certainly one of the greatest and quite invaluable advantages which we gain from Schopenhauer, that he occasionally forces our sensations back into older, mightier modes of contemplating the world and man, to which no other path would so easily lead us. The gain to history and justice is very great – I do not think that any one would so easily succeed now in doing justice to Christianity and its Asiatic relations without Schopenhauer's assistance, which is specially impossible from the basis of still existing Christianity. Only after this great *success of justice*, only after we have corrected so essential a point as the historical mode of contemplation which the age of enlightenment brought with it, may we again bear onward the banner of enlightenment, the banner with the three names, Petrarch, Erasmus, Voltaire. We have turned reaction into progress.

27.

A Substitute for Religion. – It is believed that something good is said of philosophy when it is put forward as a substitute for religion for the people. As a matter of fact, in the spiritual economy there is need, at times, of an *intermediary* order of thought: the transition from religion to scientific contemplation is a violent, dangerous leap, which is not to be recommended. To this extent the recommendation is justifiable. But one should eventually learn that the needs which have been satisfied by religion and are now to be satisfied by philosophy are not unchangeable;

these themselves can be *weakened* and *eradicated*. Think, for instance, of the Christian's distress of soul, his sighing over inward corruption, his anxiety for salvation – all notions which originate only in errors of reason and deserve not satisfaction but destruction. A philosophy can serve either to *satisfy* those needs or to *set them aside*; for they are acquired, temporally limited needs, which are based upon suppositions contradictory to those of science. Here, in order to make a transition, art is far rather to be employed to relieve the mind over-burdened with emotions; for those notions receive much less support from it than from a metaphysical philosophy. It is easier, then, to pass over from art to a really liberating philosophical science.

28.

Ill-famed Words. – Away with those wearisomely hackneyed terms Optimism and Pessimism! For the occasion for using them becomes less and less from day to day; only the chatterboxes still find them so absolutely necessary. For why in all the world should any one wish to be an optimist unless he had a God to defend who *must* have created the best of worlds if he himself be goodness and perfection – what thinker, however, still needs the hypothesis of a God? But every occasion for a pessimistic confession of faith is also lacking when one has no interest in being annoyed at the advocates of God (the theologians, or the theologising philosophers), and in energetically defending the opposite view, that evil reigns, that pain is greater than pleasure, that the world is a bungled piece of work, the manifestation of an ill-will to life. But who still bothers about the theologians now – except the theologians? Apart from all theology and its contentions, it is quite clear that the world is not good and not bad (to say nothing of its being the best or the worst), and that the terms ' good' and 'bad' have only significance with respect to man, and indeed, perhaps, they are not justified even here in the way they are usually employed; in any case we must get rid of both the calumniating and the glorifying conception of the world.

29.

Intoxicated by the Scent of the Blossoms. – It is supposed that the ship of humanity has always a deeper draught, the heavier it is laden;

it is believed that the deeper a man thinks, the more delicately he feels, the higher he values himself, the greater his distance from the other animals – the more he appears as a genius amongst the animals – all the nearer will he approach the real essence of the world and its knowledge; this he actually does too, through science, but he *means* to do so still more through his religions and arts. These certainly are blossoms of the world, but by no means any *nearer to the root of the world* than the stalk; it is not possible to understand the nature of things better through them, although almost every one believes he can. *Error* has made man so deep, sensitive, and inventive that he has put forth such blossoms as religions and arts. Pure knowledge could not have been capable of it. Whoever were to unveil for us the essence of the world would give us all the most disagreeable disillusionment. Not the world as thing-in-itself, but the world as representation (as error) is so full of meaning, so deep, so wonderful, bearing happiness and unhappiness in its bosom. This result leads to a philosophy of the logical denial of the world, which, however, can be combined with a practical world-affirming just as well as with its opposite.

30.

Bad Habits in Reasoning. – The usual false conclusions of mankind are these: a thing exists, therefore it has a right to exist. Here there is inference from the ability to live to its suitability; from its suitability to its rightfulness. Then: an opinion brings happiness; therefore it is the true opinion. Its effect is good; therefore it is itself good and true. To the effect is here assigned the predicate beneficent, good, in the sense of the useful, and the cause is then furnished with the same predicate good, but here in the sense of the logically valid. The inversion of the sentences would read thus: an affair cannot be carried through, or maintained, therefore it is wrong; an opinion causes pain or excites, therefore it is false. The free spirit who learns only too often the faultiness of this mode of reasoning, and has to suffer from its consequences, frequently gives way to the temptation to draw the very opposite conclusions, which, in general, are naturally just as false: an affair cannot be carried through, therefore it is good; an opinion is distressing and disturbing, therefore it is true.

31.

The Illogical Necessary. – One of those things that may drive a thinker into despair is the recognition of the fact that the illogical is necessary for man, and that out of the illogical comes much that is good. It is so firmly rooted in the passions, in language, in art, in religion, and generally in everything that gives value to life, that it cannot be withdrawn without thereby hopelessly injuring these beautiful things. It is only the all-too-naive people who can believe that the nature of man can be changed into a purely logical one; but if there were degrees of proximity to this goal, how many things would not have to be lost on this course! Even the most rational man has need of nature again from time to time, i.e. his *illogical fundamental attitude* towards all things.

32.

Injustice Necessary. – All judgements on the value of life are illogically developed, and therefore unjust. The inexactitude of the judgement lies, firstly, in the manner in which the material is presented, namely very imperfectly; secondly, in the manner in which the conclusion is formed out of it; and thirdly, in the fact that every separate element of the material is again the result of vitiated recognition, and this, too, of necessity. For instance, no experience of an individual, however near he may stand to us, can be perfect, so that we could have a logical right to make a complete estimate of him; all estimates are rash, and must be so. Finally, the standard by which we measure, our nature, is not of unalterable dimensions – we have moods and vacillations, and yet we should have to recognise ourselves as a fixed standard in order to estimate correctly the relation of any thing whatever to ourselves. From this it will, perhaps, follow that we should make no judgements at all; if one could only live without making estimations, without having likes and dislikes! For all dislike is connected with an estimation, as well as all inclination. An impulse towards or away from anything without a feeling that something advantageous is desired, something injurious avoided, an impulse without any kind of conscious valuation of the worth of the aim does not exist in man. We are from the beginning illogical, and therefore unjust beings, *and can recognise this*; it is one of the greatest and most inexplicable discords of existence.

33.

Error about Life necessary for Life. – Every belief in the value and worthiness of life is based on vitiated thought; it is only possible through the fact that sympathy for the general life and suffering of mankind is very weakly developed in the individual. Even the rarer people who think outside themselves do not contemplate this general life, but only a limited part of it. If one understands how to direct one's attention chiefly to the exceptions – I mean to the highly gifted and the rich souls – if one regards the production of these as the aim of the whole world-development and rejoices in its operation, then one may believe in the value of life, because one thereby *overlooks* the other men – one consequently thinks fallaciously. So too, when one directs one's attention to all mankind, but only considers *one* species of impulses in them, the less egoistical ones, and excuses them with regard to the other instincts, one may then again entertain hopes of mankind in general and believe so far in the value of life, consequently in this case also through fallaciousness of thought. Let one, however, behave in this or that manner: with such behaviour one is an *exception* amongst men. Now, most people bear life without any considerable grumbling, and consequently *believe* in the value of existence, but precisely because each one is solely self-seeking and self-affirming, and does not step out of himself like those exceptions; everything extra-personal is imperceptible to them, or at most seems only a faint shadow. Therefore on this alone is based the value of life for the ordinary everyday man, that he regards himself as more important than the world. The great lack of imagination from which he suffers is the reason why he cannot enter into the feelings of other beings, and therefore sympathises as little as possible with their fate and suffering. He, on the other hand, who really *could* sympathise therewith, would have to despair of the value of life; were he to succeed in comprehending and feeling in himself the general consciousness of mankind, he would collapse with a curse on existence; for mankind as a whole has *no* goals, consequently man, in considering his whole course, cannot find in it his comfort and support, but his despair. If, in all that he does, he considers the final aimlessness of man, his own activity assumes in his eyes the character of wastefulness. But to feel one's self just as much wasted as humanity (and not only as an individual) as we see the single blossom of nature wasted, is a feeling above all other feelings. But who is capable of it? Assuredly only a poet, and poets always know how to console themselves.

34.

For Tranquillity. – But does not our philosophy thus become a tragedy? Does not truth become hostile to life, to improvement? A question seems to weigh upon our tongue and yet hesitate to make itself heard: whether one can consciously remain in untruthfulness? Or, supposing one were *obliged* to do this, would not death be preferable? For there is no longer any 'must'; morality, in so far as it had any 'must' or 'shalt', has been destroyed by our mode of contemplation, just as religion has been destroyed. Knowledge can only allow pleasure and pain, benefit and injury to subsist as motives; but how will these motives agree with the sense of truth? They also contain errors (for, as already said, inclination and aversion, and their very incorrect determinations, practically regulate our pleasure and pain). The whole of human life is deeply immersed in untruthfulness; the individual cannot draw it up out of this well, without thereby taking a deep dislike to his whole past, without finding his present motives – those of honour, for instance – inconsistent, and without opposing scorn and disdain to the passions which conduce to happiness in the future. Is it true that there remains but one sole way of thinking which brings after it despair as a personal experience, as a theoretical result, a philosophy of dissolution, disintegration, and self-destruction? I believe that the decision with regard to the after-effects of the knowledge will be given through the *temperament* of a man; I could imagine another after-effect, just as well as that one described, which is possible in certain natures, by means of which a life would arise much simpler, freer from emotions than is the present one, so that though at first, indeed, the old motives of passionate desire might still have strength from old hereditary habit, they would gradually become weaker under the influence of purifying knowledge. One would live at last amongst men, and with one's self as with *Nature*, without praise, reproach, or agitation, feasting one's eyes, as if it were a *play*, upon much of which one was formerly afraid. One would be free from the emphasis, and would no longer feel the goading, of the thought that one is not only nature or more than nature. Certainly, as already remarked, a good temperament would be necessary for this, an even, mild, and naturally joyous soul, a disposition which would not always need to be on its guard against spite and sudden outbreaks, and would not convey in its utterances anything of a grumbling or sudden nature – those well-known vexatious qualities of old dogs and men who have been long chained up. On the contrary, a man from whom the ordinary fetters of life have so far fallen that he continues to live only for the sake of ever better knowledge must be able to renounce without envy and regret: much, indeed almost everything that is precious to other men, he must regard as the *all-sufficing* and the most desirable condition; the free, fearless soaring over men, customs, laws, and the traditional valuations of things. The joy of this condition he imparts willingly, and he *has* perhaps nothing else to impart – wherein, to be sure, there is more privation and renunciation. If, nevertheless, more is demanded from him, he will point with a friendly shake of his head to his brother, the free man of action, and will perhaps not conceal a little derision, for as regards this 'freedom' it is a very peculiar case.

SECOND DIVISION.

THE HISTORY OF THE MORAL SENTIMENTS.

35.

Advantages of Psychological Observation. – That reflection on the human, all-too-human – or, according to the learned expression, psychological observation – is one of the means by which one may lighten the burden of life, that exercise in this art produces presence of mind in difficult circumstances, in the midst of tiresome surroundings, even that from the most thorny and unpleasant periods of one's own life one may gather maxims and thereby feel a little better: all this was believed, was known in former centuries. Why was it forgotten by our century, when in Germany at least, even in all Europe, the poverty of psychological observation betrays itself by many signs? Not exactly in novels, tales, and philosophical treatises – they are the work of exceptional individuals – rather in the judgements on public events and personalities; but above all there is a lack of the art of psychological analysis and summing-up in every rank of society, in which a great deal is talked about men, but nothing about *man*. Why do we allow the richest and most harmless subject of conversation to escape us? Why are not the great masters of psychological maxims more read? For, without any exaggeration, the educated man in Europe who has read La Rochefoucauld and his kindred in mind and art, is rarely found, and still more rare is he who knows them and does not blame them. It is probable, however, that even this exceptional reader will find much less pleasure in them than the form of this artist should afford him; for even the clearest head is not capable of rightly estimating the art of shaping and polishing maxims unless he has really been brought up to it and has competed in it. Without this practical teaching one deems this shaping and polishing to be easier than it is; one has not a sufficient perception of fitness and charm. For this reason the present readers of maxims find in them a comparatively small pleasure, hardly a mouthful of pleasantness, so that they resemble the people who generally look at cameos, who praise because they cannot love, and are very ready to admire, but still more ready to run away.

36.

Objection. – Or should there be a counter-reckoning to that theory that places psychological observation amongst the means of charming, curing, and relieving existence? Should one have sufficiently convinced one's self of the unpleasant consequences of this art to divert from it designedly the attention of him who is educating himself in it? As a matter of fact, a certain blind belief in the goodness of human nature, an innate aversion to the analysis of human actions, a kind of shamefacedness with respect to the nakedness of the soul may really be more desirable for the general wellbeing of a man than that quality, useful in isolated cases, of psychological sharp-sightedness; and perhaps the belief in goodness, in virtuous men and deeds, in an abundance of impersonal goodwill in the world, has made men better inasmuch as it has made them less distrustful. When one imitates Plutarch's heroes with enthusiasm, and turns with disgust from a suspicious examination of the motives for their actions, it is not truth which benefits thereby, but the welfare of human society; the psychological mistake and, generally speaking, the insensibility on this matter helps humanity forwards, while the recognition of truth gains more through the stimulating power of hypothesis than La Rochefoucauld has said in his preface to the first edition of his '*Sentences et maximes morales!*' . . . '*Ce que le monde nomme vertu n'est d'ordinaire qu'un fantôme formé par nos passions, à qui on donne un nom honnête pour faire impunément ce qu'on veut.*' La Rochefoucauld and those other French masters of soul-examination (who have lately been joined by a German, the author of *Psychological Observations*[3]) resemble good marksmen who again and again hit the bull's-eye; but it is the bull's-eye of human nature. Their art arouses astonishment; but in the end a spectator who is not led by the spirit of science, but by humane intentions, will probably execrate an art which appears to implant in the soul the sense of the disparagement and suspicion of mankind.

---

3 Dr Paul Rée.– J. M. K.

37.

Nevertheless. – However it may be with reckoning and counter-reckoning, in the present condition of philosophy the awakening of moral observation is necessary. Humanity can no longer be spared the cruel sight of the psychological dissecting-table with its knives and forceps. For here rules that science which inquires into the origin and history of the so-called moral sentiments, and which, in its progress, has to draw up and solve complicated sociological problems: the older philosophy knows the latter one not at all, and has always avoided the examination of the origin and history of moral sentiments on any feeble pretext. With what consequences it is now very easy to see, after it has been shown by many examples how the mistakes of the greatest philosophers generally have their starting-point in a wrong explanation of certain human actions and sensations, just as on the ground of an erroneous analysis – for instance, that of the so-called unselfish actions – a false ethic is built up; then, to harmonise with this again, religion and mythological confusion are brought in to assist, and finally the shades of these dismal spirits fall also over physics and the general mode of regarding the world. If it is certain, however, that superficiality in psychological observation has laid, and still lays, the most dangerous snares for human judgements and conclusions, then there is need now of that endurance of work which does not grow weary of piling stone upon stone, pebble on pebble; there is need of courage not to be ashamed of such humble work and to turn a deaf ear to scorn. And this is also true – numberless single observations on the human and all-too-human have first been discovered, and given utterance to, in circles of society which were accustomed to offer sacrifice therewith to a clever desire to please, and not to scientific knowledge – and the odour of that old home of the moral maxim, a very seductive odour, has attached itself almost inseparably to the whole species, so that on its account the scientific man involuntarily betrays a certain distrust of this species and its earnestness. But it is sufficient to point to the consequences, for already it begins to be seen what results of a serious kind spring from the ground of psychological observation. What, after all, is the principal axiom to which the boldest and coldest thinker, the author of the book *On the Origin of Moral Sensations*[4] has attained by means of his incisive and decisive analyses of human actions? 'The moral man,' he says, 'is no nearer to the intelligible (metaphysical) world than is the physical man.' This theory, hardened and sharpened under the hammer-blow of historical knowledge, may some time or other, perhaps in some future period, serve as the axe which is applied to the root of the 'metaphysical need' of man – whether *more* as a blessing than a curse to the general welfare it is not easy to say, but in any case as a theory with the most important consequences, at once fruitful and terrible, and looking into the world with that Janus-face which all great knowledge possesses.

38.

How Far Useful. – It must remain for ever undecided whether psychological observation is advantageous or disadvantageous to man; but it is certain that it is necessary, because science cannot do without it. Science, however, has no consideration for ultimate purposes, any more than Nature has, but just as the latter occasionally achieves things of the greatest suitableness without intending to do so, so also true science, as the *imitator of nature in ideas*, will occasionally and in many ways further the usefulness and welfare of man – *but also without intending to do so.*

But whoever feels too chilled by the breath of such a reflection has perhaps too little fire in himself; let him look around him meanwhile and he will become aware of illnesses which have need of ice-poultices, and of men who are so 'kneaded together' of heat and spirit that they can hardly find an atmosphere that is cold and biting enough. Moreover, as individuals and nations that are too serious have need of frivolities, as others too mobile and excitable have need occasionally of heavily oppressing burdens for the sake of their health, should not we, the more *intellectual* people of this age, that grows visibly more and more inflamed, seize all quenching and cooling means that exist, in order that we may at least remain as constant, harmless, and moderate as we still are, and thus, perhaps, serve some time or other as mirror and self-contemplation for this age?

4 Dr Paul Rée.– J. M. K.

39.

The Fable of Intelligible Freedom. – The history of the sentiments by means of which we make a person responsible consists of the following principal phases. First, all single actions are called good or bad without any regard to their motives, but only on account of the useful or injurious consequences which result for the community. But soon the origin of these distinctions is forgotten, and it is deemed that the qualities 'good' or 'bad' are contained in the action itself without regard to its consequences, by the same error according to which language describes the stone as hard, the tree as green – with which, in short, the result is regarded as the cause. Then the goodness or badness is implanted in the motive, and the action in itself is looked upon as morally ambiguous. Mankind even goes further, and applies the predicate good or bad no longer to single motives, but to the whole nature of an individual, out of whom the motive grows as the plant grows out of the earth. Thus, in turn, man is made responsible for his operations, then for his actions, then for his motives, and finally for his nature. Eventually it is discovered that even this nature cannot be responsible, inasmuch as it is an absolutely necessary consequence concreted out of the elements and influences of past and present things – that man, therefore, cannot be made responsible for anything, neither for his nature, nor his motives, nor his actions, nor his effects. It has therewith come to be recognised that the history of moral valuations is at the same time the history of an error, the error of responsibility, which is based upon the error of the freedom of will. Schopenhauer thus decided against it: because certain actions bring ill humour ('consciousness of guilt') in their train, there must be a responsibility; for there would be no reason for this ill humour if not only all human actions were not done of necessity – which is actually the case and also the belief of this philosopher – but man himself from the same necessity is precisely the being that he is – which Schopenhauer denies. From the fact of that ill humour Schopenhauer thinks he can prove a liberty which man must somehow have had, not with regard to actions, but with regard to nature; liberty, therefore, to be thus or otherwise, not to act thus or otherwise. From the *esse*, the sphere of freedom and responsibility, there results, in his opinion, the *operari*, the sphere of strict causality, necessity, and irresponsibility. This ill humour is apparently directed to the *operari* – in so far it is erroneous – but in reality it is directed to the *esse*, which is the deed of a free will, the fundamental cause of the existence of an individual, man becomes that which he wishes to be, his will is anterior to his existence. Here the mistaken conclusion is drawn that from the fact of the ill humour, the justification, the reasonable *admissableness* of this ill humour is presupposed; and starting from this mistaken conclusion, Schopenhauer arrives at his fantastic sequence of the so-called intelligible freedom. But the ill humour after the deed is not necessarily reasonable, indeed it is assuredly not reasonable, for it is based upon the erroneous presumption that the action need not have inevitably followed. Therefore, it is only because man *believes* himself to be free, not because he is free, that he experiences remorse and pricks of conscience. Moreover, this ill humour is a habit that can be broken off; in many people it is entirely absent in connection with actions where others experience it. It is a very changeable thing, and one which is connected with the development of customs and culture, and probably only existing during a comparatively short period of the world's history. Nobody is responsible for his actions, nobody for his nature; to judge is identical with being unjust. This also applies when an individual judges himself. The theory is as clear as sunlight, and yet every one prefers to go back into the shadow and the untruth, for fear of the consequences.

40.

The Super-Animal. – The beast in us wishes to be deceived; morality is a lie of necessity in order that we may not be torn in pieces by it. Without the errors which lie in the assumption of morality, man would have remained an animal. Thus, however, he has considered himself as something higher and has laid strict laws upon himself. Therefore he hates the grades which have remained nearer to animalness, whereby the former scorn of the slave, as a not-yet-man, is to be explained as a fact.

41.

The Unchangeable Character. – That the character is unchangeable is not true in a strict sense; this favourite theory means, rather, that during the short lifetime of an individual the new influencing motives cannot penetrate deeply enough to destroy the ingrained marks of many thousands of years. But if one were to imagine a man of eighty thousand years, one would have in him an absolutely changeable character, so that a number of different individuals would gradually develop out of him. The shortness of human life misleads us into forming many erroneous ideas about the qualities of man.

42.

The Order of Possessions and Morality. – The once-accepted hierarchy of possessions, according as this or the other is coveted by a lower, higher, or highest egoism, now decides what is moral or immoral. To prefer a lesser good (for instance, the gratification of the senses) to a more highly valued good (for instance, health) is accounted immoral, and also to prefer luxury to liberty. The hierarchy of possessions, however, is not fixed and equal at all times; if any one prefers vengeance to justice he is moral according to the standard of an earlier civilisation, but immoral according to the present one. To be 'immoral', therefore, denotes that an individual has not felt, or not felt sufficiently strongly, the higher, finer, spiritual motives which have come in with a new culture; it marks one who has remained behind, but only according to the difference of degrees. The order of possessions itself is not raised and lowered according to a moral point of view; but each time that it is fixed it supplies the decision as to whether an action is moral or immoral.

43.

Cruel People as Those who have Remained Behind – People who are cruel nowadays must be accounted for by us as the grades of earlier civilisations which have survived; here are exposed those deeper formations in the mountain of humanity which usually remain concealed. They are backward people whose brains, through all manner of accidents in the course of inheritance, have not been developed in so delicate and manifold a way. They show us what we all *were* and horrify us, but they themselves are as little responsible as is a block of granite for being granite. There must, too, be grooves and twists in our brains which answer to that condition of mind, as in the form of certain human organs there are supposed to be traces of a fish-state. But these grooves and twists are no longer the bed through which the stream of our sensation flows.

44.

Gratitude and Revenge. – The reason why the powerful man is grateful is this: his benefactor, through the benefit he confers, has mistaken and intruded into the sphere of the powerful man – how the latter, in return, penetrates into the sphere of the benefactor by the act of gratitude. It is a milder form of revenge. Without the satisfaction of gratitude, the powerful man would have shown himself powerless, and would have been reckoned as such ever after. Therefore every society of the good, which originally meant the powerful, places gratitude amongst the first duties. Swift propounded the maxim that men were grateful in the same proportion as they were revengeful.

45.

The Twofold Early History of Good and Evil. – The conception of good and evil has a twofold early history, namely *once* in the soul of the ruling tribes and castes. Whoever has the power of returning good for good, evil for evil, and really practises requital, and who is, therefore, grateful and revengeful, is called good; whoever is powerless, and unable to requite, is reckoned as bad. As a good man one is reckoned among the 'good', a community which has common feelings because the single individuals are bound to one another by the sense of requital. As a bad man one belongs to the 'bad', to a party of subordinate, powerless people who have no common feeling. The good are a caste, the bad are a mass like dust. Good and bad have for a long time meant the same thing as noble and base, master and slave. On the other hand, the enemy is not looked upon as evil, he can requite. In Homer the Trojan and the Greek are both good. It is not the one who injures us, but the one who is despicable, who is called bad. Good is inherited in the community of the good; it is impossible that a bad man could spring from such good soil. If, nevertheless, one of the good ones does something which is unworthy of the good, refuge is sought in excuses; the guilt is thrown upon a god, for instance; it is said that he has struck the good man with blindness and madness. –

Then in the soul of the oppressed and powerless. Here every other man is looked upon as hostile, inconsiderate, rapacious, cruel, cunning, be he noble or base; evil is the distinguishing word for man, even for every conceivable living creature, e.g. for a god; human, divine, is the same thing as devilish, evil. The signs of goodness, helpfulness, pity, are looked upon with fear as spite, the prelude to a terrible result, stupefaction and outwitting – in short, as refined malice. With such a disposition in the individual a community could hardly exist, or at most it could exist only in its crudest form, so that in all places where this conception of good and evil obtains, the downfall of the single individuals, of their tribes and races, is at hand. Our present civilisation has grown up on the soil of the *ruling* tribes and castes.

46.

Sympathy Stronger than Suffering. – There are cases when sympathy is stronger than actual suffering. For instance, we are more pained when one of our friends is guilty of something shameful than when we do it ourselves. For one thing, we have more faith in the purity of his character than he has himself; then our love for him, probably on account of this very faith, is stronger than his love for himself. And even if his egoism suffers more thereby than our egoism, inasmuch as it has to bear more of the bad consequences of his fault, the un-egoistic in us – this word is not to be taken too seriously, but only as a modification of the expression – is more deeply wounded by his guilt than is the un-egoistic in him.

47.

Hypochondria. – There are people who become hypochondriacal through their sympathy and concern for another person; the kind of sympathy which results therefrom is nothing but a disease. Thus there is also a Christian hypochondria, which afflicts those solitary, religiously-minded people who keep constantly before their eyes the sufferings and death of Christ.

48.

Economy of Goodness. – Goodness and love, as the most healing herbs and powers in human intercourse, are such costly discoveries that one would wish as much economy as possible to be exercised in the employment of these balsamic means; but this is impossible. The economy of goodness is the dream of the most daring Utopians.

49.

Goodwill. – Amongst the small, but countlessly frequent and therefore very effective, things to which science should pay more attention than to the great, rare things, is to be reckoned goodwill; I mean that exhibition of a friendly disposition in intercourse, that smiling eye, that clasp of the hand, that cheerfulness with which almost all human actions are usually accompanied. Every teacher, every official, adds this to whatever is his duty; it is the perpetual occupation of humanity, and at the same time the waves of its light, in which everything grows; in the narrowest circle, namely, within the family, life blooms and flourishes only through that goodwill. Kindliness, friendliness, the courtesy of the heart, are ever-flowing streams of un-egoistic impulses, and have given far more powerful assistance to culture than even those much more famous demonstrations which are called pity, mercy, and self-sacrifice. But they are thought little of, and, as a matter of fact, there is not much that is un-egoistic in them. The *sum* of these small doses is nevertheless mighty, their united force is amongst the strongest forces. Thus one finds much more happiness in the world than sad eyes see, if one only reckons rightly, and does not forget all those moments of comfort in which every day is rich, even in the most harried of human lives.

50.

The Wish to arouse Pity. – In the most remarkable passage of his auto portrait (first printed in 1658), La Rochefoucauld assuredly hits the nail on the head when he warns all sensible people against pity, when he advises them to leave that to those orders of the people who have need of passion (because it is not ruled by reason), and to reach the point of helping the suffering and acting energetically in an accident;

while pity, according to his (and Plato's) judgement, weakens the soul. Certainly we should *exhibit* pity, but take good care not to *feel* it, for the unfortunate are so *stupid* that to them the exhibition of pity is the greatest good in the world. One can, perhaps, give a more forcible warning against this feeling of pity if one looks upon that need of the unfortunate not exactly as stupidity and lack of intellect, a kind of mental derangement which misfortune brings with it (and as such, indeed, La Rochefoucauld appears to regard it), but as something quite different and more serious. Observe children, who cry and scream *in order* to be pitied, and therefore wait for the moment when they will be noticed; live in intercourse with the sick and mentally oppressed, and ask yourself whether that ready complaining and whimpering, that making a show of misfortune, does not, at bottom, aim at *making the spectators miserable*; the pity which the spectators then exhibit is in so far a consolation for the weak and suffering in that the latter recognise therein that they *possess still one power*, in spite of their weakness, *the power of giving pain*. The unfortunate derives a sort of pleasure from this feeling of superiority, of which the exhibition of pity makes him conscious; his imagination is exalted, he is still powerful enough to give the world pain. Thus the thirst for pity is the thirst for self-gratification, and that, moreover, at the expense of his fellow-men; it shows man in the whole inconsiderateness of his own dear self, but not exactly in his 'stupidity', as La Rochefoucauld thinks. In society-talk three-fourths of all questions asked and of all answers given are intended to cause the interlocutor a little pain; for this reason so many people pine for company; it enables them to feel their power. There is a powerful charm of life in such countless but very small doses in which malice makes itself felt, just as goodwill, spread in the same way throughout the world, is the ever-ready means of healing. But are there many honest people who will admit that it is pleasing to give pain? That one not infrequently amuses one's self – and amuses one's self very well – in causing mortifications to others, at least in thought, and firing off at them the grape-shot of petty malice? Most people are too dishonest, and a few are too good, to know anything of this *pudendum*; these will always deny that Prosper Merimée is right when he says, '*Sachez aussi qu'il n'y a rien de plus commun que de faire le mal pour le plaisir de le faire.*'

51.

How Appearance becomes Actuality. – The actor finally reaches such a point that even in the deepest sorrow he cannot cease from thinking about the impression made by his own person and the general scenic effect; for instance, even at the funeral of his child, he will weep over his own sorrow and its expression like one of his own audience. The hypocrite, who always plays one and the same part, ceases at last to be a hypocrite; for instance, priests, who as young men are generally conscious or unconscious hypocrites, become at last natural, and are then really without any affectation, just priests; or if the father does not succeed so far, perhaps the son does, who makes use of his father's progress and inherits his habits. If any one long and obstinately desires to *appear* something, he finds it difficult at last to *be* anything else. The profession of almost every individual, even of the artist, begins with hypocrisy, with an imitating from without, with a copying of the effective. He who always wears the mask of a friendly expression must eventually obtain a power over well-meaning dispositions without which the expression of friendliness is not to be compelled – and finally, these, again, obtain a power over him, he *is* well-meaning.

52.

The Point of Honour in Deception. – In all great deceivers one thing is noteworthy, to which they owe their power. In the actual act of deception, with all their preparations, the dreadful voice, expression, and mien, in the midst of their effective scenery they are overcome by their *belief in themselves*; it is this, then, which speaks so wonderfully and persuasively to the spectators. The founders of religions are distinguished from those great deceivers in that they never awake from their condition of self-deception; or at times, but very rarely, they have an enlightened moment when doubt overpowers them; they generally console themselves, however, by ascribing these enlightened moments to the influence of the Evil One. There must be self-deception in order that this and that may *produce* great *effects*. For men believe in the truth of everything that is visibly, strongly believed in.

53.

The Nominal Degrees of Truth. – One of the commonest mistakes is this: because some one is truthful and honest towards us, he must speak the truth. Thus the child believes in its parents' judgement, the Christian in the assertions of the Founder of the Church. In the same way men refuse to admit that all those things which men defended in former ages with the sacrifice of life and happiness were nothing but errors; it is even said, perhaps, that they were degrees of the truth. But what is really meant is that when a man has honestly believed in something, and has fought and died for his faith, it would really be too *unjust* if he had only been inspired by an error. Such a thing seems a contradiction of eternal justice; therefore the heart of sensitive man ever enunciates against his head the axiom: between moral action and intellectual insight there must absolutely be a necessary connection. It is unfortunately otherwise; for there is no eternal justice.

54.

Falsehood. – Why do people mostly speak the truth in daily life? Assuredly not because a god has forbidden falsehood. But, firstly, because it is more convenient, as falsehood requires invention, deceit, and memory. (As Swift says, he who tells a lie is not sensible how great a task he undertakes; for in order to uphold one lie he must invent twenty others.) Therefore, because it is advantageous in upright circumstances to say straight out, 'I want this, I have done that,' and so on; because, in other words, the path of compulsion and authority is surer than that of cunning. But if a child has been brought up in complicated domestic circumstances, he employs falsehood, naturally and unconsciously says whatever best suits his interests; a sense of truth and a hatred of falsehood are quite foreign and unknown to him, and so he lies in all innocence.

55.

Throwing Suspicion on Morality for Faith's Sake. – No power can be maintained when it is only represented by hypocrites; no matter how many 'worldly' elements the Catholic Church possesses, its strength lies in those still numerous priestly natures who render life hard and full of meaning for themselves, and whose glance and worn bodies speak of nocturnal vigils, hunger, burning prayers, and perhaps even of scourging; these move men and inspire them with fear. What if it were *necessary* to live thus? This is the terrible question which their aspect brings to the lips. Whilst they spread this doubt they always uprear another pillar of their power; even the free-thinker does not dare to withstand such unselfishness with hard words of truth, and to say, 'Thyself deceived, deceive not others!' Only the difference of views divides them from him, certainly no difference of goodness or badness; but men generally treat unjustly that which they do not like. Thus we speak of the cunning and the infamous art of the Jesuits, but overlook the self-control which every individual Jesuit practises, and the fact that the lightened manner of life preached by Jesuit books is by no means for their benefit, but for that of the laity. We may even ask whether, with precisely similar tactics and organisation, we enlightened ones would make equally good tools, equally admirable through self-conquest, indefatigableness, and renunciation.

56.

Victory of Knowledge over Radical Evil. – It is of great advantage to him who desires to be wise to have witnessed for a time the spectacle of a thoroughly evil and degenerate man; it is false, like the contrary spectacle, but for whole long periods it held the mastery, and its roots have even extended and ramified themselves to us and our world. In order to understand *ourselves* we must understand *it*, but then, in order to mount higher we must rise above it. We recognise, then, that there exist no sins in the metaphysical sense; but, in the same sense, also no virtues; we recognise that the entire domain of ethical ideas is perpetually tottering, that there are higher and deeper conceptions of good and evil, of moral and immoral. He who does not desire much more from things than a knowledge of them easily makes peace with his soul, and will make a mistake (or commit a sin, as the world calls it) at the most from ignorance, but hardly from covetousness. He will no longer wish to excommunicate and exterminate desires; but his only, his wholly dominating ambition, to *know* as well as possible at all times, will make him cool and will soften all the savageness in his disposition. Moreover, he has been freed from a number of tormenting conceptions, he has no more feeling at the mention of the words 'punishments of hell', 'sinfulness', ' incapacity for good', he recognises in them only the vanishing shadow-pictures of false views of the world and of life.

57.

Morality as the Self-Disintegration of Man. – A good author, who really has his heart in his work, wishes that some one could come and annihilate him by representing the same thing in a clearer way and answering without more ado the problems therein proposed. The loving girl wishes she could prove the self-sacrificing faithfulness of her love by the unfaithfulness of her beloved. The soldier hopes to die on the field of battle for his victorious fatherland; for his loftiest desires triumph in the victory of his country. The mother gives to the child that of which she deprives herself – sleep, the best food, sometimes her health and fortune. But are all these unegoistic conditions? Are these deeds of morality *miracles*, because, to use Schopenhauer's expression, they are 'impossible and yet performed'? Is it not clear that in all four cases the individual loves *something of himself*, a thought, a desire, a production, better than *anything else of himself*; that he therefore divides his nature and to one part sacrifices all the rest? Is it something entirely different when an obstinate man says, 'I would rather be shot than move a step out of my way for this man'? The *desire for something* (wish, inclination, longing) is present in all the instances mentioned; to give way to it, with all its consequences, is certainly not 'un-egoistic'. In ethics man does not consider himself as *individuum* but as *dividuum*.

58.

What One may Promise. – One may promise actions, but no sentiments, for these are involuntary. Whoever promises to love or hate a person, or be faithful to him for ever, promises something which is not within his power; he can certainly promise such actions as are usually the results of love, hate, or fidelity, but which may also spring from other motives; for many ways and motives lead to one and the same action. The promise to love some one for ever is, therefore, really: So long as I love you I will act towards you in a loving way; if I cease to love you, you will still receive the same treatment from me, although inspired by other motives, so that our fellow-men will still be deluded into the belief that our love is unchanged and ever the same. One promises, therefore, the continuation of the semblance of love, when, without self-deception, one speaks vows of eternal love.

59.

Intellect and Morality. – One must have a good memory to be able to keep a given promise. One must have a strong power of imagination to be able to feel pity. So closely is morality bound to the goodness of the intellect.

60.

To wish for Revenge and to take Revenge. – To have a revengeful thought and to carry it into effect is to have a violent attack of fever, which passes off, however – but to have a revengeful thought without the strength and courage to carry it out is a chronic disease, a poisoning of body and soul which we have to bear about with us. Morality, which only takes intentions into account, considers the two cases as equal; usually the former case is regarded as the worse (because of the evil consequences which may perhaps result from the deed of revenge). Both estimates are short-sighted.

61.

The Power of Waiting. – Waiting is so difficult that even great poets have not disdained to take incapability of waiting as the motive for their works. Thus Shakespeare in Othello or Sophocles in Ajax, to whom suicide, had he been able to let his feelings cool down for one day, would no longer have seemed necessary, as the oracle intimated; he would probably have snapped his fingers at the terrible whisperings of wounded vanity, and said to himself, 'Who has not already, in my circumstances, mistaken a fool for a hero? Is it something so very extraordinary?' On the contrary, it is something very commonly human; Ajax might allow himself that consolation. Passion will not wait; the tragedy in the lives of great men frequently lies *not* in their conflict with the times and the baseness of their fellow-men, but in their incapacity of postponing their work for a year or two; they cannot wait. In all duels advising friends have one thing to decide, namely whether the parties concerned can still wait awhile; if this is not the case, then a duel is advisable, inasmuch as each of the two says, 'Either I continue to live and that other man must die immediately, or vice versa.' In such case waiting would mean a prolonged suffering of the terrible martyrdom of wounded honour in the face of the insulter, and this may entail more suffering than life is worth.

62.

Revelling in Vengeance. – Coarser individuals who feel themselves insulted, make out the insult to be as great as possible, and relate the affair in greatly exaggerated language, in order to be able to revel thoroughly in the rarely awakened feelings of hatred and revenge.

63.

The Value of Disparagement. – In order to maintain their self-respect in their own eyes and a certain thoroughness of action, not a few men, perhaps even the majority, find it absolutely necessary to run down and disparage all their acquaintances. But as mean natures are numerous, and since it is very important whether they possess that thoroughness or lose it, hence—

64.

The Man in a Passion. – We must beware of one who is in a passion against us as of one who has once sought our life; for the fact that we still live is due to the absence of power to kill – if looks would suffice, we should have been dead long ago. It is a piece of rough civilisation to force some one into silence by the exhibition of physical savageness and the inspiring of fear. That cold glance which exalted persons employ towards their servants is also a relic of that caste division between man and man, a piece of rough antiquity; women, the preservers of ancient things, have also faithfully retained this *survival* of an ancient habit.

65.

Whither Honesty can Lead. – Somebody had the bad habit of occasionally talking quite frankly about the motives of his actions, which were as good and as bad as the motives of most men. He first gave offence, then aroused suspicion, was then gradually excluded from society and declared a social outlaw, until at last justice remembered such an abandoned creature, on occasions when it would otherwise have had no eyes, or would have closed them. The lack of power to hold his tongue concerning the common secret, and the irresponsible tendency to see what no one wishes to see – himself – brought him to a prison and an early death.

66.

Punishable, but never Punished. – Our crime against criminals lies in the fact that we treat them like rascals.

67.

Sancta simplicitas of Virtue. – Every virtue has its privileges; for example, that of contributing its own little faggot to the scaffold of every condemned man.

68.

Morality and Consequences. – It is not only the spectators of a deed who frequently judge of its morality or immorality according to its consequences, but the doer of the deed himself does so. For the motives and intentions are seldom sufficiently clear and simple, and sometimes memory itself seems clouded by the consequences of the deed, so that one ascribes the deed to false motives or looks upon unessential motives as essential. Success often gives an action the whole honest glamour of a good conscience; failure casts the shadow of remorse over the most estimable deed. Hence arises the well-known practice of the politician, who thinks, 'Only grant me success, with that I bring all honest souls over to my side and make myself honest in my own eyes.' In the same way success must replace a better argument. Many educated people still believe that the triumph of Christianity over Greek philosophy is a proof of the greater truthfulness of the former – although in this case it is only the coarser and more powerful that has triumphed over the more spiritual and delicate. Which possesses the greater truth may be seen from the fact that the awakening sciences have agreed with Epicurus' philosophy on point after point, but on point after point have rejected Christianity.

69.

Love and Justice. – Why do we over-estimate love to the disadvantage of justice, and say the most beautiful things about it, as if it were something very much higher than the latter? Is it not visibly more stupid than justice? Certainly, but precisely for that reason all the *pleasanter* for every one. It is blind, and possesses an abundant cornucopia, out of which it distributes its gifts to all, even if they do not deserve them, even if they express no thanks for them. It is as impartial as the rain, which, according to the Bible and experience, makes not only the unjust, but also occasionally the just wet through to the skin.

70.

Execution. – How is it that every execution offends us more than does a murder? It is the coldness of the judges, the painful preparations, the conviction that a human being is here being used as a warning to scare others. For the guilt is not punished, even if it existed – it lies with educators, parents, surroundings, in ourselves, not in the murderer – I mean the determining circumstances.

71.

Hope. – Pandora brought the box of ills and opened it. It was the gift of the gods to men, outwardly a beautiful and seductive gift, and called the Casket of Happiness. Out of it flew all the evils, living winged creatures, thence they now circulate and do men injury day and night. One single evil had not yet escaped from the box, and by the will of Zeus Pandora closed the lid and it remained within. Now for ever man has the casket of happiness in his house and thinks he holds a great treasure; it is at his disposal, he stretches out his hand for it whenever he desires; for he does not know the box which Pandora brought was the casket of evil, and he believes the ill which remains within to be the greatest blessing – it is hope. Zeus did not wish man, however much he might be tormented by the other evils, to fling away his life, but to go on letting himself be tormented again and again. Therefore he gives man hope – in reality it is the worst of all evils, because it prolongs the torments of man.

72.

The Degree of Moral Inflammability Unknown. – According to whether we have or have not had certain disturbing views and impressions – for instance, an unjustly executed, killed, or martyred father; a faithless wife; a cruel hostile attack – it depends whether our passions reach fever heat and influence our whole life or not. No one knows to what he may be driven by circumstances, pity, or indignation; he does not know the degree of his own inflammability. Miserable little circumstances make us miserable; it is generally not the quantity of experiences, but their quality, on which lower and higher man depends, in good and evil.

73

The Martyr in Spite of Himself. – There was a man belonging to a party who was too nervous and cowardly ever to contradict his comrades; they made use of him for everything, they demanded everything from him, because he was more afraid of the bad opinion of his companions than of death itself; his was a miserable, feeble soul. They recognised this, and on the ground of these qualities they made a hero of him, and finally even a martyr. Although the coward inwardly always said No, with his lips he always said Yes, even on the scaffold, when he was about to die for the opinions of his party; for beside him stood one of his old companions, who so tyrannised over him by word and look that he really suffered death in the most respectable manner, and has ever since been celebrated as a martyr and a great character.

74.

The Every-day Standard. – One will seldom go wrong if one attributes extreme actions to vanity, average ones to habit, and petty ones to fear.

75.

Misunderstanding Concerning Virtue. Whoever has known immorality in connection with pleasure, as is the case with a man who has a pleasure-seeking youth behind him, imagines that virtue must be connected with absence of pleasure. Whoever, on the contrary, has been much plagued by his passions and vices, longs to find in virtue peace and the soul's happiness. Hence it is possible for two virtuous persons not to understand each other at all.

76.

The Ascetic. – The ascetic makes a necessity of virtue.

77.

Transferring Honour from the Person to the Thing. – Deeds of love and sacrifice for the benefit of one's neighbour are generally honoured, wherever they are manifested. Thereby we multiply the valuation of things which are thus loved, or for which we sacrifice ourselves, although perhaps they are not worth much in themselves. A brave army is convinced of the cause for which it fights.

78.

Ambition a Substitute for the Moral Sense. – The moral sense must not be lacking in those natures which have no ambition. The ambitious manage without it, with almost the same results. For this reason the sons of unpretentious, unambitious families, when once they lose the moral sense, generally degenerate very quickly into complete scamps.

79.

Vanity Enriches. – How poor would be the human mind without vanity! Thus, however, it resembles a well-stocked and constantly replenished bazaar which attracts buyers of every kind. There they can find almost everything, obtain almost everything, provided that they bring the right sort of coin, namely admiration.

80.

Old Age and Death. – Apart from the commands of religion, the question may well be asked. Why is it more worthy for an old man who feels his powers decline, to await his slow exhaustion and extinction than with full consciousness to set a limit to his life? Suicide in this case is a perfectly natural, obvious action, which should justly arouse respect as a triumph of reason, and did arouse it in those times when the heads of Greek philosophy and the sturdiest patriots used to seek death through suicide. The seeking, on the contrary, to prolong existence from day to day, with anxious consultation of doctors and painful mode of living, without the power of drawing nearer to the actual aim of life, is far less worthy. Religion is rich in excuses to reply to the demand for suicide, and thus it ingratiates itself with those who wish to cling to life.

81.

Errors of the Sufferer and the Doer. – When a rich man deprives a poor man of a possession (for instance, a prince taking the sweetheart of a plebeian), an error arises in the mind of the poor man; he thinks that the rich man must be utterly infamous to take away from him the little that he has. But the rich man does not estimate so highly the value of a *single* possession, because he is accustomed to have many; hence he cannot imagine himself in the poor man's place, and does not commit nearly so great a wrong as the latter supposes. They each have a mistaken idea of the other. The injustice of the powerful, which, more than anything else, rouses indignation in history, is by no means so great as it appears. Alone the mere inherited consciousness of being a higher creation, with higher claims, produces a cold temperament, and leaves the conscience quiet; we all of us feel no injustice when the difference is very great between ourselves and another creature, and kill a fly, for instance, without any pricks of conscience. Therefore it was no sign of badness in Xerxes (whom even all Greeks describe as superlatively noble) when he took a son away from his father and had him cut in pieces, because he had expressed a nervous, ominous distrust of the whole campaign; in this case the individual is put out of the way like an unpleasant insect; he is too lowly to be allowed any longer to cause annoyance to a ruler of the world. Yes, every cruel man is not so cruel as the ill-treated one imagines; the idea of pain is not the same as its endurance. It is the same thing in the case of unjust judges, of the journalist who leads public opinion astray by small dishonesties. In all these cases cause and effect are surrounded by entirely different groups of feelings and thoughts; yet one unconsciously takes it for granted that doer and sufferer think and feel alike, and according to this supposition we measure the guilt of the one by the pain of the other.

82.

The Skin of the Soul. – As the bones, flesh, entrails, and blood-vessels are enclosed within a skin, which makes the aspect of man endurable, so the emotions and passions of the soul are enwrapped with vanity – it is the skin of the soul.

83.

The Sleep of Virtue. – When virtue has slept, it will arise again all the fresher.

84.

The Refinement of Shame. – People are not ashamed to think something foul, but they are ashamed when they think these foul thoughts are attributed to them.

85.

Malice is Rare. – Most people are far too much occupied with themselves to be malicious.

86.

The Tongue in the Balance. – We praise or blame according as the one or the other affords more opportunity for exhibiting our power of judgement.

87.

St. Luke xviii. 14, Improved. – He that humbleth himself wishes to be exalted.

88.

The Prevention of Suicide. – There is a certain right by which we may deprive a man of life, but none by which we may deprive him of death; this is mere cruelty.

89.

Vanity. – We care for the good opinion of men, firstly because they are useful to us, and then because we wish to please them (children their parents, pupils their teachers, and well-meaning people generally their fellow-men). Only where the good opinion of men is of importance to some one, apart from the advantage thereof or his wish to please, can we speak of vanity. In this case the man wishes to please himself, but at the expense of his fellow-men, either by misleading them into holding a false opinion about him, or by aiming at a degree of 'good opinion' which must be painful to every one else (by arousing envy). The individual usually wishes to corroborate the opinion he holds of himself by the opinion of others, and to strengthen it in his own eyes; but the strong habit of authority – a habit as old as man himself – induces many to support by authority their belief in themselves: that is to say, they accept it first from others; they trust the judgement of others more than their own. The interest in himself, the wish to please himself, attains to such a height in a vain man that he misleads others into having a false, all too elevated estimation of him, and yet nevertheless sets store by their authority – thus causing an error and yet believing in it. It must be confessed, therefore, that vain people do not wish to please others so much as themselves, and that they go so far therein as to neglect their advantage, for they often endeavour to prejudice their fellow men unfavourably, inimicably, enviously, consequently injuriously against themselves, merely in order to have pleasure in themselves, personal pleasure.

90.

The Limits of Human Love. – A man who as declared that another is an idiot and a bad companion, is angry when the latter eventually proves himself to be otherwise.

91.

Moralité larmoyante. – What a great deal of pleasure morality gives! Only think what a sea of pleasant tears has been shed over descriptions of noble and unselfish deeds! This charm of life would vanish if the belief in absolute irresponsibility were to obtain supremacy.

92.

The Origin of Justice. – Justice (equity) has its origin amongst powers which are fairly equal, as Thucydides (in the terrible dialogue between the Athenian and Melian ambassadors) rightly comprehended: that is to say, where there is no clearly recognisable supremacy, and where a conflict would be useless and would injure both sides, there arises the thought of coming to an understanding and settling the opposing claims; the character of *exchange* is the primary character of justice. Each party satisfies the other, as each obtains what he values more than the other. Each one receives that which he desires, as his own henceforth, and whatever is desired is received in return. Justice, therefore, is recompense and exchange based on the hypothesis of a fairly equal degree of power – thus, originally, revenge belongs to the province of justice, it is an exchange. Also gratitude. Justice naturally is based on the point of view of a judicious self-preservation, on the egoism, therefore, of that reflection, 'Why should I injure myself uselessly and perhaps not attain my aim after all?' So much about the *origin* of justice. Because man, according to his intellectual custom, has *forgotten* the original purpose of so-called just and reasonable actions, and particularly because for hundreds of years children have been taught to admire and imitate such actions, the idea has gradually arisen that such an action is un-egoistic; upon this idea, however, is based the high estimation in which it is held: which, moreover, like all valuations, is constantly growing, for something that is valued highly is striven after, imitated, multiplied, and increases, because the value of the output of toil and enthusiasm of each individual is added to the value of the thing itself. How little moral would the world look without this forgetfulness! A poet might say that God had placed forgetfulness as door-keeper in the temple of human dignity.

93.

The Right of the Weaker. – When any one submits under certain conditions to a greater power, as a besieged town for instance, the counter-condition is that one can destroy one's self, burn the town, and so cause the mighty one a great loss. Therefore there is a kind of *equalisation* here, on the basis of which rights may be determined. The enemy has his advantage in maintaining it. In so far there are also rights between slaves and masters, that is, precisely so far as the possession of the slave is useful and important to his master. The *right* originally extends *so far as* one *appears* to be valuable to the other, essentially unlosable, unconquerable, and so forth. In so far the weaker one also has rights, but lesser ones. Hence the famous *unusquisque tantum juris habet, quantum, potentia valet* (or more exactly, *quantum, potentia valere creditur*).

94.

The Three Phases of Hitherto Existing Morality. – It is the first sign that the animal has become man when its actions no longer have regard only to momentary welfare, but to what is enduring, when it grows *useful* and *practical*; there the free rule of reason first breaks out. A still higher step is reached when he acts according to the principle of *honour*; by this means he brings himself into order, submits to common feelings, and that exalts him still higher over the phase in which he was led only by the idea of usefulness from a personal point of view; he respects and wishes to be respected, i.e. he understands usefulness as dependent upon what he thinks of others and what others think of him. Eventually he acts, on the highest step of the *hitherto* existing morality, according to *his* standard of things and men; he himself decides for himself and others what is honourable, what is useful; he has become the law-giver of opinions, in accordance with the ever more highly developed idea of what is useful and honourable. Knowledge enables him to place that which is most useful, that is to say the general, enduring usefulness, above the personal, the honourable recognition of general, enduring validity above the momentary; he lives and acts as a collective individual.

95.

The Morality of the Mature Individual. – The impersonal has hitherto been looked upon as the actual distinguishing mark of moral action; and it has been pointed out that in the beginning it was in consideration of the common good that all impersonal actions were praised and distinguished. Is not an important change in these views impending, now when it is more and more recognised that it is precisely in the most *personal* possible considerations that the common good is the greatest, so that a *strictly personal* action now best illustrates the present idea of morality, as utility for the mass? To make a whole *personality* out of ourselves, and in all that we do to keep that personality's *highest good* in view, carries us further than those sympathetic emotions and actions for the benefit of others. We all still suffer, certainly, from the too small consideration of the personal in us; it is badly developed – let us admit it; rather has our mind been forcibly drawn away from it and offered as a sacrifice to the State, to science, or to those who stand in need of help, as if it were the bad part which must be sacrificed. We are still willing to work for our fellow-men, but only so far as we find our own greatest advantage in this work, no more and no less. It is only a question of what we understand as *our advantage*, the unripe, undeveloped, crude individual will understand it in the crudest way.

96.

Custom and Morality. – To be moral, correct, and virtuous is to be obedient to an old-established law and custom. Whether we submit with difficulty or willingly is immaterial, enough that we do so. He is called 'good' who, as if naturally, after long precedent, easily and willingly, therefore, does what is right, according to whatever this may be (as, for instance, taking revenge, if to take revenge be considered as right, as amongst the ancient Greeks). He is called good because he is good 'for something'; but as goodwill, pity, consideration, moderation, and such like, have come, with the change in manners, to be looked upon as 'good for something', as useful, the good-natured and helpful have, later on, come to be distinguished specially as 'good'. (In the beginning other and more important kinds of usefulness stood in the foreground.) To be evil is to be 'not moral' (immoral), to be immoral is to be in opposition to tradition, however sensible or stupid it may be; injury to the community (the 'neighbour' being understood thereby) has, however, been looked upon by the social laws of all different ages as being eminently the actual 'immorality', so that now at the word 'evil' we immediately think of voluntary injury to one's neighbour. The fundamental antithesis which has taught man the distinction between moral and immoral, between good and evil, is not the 'egoistic' and 'unegoistic', but the being bound to the tradition, law, and solution thereof. How the tradition has *arisen* is immaterial, at all events without regard to good and evil or any immanent categorical imperative, but above all for the purpose of preserving a *community*, a generation, an association, a people; every superstitious custom that has arisen on account of some falsely explained accident, creates a tradition, which it is moral to follow; to separate one's self from it is dangerous, but more dangerous for the *community* than for the individual (because the Godhead punishes the community for every outrage and every violation of its rights, and the individual only in proportion). Now every tradition grows continually more venerable, the farther off lies its origin, the more this is lost sight of; the veneration paid it accumulates from generation to generation, the tradition at last becomes holy and excites awe; and thus in any case the morality of piety is a much older morality than that which requires un-egoistic actions.

97.

Pleasure in Traditional Custom. – An important species of pleasure, and therewith the source of morality, arises out of habit. Man does what is habitual to him more easily, better, and therefore more willingly; he feels a pleasure therein, and knows from experience that the habitual has been tested, and is therefore useful; a custom that we can live with is proved to be wholesome and advantageous in contrast to all new and not yet tested experiments. According to this, morality is the union of the pleasant and the useful; moreover, it requires no reflection. As soon as man can use compulsion, he uses it to introduce and enforce his *customs*; for in his eyes they are proved as the wisdom of life. In the same way a company of individuals compels each single one to adopt the same customs. Here the inference is wrong; because we feel at ease with a morality, or at least because we are able to carry on existence with it, therefore this morality is necessary, for it seems to be the *only* possibility of feeling at ease; the ease of life seems to grow out of it alone. This comprehension of the habitual as a necessity of existence is pursued even to the smallest details of custom – as insight into genuine causality is very small with lower peoples and civilisations, they take precautions with superstitious fear that everything should go in its same groove; even where custom is difficult, hard, and burdensome, it is preserved on account of its apparent highest usefulness. It is not known that the same degree of well-being can also exist with other customs, and that even higher degrees may be attained. We become aware, however, that all customs, even the hardest, grow pleasanter and milder with time, and that the severest way of life may become a habit and therefore a pleasure.

98.

Pleasure and Social Instinct. – Out of his relations with other men, man obtains a new species of *pleasure* in addition to those pleasurable sensations which he derives from himself; whereby he greatly increases the scope of enjoyment. Perhaps he has already taken too many of the pleasures of this sphere from animals, which visibly feel pleasure when they play with each other, especially the mother with her young. Then consider the sexual relations, which make almost every female interesting to a male with regard to pleasure, and *vice versa*. The feeling of pleasure on the basis of human relations generally makes man better; joy in common, pleasure enjoyed together is increased, it gives the individual security, makes him good-tempered, and dispels mistrust and envy, for we feel ourselves at ease and see others at ease. *Similar manifestations of pleasure* awaken the idea of the same sensations, the feeling of being like something; a like effect is produced by common sufferings, the same bad weather, dangers, enemies. Upon this foundation is based the oldest alliance, the object of which is the mutual obviating and averting of a threatening danger for the benefit of each individual. And thus the social instinct grows out of pleasure.

99.

The Innocent Side of so-called Evil Actions. – All 'evil' actions are prompted by the instinct of preservation, or, more exactly, by the desire for pleasure and the avoidance of pain on the part of the individual; thus prompted, but not evil. 'To cause pain *per se*' *does not exist*, except in the brains of philosophers, neither does 'to give pleasure *per se*' (pity in Schopenhauer's meaning). In the social condition *before* the State we kill the creature, be it ape or man, who tries to take from us the fruit of a tree when we are hungry and approach the tree, as we should still do with animals in inhospitable countries. The evil actions which now most rouse our indignation, are based upon the error that he who causes them has a free will, that he had the option, therefore, of not doing us this injury. This belief in option arouses hatred, desire for revenge, spite, and the deterioration of the whole imagination, while we are much less angry with an animal because we consider it irresponsible. To do injury, not from the instinct of preservation, but as *requital*, is the consequence of a false judgement and therefore equally innocent. The individual can in the condition which lies before the State, act sternly and cruelly towards other creatures for the purpose of *terrifying*, to establish his existence firmly by such terrifying proofs of his power. Thus act the violent, the mighty, the original founders of States, who subdue the weaker to themselves. They have the right to do so, such as the State still takes for itself; or rather, there is no right that can hinder this. The ground for all morality can only be made ready when a stronger individual or a collective individual, for instance society or the State, subdues the single individuals, draws them out of their singleness, and forms them into an association. *Compulsion* precedes morality, indeed morality itself is compulsion for a time, to which one submits for the avoidance of pain. Later on it becomes custom – later still, free obedience, and finally almost instinct – then, like everything long accustomed and natural, it is connected with pleasure – and is henceforth called *virtue*.

100.

Shame. – Shame exists everywhere where there is a 'mystery'; this, however, is a religious idea, which was widely extended in the older times of human civilisation. Everywhere were found bounded domains to which access was forbidden by divine right, except under certain conditions; at first locally, as, for example, certain spots that ought not to be trodden by the feet of the uninitiated, in the neighbourhood of which these latter experienced horror and fear. This feeling was a good deal carried over into other relations, for instance, the sex relations, which, as a privilege and αδυτον of riper years, had to be withheld from the knowledge of the young for their advantage, relations for the protection and sanctification of which many gods were invented and were set up as guardians in the nuptial chamber. (In Turkish this room is on this account called harem, 'sanctuary', and is distinguished with the same name, therefore, that is used for the entrance courts of the mosques.) Thus the kingdom is as a centre from which radiate power and glory, to the subjects a mystery full of secrecy and shame, of which many after-effects may still be felt among nations which otherwise do not by any means belong to the bashful type. Similarly, the whole world of inner conditions, the so-called 'soul', is still a mystery for all who are not philosophers, after it has been looked upon for endless ages as of divine origin and as worthy of divine intercourse; according to this it is an αδυτον and arouses shame.

101.

Judge not. – In considering earlier periods, care must be taken not to fall into unjust abuse. The injustice in slavery, the cruelty in the suppression of persons and nations, is not to be measured by our standard. For the instinct of justice was not then so far developed. Who dares to reproach the Genevese Calvin with the burning of the physician Servet? It was an action following and resulting from his convictions, and in the same way the Inquisition had a good right; only the ruling views were false, and produced a result which seems hard to us because those views have now grown strange to us. Besides, what is the burning of a single individual compared with eternal pains of hell for almost all! And yet this idea was universal at that time, without essentially injuring by its dreadfulness the conception of a God. With us, too, political sectarians are hardly and cruelly treated, but because one is accustomed to believe in the necessity of the State, the cruelty is not so deeply felt here as it is where we repudiate the views. Cruelty to animals in children and Italians is due to ignorance, i.e. the animal, through the interests of Church teaching, has been placed too far behind man. Much that is dreadful and inhuman in history, much that one hardly likes to believe, is mitigated by the reflection that the one who commands and the one who carries out are different persons – the former does not behold the right and therefore does not experience the strong impression on the imagination; the latter obeys a superior and therefore feels no responsibility. Most princes and military heads, through lack of imagination, easily appear hard and cruel without really being so. *Egoism is not evil,* because the idea of the 'neighbour' – the word is of Christian origin and does not represent the truth – is very weak in us; and we feel ourselves almost as free and irresponsible towards him as towards plants and stones. We have yet to *learn* that others suffer, and this can never be completely learnt.

102.

'Man always Acts Rightly.' – We do not complain of nature as immoral because it sends a thunderstorm and makes us wet – why do we call those who injure us immoral? Because in the latter case we take for granted a free will functioning voluntarily; in the former we see necessity. But this distinction is an error. Thus we do not call even intentional injury immoral in all circumstances; for instance, we kill a fly unhesitatingly and intentionally, only because its buzzing annoys us; we punish a criminal intentionally and hurt him in order to protect ourselves and society. In the first case it is the individual who, in order to preserve himself, or even to protect himself from worry, does intentional injury; in the second case it is the State. All morals allow intentional injury *in the case of necessity*, that is, when it is a matter of *self-preservation*! But these two points of view suffice to explain all evil actions committed by men against men, we are desirous of obtaining pleasure or avoiding pain; in any case it is always a question of self-preservation. Socrates and Plato are right: whatever man does he always does well, that is, he does that which seems to him good (useful) according to the degree of his intellect, the particular standard of his reasonableness.

103.

The Harmlessness of Malice. – The aim of malice is *not* the suffering of others in itself, but our own enjoyment; for instance, as the feeling of revenge, or stronger nervous excitement. All teasing, even, shows the pleasure it gives to exercise our power on others and bring it to an enjoyable feeling of preponderance. Is it *immoral* to taste pleasure at the expense of another's pain? Is malicious joy[5] devilish, as Schopenhauer says? We give ourselves pleasure in nature by breaking off twigs, loosening stones, fighting with wild animals, and do this in

5 This is the untranslatable word *Schadenfreude*, which means joy at the misfortune of others. – J. M. K.

order to become thereby conscious of our strength. Is the knowledge, therefore, that another suffers through us, the same thing concerning which we otherwise feel irresponsible, supposed to make us immoral? But if we did not know this we would not thereby have the enjoyment of our own superiority, which can only *manifest* itself by the suffering of others, for instance in teasing. All pleasure *per se* is neither good nor evil; whence should come the decision that in order to have pleasure ourselves we may not cause displeasure to others? From the point of view of usefulness alone, that is, out of consideration for the *consequences*, for *possible* displeasure, when the injured one or the replacing State gives the expectation of resentment and revenge: this only can have been the original reason for denying ourselves such actions. *Pity* aims just as little at the pleasure of others as malice at the pain of others *per se*. For it contains at least two (perhaps many more) elements of a personal pleasure, and is so far self-gratification; in the first place as the pleasure of emotion, which is the kind of pity that exists in tragedy, and then, when it impels to action, as the pleasure of satisfaction in the exercise of power. If, besides this, a suffering person is very dear to us, we lift a sorrow from ourselves by the exercise of sympathetic actions. Except by a few philosophers, pity has always been placed very low in the scale of moral feelings, and rightly so.

104.

Self-defence. – If self-defence is allowed to pass as moral, then almost all manifestations of the so-called immoral egoism must also stand; men injure, rob, or kill in order to preserve or defend themselves, to prevent personal injury; they lie where cunning and dissimulation are the right means of self-preservation. *Intentional injury*, when our existence or safety (preservation of our comfort) is concerned, is conceded to be moral; the State itself injures, according to this point of view, when it punishes. In unintentional injury, of course, there can be nothing immoral, that is ruled by chance. Is there, then, a kind of intentional injury where our existence or the preservation of our comfort is *not* concerned? Is there an injuring out of pure *malice*, for instance in cruelty? If one does not know how much an action hurts, it is no deed of malice; thus the child is not malicious towards the animal, not evil; he examines and destroys it like a toy. But do we ever know entirely how an action hurts another? As far as our nervous system extends we protect ourselves from pain; if it extended farther, to our fellow-men, namely, we should do no one an injury (except in such cases as we injure ourselves, where we cut ourselves for the sake of cure, tire and exert ourselves for the sake of health). We *conclude* by analogy that something hurts somebody, and through memory and the strength of imagination we may suffer from it ourselves. But still what a difference there is between toothache and the pain (pity) that the sight of toothache calls forth! Therefore, in injury out of so-called malice the *degree* of pain produced is always unknown to us; but inasmuch as there is *pleasure* in the action (the feeling of one's own power, one's own strong excitement), the action is committed, in order to preserve the comfort of the individual, and is regarded, therefore, from a similar point of view as defence and falsehood in necessity. No life without pleasure; the struggle for pleasure is the struggle for life. Whether the individual so fights this fight that men call him good, or so that they call him evil, is determined by the measure and the constitution of his *intellect*.

105.

Recompensing Justice. – Whoever has completely comprehended the doctrine of absolute irresponsibility can no longer include the so-called punishing and recompensing justice in the idea of justice, should this consist of giving to each man his due. For he who is punished does not deserve the punishment, he is only used as a means of henceforth warning away from certain actions; equally so, he who is rewarded does not merit this reward, he could not act otherwise than he did. Therefore the reward is meant only as an encouragement to him and others, to provide a motive for subsequent actions; words of praise are flung to the runners on the course, not to the one who has reached the goal. Neither punishment nor reward is anything that comes to one as *one's own*; they are given from motives of usefulness, without one having a right to claim them. Hence we must say, 'The wise man gives no reward because the deed has been well done,' just as we have said, 'The wise man does not punish because evil has been committed, but in order that evil shall not be committed.' If punishment and reward no longer existed, then the strongest motives which deter men from certain actions and impel them to certain other actions, would also no longer exist; the needs of mankind require their continuance; and inasmuch as punishment and reward, blame and praise, work most sensibly on vanity, the same need requires the continuance of vanity.

106.

At the Waterfall. – In looking at a waterfall we imagine that there is freedom of will and fancy in the countless turnings, twistings, and breakings of the waves; but everything is compulsory, every movement can be mathematically calculated. So it is also with human actions; one would have to be able to calculate every single action beforehand if one were all-knowing; equally so all progress of knowledge, every error, all malice. The one who acts certainly labours under the illusion of voluntariness; if the world's wheel were to stand still for a moment and an all-knowing, calculating reason were there to make use of this pause, it could foretell the future of every creature to the remotest times, and mark out every track upon which that wheel would continue to roll. The delusion of the acting agent about himself, the supposition of a free will, belongs to this mechanism which still remains to be calculated.

107.

Irresponsibility and Innocence. – The complete irresponsibility of man for his actions and his nature is the bitterest drop which he who understands must swallow if he was accustomed to see the patent of nobility of his humanity in responsibility and duty. All his valuations, distinctions, disinclinations, are thereby deprived of value and become false – his deepest feeling for the sufferer and the hero was based on an error; he may no longer either praise or blame, for it is absurd to praise and blame nature and necessity. In the same way as he loves a fine work of art, but does not praise it, because it can do nothing for itself; in the same way as he regards plants, so must he regard his own actions and those of mankind. He can admire strength, beauty, abundance, in themselves; but must find no merit therein – the chemical progress and the strife of the elements, the torments of the sick person who thirsts after recovery, are all equally as little merits as those struggles of the soul and states of distress in which we are torn hither and thither by different impulses until we finally decide for the strongest – as we say (but in reality it is the strongest motive which decides for us). All these motives, however, whatever fine names we may give them, have all grown out of the same root, in which we believe the evil poisons to be situated; between good and evil actions there is no difference of species, but at most of degree. Good actions are sublimated evil ones; evil actions are vulgarised and stupefied good ones. The single longing of the individual for self-gratification (together with the fear of losing it) satisfies itself in all circumstances: man may act as he can, that is as he must, be it in deeds of vanity, revenge, pleasure, usefulness, malice, cunning; be it in deeds of sacrifice, of pity, of knowledge. The degrees of the power of judgement determine whither any one lets himself be drawn through this longing; to every society, to every individual, a scale of possessions is continually present, according to which he determines his actions and judges those of others. But this standard changes constantly; many actions are called evil and are only stupid, because the degree of intelligence which decided for them was very low. In a certain sense, even, *all* actions are still stupid; for the highest degree of human intelligence which can now be attained will assuredly be yet surpassed, and then, in a retrospect, all our actions and judgements will appear as limited and hasty as the actions and judgements of primitive wild peoples now appear limited and hasty to us. To recognise all this may be deeply painful, but consolation comes after; such pains are the pangs of birth. The butterfly wants to break through its chrysalis: it rends and tears it, and is then blinded and confused by the unaccustomed light, the kingdom of liberty. In such people as are *capable* of such sadness – and how few are! – the first experiment made is to see whether *mankind can change itself* from a *moral* into a *wise* mankind. The sun of a new gospel throws its rays upon the highest point in the soul of each single individual, then the mists gather thicker than ever, and the brightest light and the dreariest shadow lie side by side. Everything is necessity – so says the new knowledge, and this knowledge itself is necessity. Everything is innocence, and knowledge is the road to insight into this innocence.

Are pleasure, egoism, vanity *necessary* for the production of the moral phenomena and their highest result, the sense for truth and justice in knowledge; were error and the confusion of the imagination the only means through which mankind could raise itself gradually to this degree of self-enlightenment and self-liberation – who would dare to undervalue these means? Who would dare to be sad if he perceived the goal to which those roads led? Everything in the domain of morality has evolved, is changeable, unstable, everything is dissolved, it is true; but *everything is also streaming towards one goal*. Even if the inherited habit of erroneous valuation, love and hatred, continue to reign in us, yet under the influence of growing knowledge it will become weaker; a new habit, that of comprehension, of not loving, not hating, of overlooking, is gradually implanting itself in us upon the same ground, and in thousands of years will perhaps be powerful enough to give humanity the strength to produce wise, innocent (consciously innocent) men, as it now produces unwise, guilt-conscious men – *that is the necessary preliminary step, not its opposite*.

THIRD DIVISION.
THE RELIGIOUS LIFE.

108.

The Double Fight against Evil. When misfortune overtakes us we can either pass over it so lightly that its cause is removed, or so that the result which it has on our temperament is altered, through a changing, therefore, of the evil into a good, the utility of which is perhaps not visible until later on. Religion and art (also metaphysical philosophy) work upon the changing of the temperament, partly through the changing of our judgement on events (for instance, with the help of the phrase 'whom the Lord loveth He chasteneth'), partly through the awakening of a pleasure in pain, in emotion generally (whence the tragic art takes its starting-point). The more a man is inclined to twist and arrange meanings the less he will grasp the causes of evil and disperse them; the momentary mitigation and influence of a narcotic, as for example in toothache, suffices him even in more serious sufferings. The more the dominion of creeds and all arts dispense with narcotics, the more strictly men attend to the actual removing of the evil, which is certainly bad for writers of tragedy; for the material for tragedy is growing scarcer because the domain of pitiless, inexorable fate is growing ever narrower – but worse still for the priests, for they have hitherto lived on the narcotisation of human woes.

109.

Sorrow is Knowledge. – How greatly we should like to exchange the false assertions of the priests, that there is a god who desires good from us, a guardian and witness of every action, every moment, every thought, who loves us and seeks our welfare in all misfortune – how greatly we would like to exchange these ideas for truths which would be just as healing, pacifying and beneficial as those errors! But there are no such truths; at most philosophy can oppose to them metaphysical appearances (at bottom also untruths). The tragedy consists in the fact that we cannot believe those dogmas of religion and metaphysics, if we have strict methods of truth in heart and brain: on the other hand, mankind has, through development, become so delicate, irritable and suffering, that it has need of the highest means of healing and consolation; whence also the danger arises that man would bleed to death from recognised truth, or, more correctly, from discovered error. Byron has expressed this in the immortal lines:

> Sorrow is knowledge: they who know the most
> Must mourn the deepest o'er the fatal truth.
> The Tree of Knowledge is not that of Life.

For such troubles there is no better help than to recall the stately levity of Horace, at least for the worst hours and eclipses of the soul, and to say with him:

> *. . . quid aeternis minorem*
> *consiliis animum fatigas?*
> *cur non sub alta vel platano vel hac*
> *pinu jacentes.*[6]

But assuredly frivolity or melancholy of every degree is better than a romantic retrospection and desertion of the flag, an approach to Christianity in any form; for according to the present condition of knowledge it is absolutely impossible to approach it without hopelessly soiling our *intellectual conscience* and giving ourselves away to ourselves and others. Those pains may be unpleasant enough, but we cannot become leaders and educators of mankind without pain; and woe to him who would wish to attempt this and no longer have that clear conscience!

110.

The Truth in Religion. – In the period of rationalism justice was not done to the importance of religion, of that there is no doubt, but equally there is no doubt that in the reaction that followed this rationalism justice was far overstepped; for religions were treated lovingly, even amorously, and, for instance, a deeper, even the very deepest, understanding of the world was ascribed to them; which science has only to strip of its dogmatic garment in order to possess

6 Why harass with eternal designs a mind too weak to compass them? Why do we not, as we lie beneath a lofty plane-tree or this pine [drink while we may]? HOR., Odes II. ii. 11-14. – J. M. K.

the 'truth' in unmythical form. Religions should, therefore – this was the opinion of all opposers of rationalism – *sensu allegorico*, with all consideration for the understanding of the masses, give utterance to that ancient wisdom which is wisdom itself, inasmuch as all true science of later times has always led up to it instead of away from it, so that between the oldest wisdom of mankind and all later harmonies similarity of discernment and a progress of knowledge – in case one should wish to speak of such a thing – rests not upon the nature but upon the way of communicating it. This whole conception of religion and science is thoroughly erroneous, and none would still dare to profess it if Schopenhauer's eloquence had not taken it under its protection; this resonant eloquence which, however, only reached its hearers a generation later. As surely as from Schopenhauer's religious-moral interpretations of men and the world much may be gained for the understanding of the Christian and other religions, so surely also is he mistaken about the *value of religion for knowledge*. Therein he himself was only a too docile pupil of the scientific teachers of his time, who all worshipped romanticism and had forsworn the spirit of enlightenment; had he been born in our present age he could not possibly have talked about the *sensus allegoricus* of religion; he would much rather have given honour to truth, as he used to do, with the words, '*no religion, direct or indirect, either as dogma or as allegory, has ever contained a truth*'. For each has been born of fear and necessity, through the byways of reason did it slip into existence; once, perhaps, when imperilled by science, some philosophic doctrine has lied itself into its system in order that it may be found there later, but this is a theological trick of the time when a religion already doubts itself. These tricks of theology (which certainly were practised in the early days of Christianity, as the religion of a scholarly period steeped in philosophy) have led to that superstition of the *sensus allegoricus*, but yet more the habits of the philosophers (especially the half-natures, the poetical philosophers and the philosophising artists), to treat all the sensations which they discovered in *themselves* as the fundamental nature of man in general, and hence to allow their own religious feelings an important influence in the building up of their systems. As philosophers frequently philosophised under the custom of religious habits, or at least under the anciently inherited power of that 'metaphysical need', they developed doctrinal opinions which really bore a great resemblance to the Jewish or Christian or Indian religious views – a resemblance, namely, such as children usually bear to their mothers, only that in this case the fathers were not clear about that motherhood, as happens sometimes – but in their innocence romanced about a family likeness between all religion and science. In reality, between religions and real science there exists neither relationship nor friendship, nor even enmity; they live on different planets. Every philosophy which shows a religious comet's tail shining in the darkness of its last prospects makes all the science it contains suspicious; all this is presumably also religion, even though in the guise of science. Moreover, if all nations were to agree about certain religious matters, for instance the existence of a God (which, it may be remarked, is not the case with regard to this point), this would only be an argument *against* those affirmed matters, for instance the existence of a God; the *consensus gentium* and *hominum* in general can only take place in case of a huge folly. On the other hand, there is no *consensus omnium sapientium*, with regard to any single thing, with that exception mentioned in Goethe's lines:

> 'Alle die Weisesten aller der Zeiten
> Lacheln und winken und stimmen mit ein:
> Thoricht, auf Bess'rung der Thoren zu barren!
> Kinder der Klugheit, o habet die Narren
> Eben zum Narren auch, wie sich's gehort!'[7]

Spoken without verse and rhyme and applied to our case, the *consensus sapientium* consists in this: that the *consensus gentium* counts as a folly.

---

7 'All greatest sages of all latest ages
Will chuckle and slily agree,
'Tis folly to wait till a fool's empty pate
Has learnt to be knowing and free:
So children of wisdom, make use of the fools
And use them whenever you can as your tools.' – J.M.K.

111.

The Origin of the Religious Cult. – If we go back to the times in which the religious life flourished to the greatest extent, we find a fundamental conviction, which we now no longer share, and whereby the doors leading to a religious life are closed to us once for all – it concerns Nature and intercourse with her. In those times people knew nothing of natural laws; neither for earth nor for heaven is there a 'must'; a season, the sunshine, the rain may come or may not come. In short, every idea of natural causality is lacking. When one rows, it is not the rowing that moves the boat, but rowing is only a magical ceremony by which one compels a *daemon* to move the boat. All maladies, even death itself, are the result of magical influences. Illness and death never happen naturally; the whole conception of 'natural sequence' is lacking – it dawned first amongst the older Greeks, that is, in a very late phase of humanity, in the conception of *Moira*, enthroned above the gods. When a man shoots with a bow, there is still always present an irrational hand and strength; if the wells suddenly dry up, men think first of subterranean *daemons* and their tricks; it must be the arrow of a god beneath whose invisible blow a man suddenly sinks down. In India (says Lubbock) a carpenter is accustomed to offer sacrifice to his hammer, his hatchet, and the rest of his tools; in the same way a Brahmin treats the pen with which he writes, a soldier the weapons he requires in the field of battle, a mason his trowel, a labourer his plough. In the imagination of religious people all nature is a summary of the actions of conscious and voluntary creatures, an enormous complex of *arbitrariness*. No conclusion may be drawn with regard to everything that is outside of us, that anything will *be* so and so, *must* be so and so; the approximately sure, reliable are *we* – man is the *rule*, nature is *irregularity* – this theory contains the fundamental conviction which obtains in rude, religiously productive primitive civilisations. We latter-day men feel just the contrary – the richer man now feels himself inwardly, the more polyphonous is the music and the noise of his soul the more powerfully the symmetry of nature works upon him; we all recognise with Goethe the great means in nature for the appeasing of the modern soul; we listen to the pendulum swing of this greatest of clocks with a longing for rest, for home and tranquillity, as if we could absorb this symmetry into ourselves and could only thereby arrive at the enjoyment of ourselves. Formerly it was otherwise; if we consider the rude, early condition of nations, or contemplate present-day savages at close quarters, we find them most strongly influenced by *law* and by *tradition*: the individual is almost automatically bound to them, and moves with the uniformity of a pendulum. To him Nature – uncomprehended, terrible, mysterious Nature – must appear as the *sphere of liberty*, of voluntariness, of the higher power, even as a superhuman degree of existence, as God. In those times and conditions, however, every individual felt that his existence, his happiness, and that of the family and the State, and the success of all undertakings, depended on those spontaneities of nature; certain natural events must appear at the right time, others be absent at the right time. How can one have any influence on these terrible unknown things, how can one bind the sphere of liberty? Thus he asks himself, thus he inquires anxiously; is there, then, no means of making those powers as regular through tradition and law as you are yourself? The aim of those who believe in magic and miracles is to *impose a law on nature* – and, briefly, the religious cult is a result of this aim. The problem which those people have set themselves is closely related to this: how can the *weaker* race dictate laws to the *stronger*, rule it, and guide its actions (in relation to the weaker)? One would first remember the most harmless sort of compulsion, that compulsion which one exercises when one has gained any one's affection. By imploring and praying, by submission, by the obligation of regular taxes and gifts, by flattering glorifications, it is also possible to exercise an influence upon the powers of nature, inasmuch as one gains the affections; love binds and becomes bound. Then one can make compacts by which one is mutually bound to a certain behaviour, where one gives pledges and exchanges vows. But far more important is a species of more forcible compulsion, by magic and witchcraft. As with the sorcerer's help man is able to injure a more powerful enemy and keep him in fear, as the love-charm works at a distance, so the weaker man believes he can influence the mightier spirits of nature. The principal thing in all witchcraft is that we must get into our possession something that belongs to some one, hair, nails, food from their table, even their portrait, their name. With such apparatus we can then practise sorcery; for the fundamental rule is, to everything spiritual there belongs something corporeal; with the help of this we are able to bind the spirit, to injure it, and destroy it; the corporeal furnishes the handles with which we can grasp the spiritual. As man controls man, so he controls some natural spirit or other; for this has also its corporeal part by which it may be grasped. The tree and, compared with it, the seed from which it sprang – this enigmatical contrast seems to prove that the same spirit embodied itself in both forms, now small, now large. A stone that begins to roll suddenly is the body in which a spirit operates; if there is an enormous rock lying on a lonely heath it seems impossible to conceive human strength sufficient to have brought it there, consequently the stone must have moved there by itself, that is, it must be possessed by a spirit. Everything that has a body is susceptible to witchcraft, therefore also the natural spirits. If a god is bound to his image we can use the most direct compulsion against him (through refusal of sacrificial food, scourging, binding in fetters, and so on). In order to obtain by force the missing favour of their god the lower classes in China wind cords round the image of the one who has left them in the lurch, pull it down and drag it through the streets in the dust and the dirt: 'You dog of a spirit,' they say, 'we gave you a magnificent temple to live in, we gilded you prettily, we fed you well, we offered you sacrifice, and yet you are so ungrateful.' Similar forcible measures against pictures of the Saints and Virgin when they refused to do their duty in pestilence or drought, have been witnessed even during the present century in Catholic countries. Through all these magic relations to nature, countless ceremonies have been called into life; and at last, when the confusion has grown too great, an endeavour has been made to order and systematise them, in order that the favourable course of the whole progress of nature, i.e. of the great succession of the seasons, may seem to be guaranteed by a corresponding course of a system of procedure. The essence of the religious cult is to determine and confine nature to human advantage, *to impress it with a legality, therefore, which it did not originally possess*; while at the present time we wish to recognise the legality of nature in order to adapt ourselves to it. In short, then, the religious cult is based upon the representations of sorcery between man and man – and the sorcerer is older than the priest. But it is likewise based upon other and nobler representations; it premises the sympathetic relation of man to man, the presence of goodwill, gratitude, the hearing of pleaders, of treaties between enemies, the granting of pledges, and the claim to the protection of property. In very low stages of civilisation man does not stand in the relation of a helpless slave to nature, he is *not* necessarily its involuntary bondsman. In the *Greek* grade of religion, particularly in relation to the Olympian gods, there may even be imagined a common life between two castes, a nobler and more powerful one, and one less noble; but in their origin both belong to each other somehow, and are of one kind; they need not be ashamed of each other. That is the nobility of the Greek religion.

112.

At the Sight of certain Antique Sacrificial Implements. – The fact of how many feelings are lost to us may be seen, for instance, in the mingling of the *droll*, even of the *obscene*, with the religious feeling. The sensation of the possibility of this mixture vanishes, we only comprehend historically that it existed in the feasts of Demeter and Dionysus, in the Christian Easter plays and Mysteries. But we also know that which is noble in alliance with burlesque and such like, the touching mingled with the laughable, which perhaps a later age will not be able to understand.

113.

Christianity as Antiquity. – When on a Sunday morning we hear the old bells ring out, we ask ourselves, 'Is it possible! This is done on account of a Jew crucified two thousand years ago who said he was the Son of God. The proof of such an assertion is wanting.' Certainly in our times the Christian religion is an antiquity that dates from very early ages, and the fact that its assertions are still believed, when otherwise all claims are subjected to such strict examination, is perhaps the oldest part of this heritage. A God who creates a son from a mortal woman; a sage who requires that man should no longer work, no longer judge, but should pay attention to the signs of the approaching end of the world; a justice that accepts an innocent being as a substitute in sacrifice; one who commands his disciples to drink his blood; prayers for miraculous intervention; sins committed against a God and atoned for through a God; the fear of a future to which death is the portal; the form of the cross in an age which no longer knows the signification and the shame of the cross,[8] how terrible all this appears to us, as if risen from the grave of the ancient past! Is it credible that such things are still believed?

114.

What is un-Greek in Christianity. – The Greeks did not regard the Homeric gods as raised above them like masters, nor themselves as being under them like servants, as the Jews did. They only saw, as in a mirror, the most perfect examples of their own caste; an ideal, therefore, and not an opposite of their own nature. There is a feeling of relationship, a mutual interest arises, a kind of symmachy. Man thinks highly of himself when he gives himself such gods, and places himself in a relation like that of the lower nobility towards the higher; while the Italian nations hold a genuine peasant-faith, with perpetual fear of evil and mischievous powers and tormenting spirits. Wherever the Olympian gods retreated into the background, Greek life was more sombre and more anxious. Christianity, on the contrary, oppressed man and crushed him utterly, sinking him as if in deep mire; then into the feeling of absolute depravity it suddenly threw the light of divine mercy, so that the surprised man, dazzled by forgiveness, gave a cry of joy and for a moment believed that he bore all heaven within himself. All psychological feelings of Christianity work upon this unhealthy excess of sentiment, and upon the deep corruption of head and heart it necessitates; it desires to destroy, break, stupefy, confuse – only one thing it does not desire, namely *moderation*, and therefore it is in the deepest sense barbaric, Asiatic, ignoble and un-Greek.

115.

To be Religious with Advantage. – There are sober and industrious people on whom religion is embroidered like a hem of higher humanity; these do well to remain religious, it beautifies them. All people who do not understand some kind of trade in weapons – tongue and pen included as weapons – become servile; for such the

8 It may be remembered that the cross was the gallows of the ancient world. – J. M. K.

Christian religion is very useful, for then servility assumes the appearance of Christian virtues and is surprisingly beautified. People to whom their daily life appears too empty and monotonous easily grow religious; this is comprehensible and excusable, only they have no right to demand religious sentiments from those whose daily life is not empty and monotonous.[9]

116.

The Commonplace Christian. – If Christianity were right, with its theories of an avenging God, of general sinfulness, of redemption, and the danger of eternal damnation, it would be a sign of weak intellect and lack of character *not* to become a priest, apostle or hermit, and to work only with fear and trembling for one's own salvation; it would be senseless thus to neglect eternal benefits for temporary comfort. Taking it for granted that there *is belief*, the commonplace Christian is a miserable figure, a man that really cannot add two and two together, and who, moreover, just because of his mental incapacity for responsibility, did not deserve to be so severely punished as Christianity has decreed.

117.

Of the Wisdom of Christianity. – It is a clever stroke on the part of Christianity to teach the utter unworthiness, sinfulness, and despicableness of mankind so loudly that the disdain of their fellow-men is no longer possible. 'He may sin as much as he likes, he is not essentially different from me – it is I who am unworthy and despicable in every way,' says the Christian to himself. But even this feeling has lost its sharpest sting, because the Christian no longer believes in his individual despicableness; he is bad as men are generally, and comforts himself a little with the axiom, 'We are all of one kind.'

118.

Change of Front. – As soon as a religion triumphs it has for its enemies all those who would have been its first disciples.

9 This may give us one of the reasons for the religiosity still happily prevailing in England and the United States. – J. M. K.

119.

The Fate of Christianity. – Christianity arose for the purpose of lightening the heart; but now it must first make the heart heavy in order afterwards to lighten it. Consequently it will perish.

120.

The Proof of Pleasure. – The agreeable opinion is accepted as true – this is the proof of the pleasure (or, as the Church says, the proof of the strength), of which all religions are so proud when they ought to be ashamed of it. If Faith did not make blessed it would not be believed in; of how little value must it be, then!

121.

A Dangerous Game. – Whoever now allows scope to his religious feelings must also let them increase, he cannot do otherwise. His nature then gradually changes; it favours whatever is connected with and near to the religious element, the whole extent of judgement and feeling becomes clouded, overcast with religious shadows. Sensation cannot stand still; one must therefore take care.

122.

The Blind Disciples. – So long as one knows well the strength and weakness of one's doctrine, one's art, one's religion, its power is still small. The disciple and apostle who has no eyes for the weaknesses of the doctrine, the religion, and so forth, dazzled by the aspect of the master and by his reverence for him, has on that account usually more power than the master himself. Without blind disciples the influence of a man and his work has never yet become great. To help a doctrine to victory often means only so to mix it with stupidity that the weight of the latter carries off also the victory for the former.

123.

Church Disestablishment. – There is not enough religion in the world even to destroy religions.

124.

The Sinlessness of Man. – If it is understood how 'sin came into the world', namely through errors of reason by which men held each other, even the single individual held himself, to be much blacker and much worse than was actually the case, the whole sensation will be much lightened, and man and the world will appear in a blaze of innocence which it will do one good to contemplate. In the midst of nature man is always the child *per se*. This child sometimes has a heavy and terrifying dream, but when it opens its eyes it always finds itself back again in Paradise.

125.

The Irreligiousness of Artists. – Homer is so much at home amongst his gods, and is so familiar with them as a poet, that he must have been deeply irreligious; that which the popular faith gave him – a meagre, rude, partly terrible superstition – he treated as freely as the sculptor does his clay, with the same unconcern, therefore, which Aeschylus and Aristophanes possessed, and by which in later times the great artists of the Renaissance distinguished themselves, as also did Shakespeare and Goethe.

126.

The Art and Power of False Interpretations. – All the visions, terrors, torpors, and ecstasies of saints are well-known forms of disease, which are only, by reason of deep-rooted religious and psychological errors, differently *explained* by him, namely not as diseases. Thus, perhaps, the *Daimonion* of Socrates was only an affection of the ear, which he, in accordance with his ruling moral mode of thought, *expounded* differently from what would be the case now. It is the same thing with the madness and ravings of the prophets and soothsayers; it is always the degree of knowledge, fantasy, effort, morality in the head and heart of the *interpreters* which has *made* so much of it. For the greatest achievements of the people who are called geniuses and saints it is necessary that they should secure interpreters by force, who *misunderstand* them for the good of mankind.

127.

The Veneration of Insanity. – Because it was remarked that excitement frequently made the mind clearer and produced happy inspirations it was believed that the happiest inspirations and WM suggestions were called forth by the greatest excitement; and so the insane were revered as wise and oracular. This is based on a false conclusion.

128.

The Promises of Science. – The aim of modern science is: as little pain as possible, as long a life as possible – a kind of eternal blessedness, therefore; but certainly a very modest one as compared with the promises of religions.

129.

Forbidden Generosity. – There is not sufficient love and goodness in the world to permit us to give some of it away to imaginary beings.

130.

The Continuance of the Religious Cult in the Feelings. – The Roman Catholic Church, and before that all antique cults, dominated the entire range of means by which man was put into unaccustomed moods and rendered incapable of the cold calculation of judgement or the clear thinking of reason. A church quivering with deep tones; the dull, regular, arresting appeals of a priestly throng, unconsciously communicates its tension to the congregation and makes it listen almost fearfully, as if a miracle were in preparation; the influence of the architecture, which, as the dwelling of a Godhead, extends into the uncertain and makes its apparition to be feared in all its sombre spaces – who would wish to bring such things back to mankind if the necessary suppositions are no longer believed? But the *results* of all this are not lost, nevertheless; the inner world of noble, emotional', deeply contrite dispositions, full of presentiments, blessed with hope, is inborn in mankind mainly through this cult; what exists of it now in the soul was then cultivated on a large scale as it germinated, grew up and blossomed.

131.

The Painful Consequences of Religion. – However much we may think we have weaned ourselves from religion, it has nevertheless not been done so thoroughly as to deprive us of pleasure in encountering religious sensations and moods in music, for instance; and if a philosophy shows us the justification of metaphysical hopes and the deep peace of soul to be thence acquired, and speaks, for instance, of the 'whole, certain gospel in the gaze of Raphael's Madonnas', we receive such statements and expositions particularly warmly; here the philosopher finds it easier to prove; that which he desires to give corresponds to a heart that desires to receive. Hence it may be observed how the less thoughtful free spirits really only take offence at the dogmas, but are well acquainted with the charm of religious sensations; they are sorry to lose hold of the latter for the sake of the former. Scientific philosophy must be very careful not to smuggle in errors on the ground of that need – a need which has grown up and is consequently temporary – even logicians speak of 'presentiments' of truth in ethics and in art (for instance, of the suspicion that 'the nature of things is one'), which should be forbidden to them. Between the carefully established truths and such 'presaged' things there remains the unbridgable chasm that those are due to intellect and these to requirement. Hunger does not prove that food *exists* to satisfy it, but that it desires food. To 'presage' does not mean the acknowledgment of the existence of a thing in any one degree, but its possibility, in so far as it is desired or feared; 'presage' does not advance one step into the land of certainty. We believe involuntarily that the portions of a philosophy which are tinged with religion are better proved than others; but actually it is the contrary, but we have the inward desire that it may be so, that that which makes blessed, therefore, may be also the true. This desire misleads us to accept bad reasons for good ones.

132.

Of the Christian Need of Redemption. – With careful reflection it must be possible to obtain an explanation free from mythology of that process in the soul of a Christian which is called the need of redemption, consequently a purely psychological explanation. Up to the present, the psychological explanations of religious conditions and processes have certainly been held in some disrepute, inasmuch as a theology which called itself free carried on its unprofitable practice in this domain; for here from the beginning (as the mind of its founder, Schleiermacher, gives us reason to suppose) the preservation of the Christian religion and the continuance of Christian theology was kept in view; a theology which was to find a new anchorage in the psychological analyses of religious 'facts', and above all a new occupation. Unconcerned about such predecessors we hazard the following interpretation of the phenomenon in question. Man is conscious of certain actions which stand far down in the customary rank of actions; he even discovers in himself a tendency towards similar actions, a tendency which appears to him almost as unchangeable as his whole nature. How willingly would he try himself in that other species of actions which in the general valuation are recognised as the loftiest and highest, how gladly would he feel himself to be full of the good consciousness which should follow an unselfish mode of thought! But unfortunately he stops short at this wish, and the discontent at not being able to satisfy it is added to all the other discontents which his lot in life or the consequences of those above-mentioned evil actions have aroused in him; so that a deep ill-humour is the result, with the search for a physician who could remove this and all its causes. This condition would not be felt so bitterly if man would only compare himself frankly with other men – then he would have no reason for being dissatisfied with himself to a particular extent, he would only bear his share of the common burden of human dissatisfaction and imperfection. But he compares himself with a being who is said to be capable only of those actions which are called unegoistic, and to live in the perpetual consciousness of an unselfish mode of thought, i.e. with God; it is because he gazes into this clear mirror that his image appears to him so dark, so unusually warped. Then he is alarmed by the thought of that same creature, in so far as it floats before his imagination as a retributive justice; in all possible small and great events he thinks he recognises its anger and menaces, that he even feels its scourge-strokes as judge and executioner. Who will help him in this danger, which, by the prospect of an immeasurable duration of punishment, exceeds in horror all the other terrors of the idea?

133.

Before we examine the further consequences of this mental state, let us acknowledge that it is not through his 'guilt' and 'sin' that man has got into this condition, but through a series of errors of reason; that it was the fault of the mirror if his image appeared so dark and hateful to him, and that that mirror was *his* work, the very imperfect work of human imagination and power of judgement. In the first place, a nature that is only capable of purely unegoistic actions is more fabulous than the phoenix; it cannot even be clearly imagined, just because, when closely examined, the whole idea 'unegoistic action' vanishes into air. No man *ever* did a thing which was done only for others and without any personal motive; how should he be able to do anything which had no relation to himself, and therefore without inward obligation (which must always have its foundation in a personal need)? How could the *ego* act without *ego*? A God who, on the contrary, is *all* love, as such a one is often represented, would not be capable of a single unegoistic action, whereby one is reminded of a saying of Lichtenberg's which is certainly taken from a lower sphere: 'We cannot possibly *feel* for others, as the saying is; we feel only for ourselves. This sounds hard, but it is not so really if it be rightly understood. We do not love father or mother or wife or child, but the pleasant sensations they cause us'; or, as Rochefoucauld says: '*Si on croit aimer sa maitresse pour l'amour d'elle, on est bien trompé.*' To know the reason why actions of love are valued more than others, not on account of their nature, namely, but of their *usefulness*, we should compare the examinations already mentioned, *On the Origin of Moral Sentiments*. But should a man desire to be entirely like that God of Love, to do and wish everything for others and nothing for himself, the latter is impossible for the reason that he must do *very much* for himself to be able to do something for the love of others. Then it is taken for granted that the other is sufficiently egoistic to accept that sacrifice again and again, that living for him – so that the people of love and sacrifice have an interest in the continuance of those who are loveless and incapable of sacrifice, and, in order to exist, the highest morality would be obliged positively to *compel* the existence of un-morality (whereby it would certainly annihilate itself). Further: the conception of a God disturbs and humbles so long as it is believed in; but as to how it arose there can no longer be any doubt in the present state of the science of comparative ethnology; and with a comprehension of this origin all belief falls to the ground. The Christian who compares his nature with God's is like Don Quixote, who under-valued his own bravery because his head was full of the marvellous deeds of the heroes of the chivalric romances – the standard of measurement in both cases belongs to the domain of fable. But if the idea of God is removed, so is also the feeling of 'sin' as a trespass against divine laws, as a stain in a creature vowed to God. Then, perhaps, there still remains that dejection which is intergrown and connected with the fear of the punishment of worldly justice or of the scorn of men; the dejection of the pricks of conscience, the sharpest thorn in the consciousness of sin, is always removed if we recognise that though by our own deed we have sinned against human descent, human laws and ordinances, still that we have not imperilled the 'eternal salvation of the Soul' and its relation to the Godhead. And if man succeeds in gaining philosophic conviction of the absolute necessity of all actions and their entire irresponsibility, and absorbing this into his flesh and blood, even those remains of the pricks of conscience vanish.

134.

Now if the Christian, as we have said, has fallen into the way of self-contempt in consequence of certain errors through a false, unscientific interpretation of his actions and sensations, he must notice with great surprise how that state of contempt, the pricks of conscience and displeasure generally, does not endure, how sometimes there come hours when all this is wafted away from his soul and he feels himself once more free and courageous. In truth, the pleasure in himself, the comfort of his own strength, together with the necessary weakening through time of every deep emotion, has usually been victorious; man loves himself once again, he feels it – but precisely this new love, this self-esteem, seems to him incredible, he can only see in it the wholly undeserved descent of a stream of mercy from on high. If he formerly believed that in every event he could recognise warnings, menaces, punishments, and every kind of manifestation of divine anger, he now finds divine goodness in all his experiences – this event appears to him to be full of love, that one a helpful hint, a third, and, indeed, his whole happy mood, a proof that God is merciful. As formerly, in his state of pain, he interpreted his actions falsely, so now he misinterprets his experiences; his mood of comfort he believes to be the working of a power operating outside of himself, the love with which he really loves himself seems to him to be divine love; that which he calls mercy, and the prologue to redemption, is actually self-forgiveness, self-redemption.

135.

Therefore: A certain false psychology, a certain kind of imaginative interpretation of motives and experiences, is the necessary preliminary for one to become a Christian and to feel the need of redemption. When this error of reason and imagination is recognised, one ceases to be a Christian.

136.

Of Christian Asceticism and Holiness. – As greatly as isolated thinkers have endeavoured to depict as a miracle the rare manifestations of morality, which are generally called asceticism and holiness, miracles which it would be almost an outrage and sacrilege to explain by the light of common sense, as strong also is the inclination towards this outrage. A mighty impulse of nature has at all times led to a protest against those manifestations; science, in so far as it is an imitation of nature, at least allows itself to rise against the supposed inexplicableness and unapproachableness of these objections. So far it has certainly not succeeded: those appearances are still unexplained, to the great joy of the above-mentioned worshippers of the morally marvellous. For, speaking generally, the unexplained *must* be absolutely inexplicable, the inexplicable absolutely unnatural, supernatural, wonderful – thus runs the demand in the souls of religious and metaphysical people (also of artists, if they should happen to be thinkers at the same time); whilst the scientist sees in this demand the 'evil principle' in itself. The general, first probability upon which one lights in the contemplation of holiness and asceticism is this, that their nature is a *complicated* one, for almost everywhere, within the physical world as well as in the moral, the apparently marvellous has been successfully traced back to the complicated, the many-conditioned. Let us venture, therefore, to isolate separate impulses from the soul of saints and ascetics, and finally to imagine them as intergrown.

137.

There is a *defiance of self*, to the sublimest manifestation of which belong many forms of asceticism. Certain individuals have such great need of exercising their power and love of ruling that, in default of other objects, or because they have never succeeded otherwise, they finally excogitate the idea of tyrannising over certain parts of their own nature, portions or degrees of themselves. Thus many a thinker confesses to views which evidently do not serve either to increase or improve his reputation; many a one deliberately calls down the scorn of others when by keeping silence he could easily have remained respected; others contradict former opinions and do not hesitate to be called inconsistent – on the contrary, they strive after this, and behave like reckless riders who like a horse best when it has grown wild, unmanageable, and covered with sweat. Thus man climbs dangerous paths up the highest mountains in order that he may laugh to scorn his own fear and his trembling knees; thus the philosopher owns to views on asceticism, humility, holiness, in the brightness of which his own picture shows to the worst possible disadvantage. This crushing of one's self, this scorn of one's own nature, this *spernere se sperni*, of which religion has made so much, is really a very high degree of vanity. The whole moral of the Sermon on the Mount belongs here; man takes a genuine delight in doing violence to himself by these exaggerated claims, and afterwards idolising these tyrannical demands of his soul. In every ascetic morality man worships one part of himself as a God, and is obliged, therefore, to diabolise the other parts.

138.

Man is not equally moral at all hours, this is well known. If his morality is judged to be the capability for great self-sacrificing resolutions and self-denial (which, when continuous and grown habitual, are called holiness), he is most moral in the *passions*; the higher emotion provides him with entirely new motives, of which he, sober and cold as usual, perhaps does not even believe himself capable. How does this happen? Probably because of the proximity of everything great and highly exciting; if man is once wrought up to a state of extraordinary suspense, he is as capable of carrying out a terrible revenge as of a terrible crushing of his need for revenge. Under the influence of powerful emotion, he desires in any case the great, the powerful, the immense; and if he happens to notice that the sacrifice of himself satisfies him as well as, or better than, the sacrifice of others, he chooses that. Actually, therefore, he only cares about discharging his emotion; in order to ease his tension he seizes the enemy's spears and buries them in his breast. That there was something great in self-denial and not in revenge had to be taught to mankind by long habit; a Godhead that sacrificed itself was the strongest, most effective symbol of this kind of greatness. As the conquest of the most difficult enemy, the sudden mastering of an affection – thus this denial *appears*; and so far it passes for the summit of morality. In reality it is a question of the confusion of one idea with another, while the temperament maintains an equal height, an equal level. Temperate men who are resting from their passions no longer understand the morality of those moments; but the general admiration of those who had the same experiences upholds them; pride is their consolation when affection and the understanding of their deed vanish. Therefore, at bottom even those actions of self-denial are not moral, inasmuch as they are not done strictly with regard to others; rather the other only provides the highly-strung temperament with an opportunity of relieving itself through that denial.

139.

In many respects the ascetic seeks to make life easy for himself, usually by complete subordination to a strange will or a comprehensive law and ritual; something like the way a Brahmin leaves nothing whatever to his own decision but refers every moment to holy precepts. This submission is a powerful means of attaining self-mastery: man is occupied and is therefore not bored, and yet has no incitement to self-will or passion; after a completed deed there is no feeling of responsibility and with it no tortures of remorse. We have renounced our own will once and for ever, and this is easier than only renouncing it occasionally; as it is also easier to give up a desire entirely than to keep it within bounds. When we remember the present relation of man to the State, we find that, even here, unconditional obedience is more convenient than conditional. The saint, therefore, makes his life easier by absolute renunciation of his personality, and we are mistaken if in that phenomenon we admire the loftiest heroism of morality. In any case it is more difficult to carry one's personality through without vacillation and unclearness than to liberate one's self from it in the above-mentioned manner; moreover, it requires far more spirit and consideration.

140.

After having found in many of the less easily explicable actions manifestations of that pleasure in *emotion per se*, I should like to recognise also in self-contempt, which is one of the signs of holiness, and likewise in the deeds of self-torture (through hunger and scourging, mutilation of limbs, feigning of madness) a means by which those natures fight against the general weariness of their life-will (their nerves); they employ the most painful irritants and cruelties in order to emerge for a time, at all events, from that dullness and boredom into which they so frequently sink through their great mental indolence and that submission to a strange will already described.

141.

The commonest means which the ascetic and saint employs to render life still endurable and amusing consists in occasional warfare with alternate victory and defeat. For this he requires an opponent, and finds it in the so-called 'inward enemy'. He principally makes use of his inclination to vanity, love of honour and rule, and of his sensual desires, that he may be permitted to regard his life as a perpetual battle and himself as a battlefield upon which good and evil spirits strive with alternating success. It is well known that sensual imagination is moderated, indeed almost dispelled, by regular sexual intercourse, whereas, on the contrary, it is rendered unfettered and wild by abstinence or irregularity. The imagination of many Christian saints was filthy to an extraordinary degree; by virtue of those theories that these desires were actual demons raging within them they did not feel themselves to be too responsible; to this feeling we owe the very instructive frankness of their self-confessions. It was to their interest that this strife should always be maintained in one degree or another, because, as we have already said, their empty life was thereby entertained. But in order that the strife might seem sufficiently important and arouse the enduring sympathy and admiration of non-saints, it was necessary that sensuality should be ever more reviled and branded, the danger of eternal damnation was so tightly bound up with these things that it is highly probable that for whole centuries Christians generated children with a bad conscience, wherewith humanity has certainly suffered a great injury. And yet here truth is all topsy-turvy, which is particularly unsuitable for truth. Certainly Christianity had said that every man is conceived and born in sin, and in the insupportable superlative-Christianity of Calderon this thought again appears, tied up and twisted, as the most distorted paradox there is, in the well-known lines –

> 'The greatest sin of man
> Is that he was ever born.'

In all pessimistic religions the act of generation was looked upon as evil in itself. This is by no means the verdict of all mankind, not even of all pessimists. For instance, Empedocles saw in all erotic things nothing shameful, diabolical, or sinful; but rather, in the great plain of disaster he saw only one hopeful and redeeming figure, that of Aphrodite; she appeared to him as a guarantee that the strife should not endure eternally, but that the sceptre should one day be given over to a gentler *daemon*. The actual Christian pessimists had, as has been said, an interest in the dominance of a diverse opinion; for the solitude and spiritual wilderness of their lives they required an ever living enemy, and a generally recognised enemy, through whose fighting and overcoming they could constantly represent themselves to the non-saints as incomprehensible, half-supernatural beings. But when at last this enemy took to flight for ever in consequence of their mode of life and their impaired health, they immediately understood how to populate their interior with new daemons. The rising and falling of the scales of pride and humility sustained their brooding minds as well as the alternations of desire and peace of soul. At that time psychology served not only to cast suspicion upon everything human, but to oppress, to scourge, to crucify; people *wished* to find themselves as bad and wicked as possible, they *sought* anxiety for the salvation of their souls, despair of their own strength. Everything natural with which man has connected the idea of evil and sin (as, for instance, he is still accustomed to do with regard to the erotic) troubles and clouds the imagination, causes a frightened glance, makes man quarrel with himself and uncertain and distrustful of himself. Even his dreams have the flavour of a restless conscience. And yet in the reality of things this suffering from what is natural is entirely without foundation, it is only the consequence of opinions *about* things. It is easily seen how men grow worse by considering the inevitably-natural as bad, and afterwards always feeling themselves made thus. It is the trump card of religion and metaphysics, which wish to have man evil and sinful by nature, to cast suspicion on nature and thus really to *make* him bad, for he learns to feel himself evil since he cannot divest himself of the clothing of nature. After living for a long natural life, he gradually comes to feel himself weighed down by such a burden of sin that supernatural powers are necessary to lift this burden, and therewith arises the so-called need of redemption, which corresponds to no real but only to an imaginary sinfulness. If we survey the separate moral demands of the earliest times of Christianity it will everywhere be found that requirements are exaggerated in order that man *cannot* satisfy them; the intention is not that he should become more moral, but that he should feel himself as *sinful as possible*. If man had not found this feeling *agreeable* – why would he have thought out such an idea and stuck to it so long? As in the antique world an immeasurable power of intellect and inventiveness was expended in multiplying the pleasure of life by festive cults, so also in the age of Christianity an immeasurable amount of intellect has been sacrificed to another endeavour – man must by all means be made to feel himself sinful and thereby be excited, *enlivened, en-souled*. To excite, enliven, en-soul at all costs – is not that the watchword of a relaxed, over-ripe, over-cultured age? The range of all natural sensations had been gone over a hundred times, the soul had grown weary, whereupon the saint and the ascetic invented a new species of stimulants for life. They presented themselves before the public eye, not exactly as an example for the many, but as a terrible and yet ravishing spectacle, which took place on that border-land between world and over-world, wherein at that time all people believed they saw now rays of heavenly light and now unholy tongues of flame glowing in the depths. The saint's eye, fixed upon the terrible meaning of this short earthly life, upon the nearness of the last decision concerning endless new spans of existence, this burning eye in a half-wasted body made men of the old world tremble to their very depths; to gaze, to turn shudderingly away, to feel anew the attraction of the spectacle and to give way to it, to drink deep of it till the soul quivered with fire and ague – that was the last *pleasure that antiquity invented* after it had grown blunted even at the sight of beast-baitings and human combats.

142.

Now to sum up. That condition of soul in which the saint or embryo saint rejoiced, was composed of elements which we all know well, only that under the influence of other than religious conceptions they exhibit themselves in other colours and are then accustomed to encounter man's blame as fully as, with that decoration of religion and the ultimate meaning of existence, they may reckon on receiving admiration and even worship – might reckon, at least, in former ages. Sometimes the saint practises that defiance of himself which is a near relative of domination at any cost and gives a feeling of power even to the most lonely; sometimes his swollen sensibility leaps from the desire to let his passions have full play into the desire to overthrow them like wild horses under the mighty pressure of a proud spirit; sometimes he desires a complete cessation of all disturbing, tormenting, irritating sensations, a waking sleep, a lasting rest in the lap of a dull, animal, and plant-like indolence; sometimes he seeks strife and arouses it within himself, because boredom has shown him its yawning countenance. He scourges his self-adoration with self-contempt and cruelty, he rejoices in the wild tumult of his desires and the sharp pain of sin, even in the idea of being lost; he understands how to lay a trap for his emotions, for instance even for his keen love of ruling, so that he sinks into the most utter abasement and his tormented soul is thrown out of joint by this contrast; and finally, if he longs for visions, conversations with the dead or with divine beings, it is at bottom a rare kind of delight that he covets, perhaps that delight in which all others are united. Novalis, an authority on questions of holiness through experience and instinct, tells the whole secret with naive joy: 'It is strange enough that the association of lust, religion, and cruelty did not long ago draw men's attention to their close relationship and common tendency.'

143.

That which gives the saint his historical value is not the thing he *is*, but the thing he *represents* in the eyes of the unsaintly. It was through the fact that errors were made about him, that the state of his soul was *falsely interpreted*, that men separated themselves from him as much as possible, as from something incomparable and strangely superhuman, that he acquired the extraordinary power which he exercised over the imagination of whole nations and whole ages. He did not know himself; he himself interpreted the writing of his moods, inclinations, and actions according to an art of interpretation which was as exaggerated and artificial as the spiritual interpretation of the Bible. The distorted and diseased in his nature, with its combination of intellectual poverty, evil knowledge, ruined health, and over-excited nerves, remained hidden from his own sight as well as from that of his spectators. He was not a particularly good man, and still less was he a particularly wise one; but he *represented* something that exceeded the human standard in goodness and wisdom. The belief in him supported the belief in the divine and miraculous, in a religious meaning of all existence, in an impending day of judgement. In the evening glory of the world's sunset, which glowed over the Christian nations, the shadowy form of the saint grew to vast dimensions, it grew to such a height that even in our own age, which no longer believes in God, there are still thinkers who believe in the saint.

144.

It need not be said that to this description of the saint which has been made from an average of the whole species, there may be opposed many a description which could give a more agreeable impression. Certain exceptions stand out from among this species, it may be through great mildness and philanthropy, it may be through the magic of unusual energy; others are attractive in the highest degree, because certain wild ravings have poured streams of light on their whole being, as is the case, for instance, with the famous founder of Christianity, who thought he was the Son of God and therefore felt himself sinless – so that through this idea – which we must not judge too hardly because the whole antique world swarms with sons of God – he reached that same goal, that feeling of complete sinlessness, complete irresponsibility, which every one can now acquire by means of science. Neither have I mentioned the Indian saints, who stand midway between the Christian saint and the Greek philosopher, and in so far represent no pure type. Knowledge, science – such as existed then – the uplifting above other men through logical discipline and training of thought, were as much fostered by the Buddhists as distinguishing signs of holiness as the same qualities in the Christian world are repressed and branded as signs of unholiness.

FOURTH DIVISION.

CONCERNING THE SOUL OF ARTISTS AND AUTHORS.

145.

The Perfect should not have Grown. – With regard to everything that is perfect we are accustomed to omit the question as to how perfection has been acquired, and we only rejoice in the present as if it had sprung out of the ground by magic. Probably with regard to this matter we are still under the effects of an ancient mythological feeling. It still *almost* seems to us (in such a Greek temple, for instance, as that of Paestum) as if one morning a god in sport had built his dwelling of such enormous masses, at other times it seems as if his spirit had suddenly entered into a stone and now desired to speak through it. The artist knows that his work is only fully effective if it arouses the belief in an improvisation, in a marvellous instantaneousness of origin; and thus he assists this illusion and introduces into art those elements of inspired unrest, of blindly groping disorder, of listening dreaming at the beginning of creation, as a means of deception, in order so to influence the soul of the spectator or hearer that it may believe in the sudden appearance of the perfect. It is the business of the science of art to contradict this illusion most decidedly, and to show up the mistakes and pampering of the intellect, by means of which it falls into the artist's trap.

146.

The Artist's Sense of Truth. – With regard to recognition of truths, the artist has a weaker morality than the thinker; he will on no account let himself be deprived of brilliant and profound interpretations of life, and defends himself against temperate and simple methods and results. He is apparently fighting for the higher worthiness and meaning of mankind; in reality he will not renounce the *most effective* suppositions for his art, the fantastical, mythical, uncertain, extreme, the sense of the symbolical, the over-valuation of personality, the belief that genius is something miraculous – he considers, therefore, the continuance of his art of creation as more important than the scientific devotion to truth in every shape, however simple this may appear.

147.

Art as Raiser of the Dead. – Art also fulfils the task of preservation and even of brightening up extinguished and faded memories; when it accomplishes this task it weaves a rope round the ages and causes their spirits to return. It is, certainly, only a phantom-life that results therefrom, as out of graves, or like the return in dreams of our beloved dead, but for some moments, at least, the old sensation lives again and the heart beats to an almost forgotten time. Hence, for the sake of the general usefulness of art, the artist himself must be excused if he does not stand in the front rank of the enlightenment and progressive civilisation of humanity; all his life long he has remained a child or a youth, and has stood still at the point where he was overcome by his artistic impulse; the feelings of the first years of life, however, are acknowledged to be nearer to those of earlier times than to those of the present century. Unconsciously it becomes his mission to make mankind more childlike; this is his glory and his limitation.

148.

Poets as the Lighteners of Life. – Poets, inasmuch as they desire to lighten the life of man, either divert his gaze from the wearisome present, or assist the present to acquire new colours by means of a life which they cause to shine out of the past. To be able to do this, they must in many respects themselves be beings who are turned towards the past, so that they can be used as bridges to far distant times and ideas, to dying or dead religions and cultures. Actually they are always and of necessity *epigoni*. There are, however, certain drawbacks to their means of lightening life – they appease and heal only temporarily, only for the moment; they even prevent men from labouring towards a genuine improvement in their conditions, inasmuch as they remove and apply palliatives to precisely that passion of discontent that induces to action.

149.

The Slow Arrow of Beauty. – The noblest kind of beauty is that which does not transport us suddenly, which does not make stormy and intoxicating impressions (such a kind easily arouses disgust), but that which slowly filters into our minds, which we take away with us almost unnoticed, and which we encounter again in our dreams; but which, however, after having long lain modestly on our hearts, takes entire possession of us, fills our eyes with tears and our hearts with longing. What is it that we long for at the sight of beauty? We long to be beautiful, we fancy it must bring much happiness with it. But that is a mistake.

150.

The Animation of Art. – Art raises its head where creeds relax. It takes over many feelings and moods engendered by religion, lays them to its heart, and itself becomes deeper, more full of soul, so that it is capable of transmitting exultation and enthusiasm, which it previously was not able to do. The abundance of religious feelings which have grown into a stream are always breaking forth again and desire to conquer new kingdoms, but the growing enlightenment has shaken the dogmas of religion and inspired a deep mistrust – thus the feeling, thrust by enlightenment out of the religious sphere, throws itself upon art, in a few cases into political life, even straight into science. Everywhere where human endeavour wears a loftier, gloomier aspect, it may be assumed that the fear of spirits, incense, and church-shadows have remained attached to it.

151.

How Rhythm Beautifies. – Rhythm casts a veil over reality; it causes various artificialities of speech and obscurities of thought; by the shadow it throws upon thought it sometimes conceals it, and sometimes brings it into prominence. As shadow is necessary to beauty, so the 'dull' is necessary to lucidity. Art makes the aspect of life endurable by throwing over it the veil of obscure thought.

152.

The Art of the Ugly Soul. – Art is confined within too narrow limits if it be required that only the orderly, respectable, well-behaved soul should be allowed to express itself therein. As in the plastic arts, so also in music and poetry: there is an art of the ugly soul side by side with the art of the beautiful soul; and the mightiest effects of art, the crushing of souls, moving of stones and humanising of beasts, have perhaps been best achieved precisely by that art.

153.

Art makes Heavy the Heart of the Thinker. – How strong metaphysical need is and how difficult nature renders our departure from it may be seen from the fact that even in the free spirit, when he has cast off everything metaphysical, the loftiest effects of art can easily produce a resounding of the long silent, even broken, metaphysical string – it may be, for instance, that at a passage in Beethoven's Ninth Symphony he feels himself floating above the earth in a starry dome with the dream of *immortality* in his heart; all the stars seem to shine round him, and the earth to sink farther and farther away. If he becomes conscious of this state, he feels a deep pain at his heart, and sighs for the man who will lead back to him his lost darling, be it called religion or metaphysics. In such moments his intellectual character is put to the test.

154.

Playing with Life. – The lightness and frivolity of the Homeric imagination was necessary to calm and occasionally to raise the immoderately passionate temperament and acute intellect of the Greeks. If their intellect speaks, how harsh and cruel does life then appear! They do not deceive themselves, but they intentionally weave lies round life. Simonides advised his countrymen to look upon life as a game; earnestness was too well-known to them as pain (the gods so gladly hear the misery of mankind made the theme of song), and they knew that through art alone misery might be turned into pleasure. As a punishment for this insight, however, they were so plagued with the love of romancing that it was difficult for them in everyday life to keep themselves free from falsehood and deceit; for all poetic nations have such a love of falsehood, and yet are innocent withal. Probably this occasionally drove the neighbouring nations to desperation.

155.

The Belief in Inspiration. – It is to the interest of the artist that there should be a belief in sudden suggestions, so-called inspirations; as if the idea of a work of art, of poetry, the fundamental thought of a philosophy shone down from heaven like a ray of grace. In reality the imagination of the good artist or thinker constantly produces good, mediocre, and bad, but his *judgement*, most clear and practised, rejects and chooses and joins together, just as we now learn from Beethoven's notebooks that he gradually composed the most beautiful melodies, and in a manner selected them, from many different attempts. He who makes less severe distinctions, and willingly abandons himself to imitative memories, may under certain circumstances become a great improvisatore; but artistic improvisation ranks low in comparison with serious and laboriously chosen artistic thoughts. All great men were great workers, unwearied not only in invention but also in rejection, reviewing, transforming, and arranging.

156.

Inspiration Again. – If the productive power has been suspended for a length of time, and has been hindered in its outflow by some obstacle, there comes at last such a sudden out-pouring, as if an immediate inspiration were taking place without previous inward working, consequently a miracle. This constitutes the familiar deception, in the continuance of which, as we have said, the interest of all artists is rather too much concerned. The capital has only *accumulated*, it has not suddenly fallen down from heaven. Moreover, such apparent inspirations are seen elsewhere, for instance in the realm of goodness, of virtue and of vice.

157.

The Suffering of Genius and its Value. – The artistic genius desires to give pleasure, but if his mind is on a very high plane he does not easily find any one to share his pleasure; he offers entertainment but nobody accepts it. This gives him, in certain circumstances, a comically touching pathos; for he has really no right to force pleasure on men. He pipes, but none will dance: can that be tragic? Perhaps. As compensation for this deprivation, however, he finds more pleasure in creating than the rest of mankind experiences in all other species of activity. His sufferings are considered as exaggerated, because the sound of his complaints is louder and his tongue more eloquent; and yet *sometimes* his sufferings are really very great; but only because his ambition and his envy are so great. The learned genius, like Kepler and Spinoza, is usually not so covetous and does not make such an exhibition of his really greater sufferings and deprivations. He can reckon with greater certainty on future fame and can afford to do without the present, whilst an artist who does this always plays a desperate game that makes his heart ache. In very rare cases, when in one and the same individual are combined the genius of power and of knowledge and the moral genius, there is added to the above-mentioned pains that species of pain which must be regarded as the most curious exception in the world; those extra and super-personal sensations which are experienced on behalf of a nation, of humanity, of all civilisation, all suffering existence, which acquire their value through the connection with particularly difficult and remote perceptions (pity in itself is worth but little). But what standard, what proof is there for its genuineness? Is it not almost imperative to be mistrustful of all who *talk* of feeling sensations of this kind?

158.

The Destiny of Greatness. – Every great phenomenon is followed by degeneration, especially in the world of art. The example of the great tempts vainer natures to superficial imitation or exaggeration; all great gifts have the fatality of crushing many weaker forces and germs, and of laying waste all nature around them. The happiest arrangement in the development of an art is for several geniuses mutually to hold one another within bounds; in this strife it generally happens that light and air are also granted to the weaker and more delicate natures.

159.

Art Dangerous for the Artist. – When art takes strong hold of an individual it draws him back to the contemplation of those times when art flourished best, and it has then a retrograde effect. The artist grows more and more to reverence sudden inspirations; he believes in gods and daemons, he spiritualises all nature, hates science, is changeable in his moods like the ancients, and longs for an overthrow of all existing conditions which are not favourable to art, and does this with the impetuosity and unreasonableness of a child. Now, in himself, the artist is already a backward nature, because he halts at a game that belongs properly to youth and childhood; to this is added the fact that he is educated back into former times. Thus there gradually arises a fierce antagonism between him and his contemporaries, and a sad ending; according to the accounts of the ancients, Homer and Aeschylus spent their last years, and died, in melancholy.

160.

Created Individuals. – When it is said that the dramatist (and the artist above all) *creates* real characters, it is a fine deception and exaggeration, in the existence and propagation of which art celebrates one of its unconscious but at the same time abundant triumphs. As a matter of fact, we do not understand much about a real, living man, and we generalise very superficially when we ascribe to him this and that character; this *very imperfect* attitude of ours towards man is represented by the poet, inasmuch as he makes into men (in this sense 'creates') outlines as *superficial* as our knowledge of man is superficial. There is a great deal of delusion about these created characters of artists; they are by no means living productions of nature, but are like painted men, somewhat too thin, they will not bear a close inspection. And when it is said that the character of the ordinary living being contradicts itself frequently, and that the one created by the dramatist is the original model conceived by nature, this is quite wrong. A genuine man is something absolutely *necessary* (even in those so-called contradictions), but we do not always recognise this necessity. The imaginary man, the phantasm, signifies something necessary, but only to those who understand a real man only in a crude, unnatural simplification, so that a few strong, oft-repeated traits, with a great deal of light and shade and half-light about them, I amply satisfy their notions. They are, therefore, ready to treat the phantasm as a genuine, necessary man, because with real men they are accustomed to regard a phantasm, an outline, an intentional abbreviation as the whole. That the painter and the sculptor express the 'idea' of man is a vain imagination and delusion; whoever says this is in subjection to the eye, for this only sees the surface, the epidermis of the human body – the inward body, however, is equally a part of the idea. Plastic art wishes to make character visible on the surface; histrionic art employs speech for the same purpose, it reflects character in sounds. Art starts from the natural *ignorance* of man about his interior condition (in body and character); it is not meant for philosophers or natural scientists.

161.

The Over-valuation of Self in the Belief in Artists and Philosophers. – We are all prone to think that the excellence of a work of art or of an artist is proved when it moves and touches us. But there *our own excellence* in judgement and sensibility must have been proved first, which is not the case. In all plastic art, who had greater power to effect a charm than Bernini, who made a greater effect than the orator that appeared after Demosthenes introduced the Asiatic style and gave it a predominance which lasted throughout two centuries? This predominance during whole centuries is not a proof of the excellence and enduring validity of a style; therefore we must not be too certain in our good opinion of any artist – this is not only belief in the truthfulness of our sensations but also in the infallibility of our judgement, whereas judgement or sensation, or even both, may be too coarse or too fine, exaggerated or crude. Neither are the blessings and blissfulness of a philosophy or of a religion proofs of its truth; just as little as the happiness which an insane person derives from his fixed idea is a proof of the reasonableness of this idea.

162.

The Cult of Genius for the sake of Vanity. – Because we think well of ourselves, but nevertheless do not imagine that we are capable of the conception of one of Raphael's pictures or of a scene such as those of one of Shakespeare's dramas, we persuade ourselves that the faculty for doing this is quite extraordinarily wonderful, a very rare case, or, if we are religiously inclined, a grace from above. Thus the cult of genius fosters our vanity, our self-love, for it is only when we think of it as very far removed from us, as a *miraculum*, that it does not wound us (even Goethe, who was free from envy, called Shakespeare a star of the farthest heavens, whereby we are reminded of the line 'die Sterne, die begehrt man nicht'[10]). But, apart from those suggestions of our vanity, the activity of a genius does not seem so radically different from the activity of a mechanical inventor, of an astronomer or historian or strategist. All these forms of activity are explicable if we realise men whose minds are active in one special direction, who make use of everything as material, who always eagerly study their own inward life and that of others, who find types and incitements everywhere, who never weary in the employment of their means. Genius does nothing but learn how to lay stones, then to build, always to seek for material and always to work upon it. Every human activity is marvellously complicated, and not only that of genius, but it is no 'miracle'. Now whence comes the belief that genius is found only in artists, orators, and philosophers, that they alone have 'intuition' (by which we credit them with a kind of magic glass by means of which they see straight into one's 'being')? It is clear that men only speak of genius where the workings of a great intellect are most agreeable to them and they have no desire to feel envious. To call any one 'divine' is as much as saying 'here we have no occasion for rivalry'. Thus it is that everything completed and perfect is stared at, and everything incomplete is undervalued. Now nobody can see how the work of an artist has *developed*; that is its advantage, for everything of which the development is seen is looked on coldly. The perfected art of representation precludes all thought of its development, it tyrannises as a present perfection. For this reason artists of representation are especially held to be possessed of genius, but not scientific men. In reality, however, the former valuation and the latter under-valuation are only puerilities of reason.

---

10 The allusion is to Goethe's lines:

Die Sterne, die begehrt man nicht,
Man freut sick ihrer Pracht.

We do not want the stars themselves,
Their brilliancy delights our hearts. – J. M. K.

163.

The Earnestness of Handicraft. – Do not talk of gifts, of inborn talents! We could mention great men of all kinds who were but little gifted. But they *obtained* greatness, became 'geniuses' (as they are called), through qualities of the lack of which nobody who is conscious of them likes to speak. They all had that thorough earnestness for work which learns first how to form the different parts perfectly before it ventures to make a great whole; they gave themselves time for this, because they took more pleasure in doing small, accessory things well than in the effect of a dazzling whole. For instance, the recipe for becoming a good novelist is easily given, but the carrying out of the recipe presupposes qualities which we are in the habit of overlooking when we say, 'I have not sufficient talent.' Make a hundred or more sketches of novel-plots, none more than two pages long, but of such clearness that every word in them is necessary; write down anecdotes every day until you learn to find the most pregnant, most effective form; never weary of collecting and delineating human types and X characters; above all, narrate things as often as possible and listen to narrations with a sharp eye and ear for the effect upon other people present; travel like a landscape painter and a designer of costumes; take from different sciences everything that is artistically effective, if it be well represented; finally, meditate on the motives for human actions, scorn not even the smallest point of instruction on this subject, and collect similar matters by day and night. Spend some ten years in these various exercises: then the creations of your study may be allowed to see the light of day. But what do most people do, on the contrary? They do not begin with the part, but with the whole. Perhaps they make one good stroke, excite attention, and ever afterwards their work grows worse and worse, for good, natural reasons. But sometimes, when intellect and character are lacking for the formation of such an artistic career, fate and necessity take the place of these qualities and lead the future master step by step through all the phases of his craft.

164.

The Danger and the Gain in the Cult of Genius. – The belief in great, superior, fertile minds is not necessarily, but still very frequently, connected with that wholly or partly religious superstition that those spirits are of superhuman origin and possess certain marvellous faculties, by means of which they obtained their knowledge in ways quite different from the rest of mankind. They are credited with having an immediate insight into the nature of the world, through a peep-hole in the mantle of the phenomenon as it were, and it is believed that, without the trouble and severity of science, by virtue of this marvellous prophetic sight, they could impart something final and decisive about mankind and the world. So long as there are still believers in miracles in the world of knowledge it may perhaps be admitted that the believers themselves derive a benefit therefrom, inasmuch as by their absolute subjection to great minds they obtain the best discipline and schooling for their own minds during the period of development. On the other hand, it may at least be questioned whether the superstition of genius, of its privileges and special faculties, is useful for a genius himself when it implants itself in him. In any case it is a dangerous sign when man shudders at his own self, be it that famous Caesarian shudder or the shudder of genius which applies to this case, when the incense of sacrifice, which by rights is offered to a God alone, penetrates into the brain of the genius, so that he begins to waver and to look upon himself as something superhuman. The slow consequences are: the feeling of irresponsibility, the exceptional rights, the belief that mere intercourse with him confers a favour, and frantic rage at any attempt to compare him with others or even to place him below them and to bring into prominence whatever is unsuccessful in his work. Through the fact that he ceases to criticise himself one pinion after another falls out of his plumage – that superstition undermines the foundation of his strength and even makes him a hypocrite after his power has failed him. For great minds it is, therefore, perhaps better when they come to an understanding about their strength and its source, when they comprehend what purely human qualities are mingled in them, what a combination they are of fortunate conditions: thus once it was continual energy, a decided application to individual aims, great personal courage, and then the good fortune of an education, which at an early period provided the best teachers, examples, and methods. Assuredly, if its aim is to make the greatest possible *effect*, abstruseness has always done much for itself and that gift of partial insanity; for at all times that power has been admired and envied by means of which men were deprived of will and imbued with the fancy that they were preceded by supernatural leaders. Truly, men are exalted and inspired by the belief that some one among them is endowed with supernatural powers, and in this respect insanity, as Plato says, has brought the greatest blessings to mankind. In a few rare cases this form of insanity may also have been the means by which an all-round exuberant nature was kept within bounds; in individual life the imaginings of frenzy frequently exert the virtue of remedies which are poisons in themselves; but in every 'genius' that believes in his own divinity the poison shows itself at last in the same proportion as the 'genius' grows old; we need but recollect the example of Napoleon, for it was most assuredly through his faith in himself and his star, and through his scorn of mankind, that he grew to that mighty unity which distinguished him from all modern men, until at last, however, this faith developed into an almost insane fatalism, robbed him of his quickness of comprehension and penetration, and was the cause of his downfall.

165.

Genius and Nullity. – It is precisely the *original* artists, those who create out of their own heads, who in certain circumstances can bring forth complete *emptiness* and husk, whilst the more dependent natures, the so-called talented ones, are full of memories of all manner of goodness, and even in a state of weakness produce something tolerable. But if the original ones are abandoned by themselves, memory renders them no assistance; they become empty.

166.

The Public. – The people really demand nothing more from tragedy than to be deeply affected, in order to have a good cry occasionally; the artist, on the contrary, who sees the new tragedy, takes pleasure in the clever technical inventions and tricks, in the management and distribution of the material, in the novel arrangement of old motives and old ideas. His attitude is the aesthetic attitude towards a work of art, that of the creator; the one first described, with regard solely to the material, is that of the people. Of the individual who stands between the two nothing need be said: he is neither 'people' nor artist, and does not know what he wants – therefore his pleasure is also clouded and insignificant.

167.

The Artistic Education of the Public. – If the same *motif* is not employed in a hundred ways by different masters, the public never learns to get beyond their interest in the subject; but at last, when it is well acquainted with the *motif* through countless different treatments, and no longer finds in it any charm of novelty or excitement, it will then begin to grasp and enjoy the various shades and delicate new inventions in its treatment.

168.

The Artist and his Followers must keep in Step. – The progress from one grade of style to another must be so slow that not only the artists but also the auditors and spectators can follow it and know exactly what is going on. Otherwise there will suddenly appear that great chasm between the artist, who creates his work upon a height apart, and the public, who cannot rise up to that height and finally sinks discontentedly deeper. For when the artist no longer raises his public it rapidly sinks downwards, and its fall is the deeper and more dangerous in proportion to the height to which genius has carried it, like the eagle, out of whose talons a tortoise that has been borne up into the clouds falls to its destruction.

169.

The Source of the Comic Element. – If we consider that for many thousands of years man was an animal that was susceptible in the highest degree to fear, and that everything sudden and unexpected had to find him ready for battle, perhaps even ready for death; that even later, in social relations, all security was based on the expected, on custom in thought and action, we need not be surprised that at everything sudden and unexpected in word and deed, if it occurs without danger or injury, man becomes exuberant and passes over into the very opposite of fear – the terrified, trembling, crouching being shoots upward, stretches itself: man laughs. This transition from momentary fear into short-lived exhilaration is called the *Comic*. On the other hand, in the tragic phenomenon, man passes quickly from great enduring exuberance into great fear; but as amongst mortals great and lasting exuberance is much rarer than the cause for fear, there is far more comedy than tragedy in the world; we laugh much oftener than we are agitated.

170.

The Artist's Ambition. – The Greek artists, the tragedians for instance, composed in order to conquer; their whole art cannot be imagined without rivalry – the good Hesiodian Eris, Ambition, gave wings to their genius. This ambition further demanded that their work should achieve the greatest excellence *in their own eyes*, as they understood excellence, *without any regard* for the reigning taste and the general opinion about excellence in a work of art; and thus it was long before Aeschylus and Euripides achieved any success, until at last they *educated* judges of art, who valued their work according to the standards which they themselves appointed. Hence they strove for victory over rivals according to their own valuation, they really wished to be more excellent; they demanded assent from without to this self-valuation, the confirmation of this verdict. To achieve honour means in this case 'to make one's self superior to others, and to desire that this should be recognised publicly'. Should the former condition be wanting, and the latter nevertheless desired, it is then called *vanity*. Should the latter be lacking and not missed, then it is named *pride*.

171.

What is Needful to a Work of Art. – Those who talk so much about the needful factors of a work of art exaggerate; if they are artists they do so *in majorem artis gloriam*, if they are laymen, from ignorance. The form of a work of art, which gives speech to their thoughts and is, therefore, their mode of talking, is always somewhat uncertain, like all kinds of speech. The sculptor can add or omit many little traits, as can also the exponent, be he an actor or, in music, a performer or conductor. These many little traits and finishing touches afford him pleasure one day and none the next, they exist more for the sake of the artist than the art; for he also has occasionally need of sweetmeats and playthings to prevent him from becoming morose with the severity and self-restraint which the representation of the dominant idea demands from him.

172.

To Cause the Master to be Forgotten. – The pianoforte player who executes the work of a master will have played best if he has made his audience forget the master, and if it seemed as if he were relating a story from his own life or just passing through some experience. Assuredly, if he is of no importance, every one will abhor the garrulity with which he talks about his own life. Therefore he must know how to influence his hearer's imagination favourably towards himself. Hereby are explained all the weaknesses and follies of 'the virtuoso'.

173.

Corriger La Fortune. – There are unfortunate accidents in the lives of great artists, which compel the painter, for instance, to sketch out his most important picture only as a passing thought, or such as obliged Beethoven to leave behind him only the insufficient pianoforte score of many great sonatas (as in the great B flat). In these cases the artist of a later day must endeavour to fill out the life of the great man – what, for instance, he would do who, as master of all orchestral effects, would call into life that symphony which has fallen into the piano-trance.

174.

Reducing. – Many things, events, or persons, cannot bear treatment on a small scale. The Laocoon group cannot be reduced to a knick-knack; great size is necessary to it. But more seldom still does anything that is naturally small bear enlargement; for which reason biographers succeed far oftener in representing a great man as small than a small one as great.

175.

Sensuousness in Present-day Art. – Artists nowadays frequently miscalculate when they count on the sensuous effect of their works, for their spectators or hearers have no longer a fully sensuous nature, and, quite contrary to the artist's intention, his work produces in them a 'holiness' of feeling which is closely related to boredom. Their sensuousness begins, perhaps, just where that of the artist ceases; they meet, therefore, only at one point at the most.

176.

Shakespeare as a Moralist. – Shakespeare meditated much on the passions, and on account of his temperament had probably a close acquaintance with many of them (dramatists are in general rather wicked men). He could, however not talk on the subject, like Montaigne, but put his observations thereon into the mouths of impassioned figures, which is contrary to nature, certainly, but makes his dramas so rich in thought that they cause all others to seem poor in comparison and readily arouse a general aversion to them. Schiller's reflections (which are almost always based on erroneous or trivial fancies) are just theatrical reflections, and as such are very effective; whereas Shakespeare's reflections do honour to his model, Montaigne, and contain quite serious thoughts in polished form, but on that account are too remote and refined for the eyes of the theatrical public, and are consequently ineffective.

177.

Securing a Good Hearing. – It is not sufficient to know how to play well; one must also know how to secure a good hearing. A violin in the hand of the greatest master gives only a little squeak when the place where it is heard is too large; the master may then be mistaken for any bungler.

178.

The Incomplete as the Effective. – Just as figures in relief make such a strong impression on the imagination because they seem in the act of emerging from the wall and only stopped by some sudden hindrance; so the relief-like, incomplete representation of a thought, or a whole philosophy, is sometimes more effective than its exhaustive amplification – more is left for the investigation of the onlooker, he is incited to the further study of that which stands out before him in such strong light and shade; he is prompted to think out the subject, and even to overcome the hindrance which hitherto prevented it from emerging clearly.

179.

Against the Eccentric. – When art arrays itself in the most shabby material it is most easily recognised as art.

180.

Collective Intellect. – A good author possesses not only his own intellect, but also that of his friends.

181.

Different Kinds of Mistakes. – The misfortune of acute and clear authors is that people consider them as shallow and therefore do not devote any effort to them; and the good fortune of obscure writers is that the reader makes an effort to understand them and places the delight in his own zeal to their credit.

182.

Relation to Science. – None of the people have any real interest in a science, who only begin to be enthusiastic about it when they themselves have made discoveries in it.

183.

The Key. – The single thought on which an eminent man sets a great value, arousing the derision and laughter of the masses, is for him a key to hidden treasures; for them, however, it is nothing *more* than a piece of old iron.

184.

Untranslatable. – It is neither the best nor the worst parts of a book which are untranslatable.

185.

Authors' Paradoxes. – The so-called paradoxes of an author to which a reader objects are often not in the author's book at all, but in the reader's head.

186.
Wit. – The wittiest authors produce a scarcely noticeable smile.

187.
Antithesis. – Antithesis is the narrow gate through which error is fondest of sneaking to the truth.

188.
Thinkers as Stylists. – Most thinkers write badly, because they communicate not only their thoughts, but also the thinking of them.

189.
Thoughts in Poetry. – The poet conveys his thoughts ceremoniously in the vehicle of rhythm, usually because they are not able to go on foot.

190.
The Sin against the Reader's Intellect. – When an author renounces his talent in order merely to put himself on a level with the reader, he commits the only deadly sin which the latter will never forgive, should he notice anything of it. One may say everything that is bad about a person, but in the manner *in which* it is said one must know how to revive his vanity anew.

191.
The Limits of Uprightness. – Even the most upright author lets fall a word too much when he wishes to round off a period.

192.
The Best Author. – The best author will be he who is ashamed to become one.

193.
Draconian Law against Authors. – One should regard authors as criminals who only obtain acquittal or mercy in the rarest cases – that would be a remedy for books becoming too rife.

194.

The Fools of Modern Culture. – The fools of mediaeval courts correspond to our *feuilleton* writers; they are the same kind of men, semi-rational, witty, extravagant, foolish, sometimes there only for the purpose of lessening the pathos of the outlook with fancies and chatter, and of drowning with their clamour the far too deep and solemn chimes of great events; they were formerly in the service of princes and nobles, now they are in the service of parties (since a large portion of the old obsequiousness in the intercourse of the people with their prince still survives in party-feeling and party-discipline). Modern literary men, however, are generally very similar to the *feuilleton* writers, they are the 'fools of modern culture', whom one judges more leniently when one does not regard them as fully responsible beings. To look upon writing as a regular profession should justly be regarded as a form of madness.

195.

After the Example of the Greeks. – It is a great hindrance to knowledge at present that, owing to centuries of exaggeration of feeling, all words have become vague and inflated. The higher stage of culture, which is under the sway (though not under the tyranny) of knowledge, requires great sobriety of feeling and thorough concentration of words – on which points the Greeks in the time of Demosthenes set an example to us. Exaggeration is a distinguishing mark of all modern writings, and even when they are simply written the expressions therein are still *felt* as *too* eccentric. Careful reflection, conciseness, coldness, plainness, even carried intentionally to the farthest limits – in a word, suppression of feeling and taciturnity – these are the only remedies. For the rest, this cold manner of writing and feeling is now very attractive, as a contrast; and to be sure there is a new danger therein. For intense cold is as good a stimulus as a high degree of warmth.

196.

Good Narrators, Bad Explainers. – In good narrators there is often found an admirable psychological sureness and logicalness, as far as these qualities can be observed in the actions of their personages, in positively ludicrous contrast to their inexperienced pyschological reasoning, so that their culture appears to be as extraordinarily high one moment as it seems regrettably defective the next. It happens far too frequently that they give an evidently false explanation of their own heroes and their actions – of this there is no doubt, however improbable the thing may appear. It is quite likely that the greatest pianoforte player has thought but little about the technical conditions and the special virtues, drawbacks, usefulness, and tractability of each finger (dactylic ethics), and makes big mistakes whenever he speaks of such things.

197.

The Writings of Acquaintances and their Readers. – We read the writings of our acquaintances (friends and enemies) in a double sense, inasmuch as our perception constantly whispers, 'That is something of himself, a remembrance of his inward being, his experiences, his talents,' and at the same time another kind of perception endeavours to estimate the profit of the work in itself, what valuation it merits apart from its author, how far it will enrich knowledge. These two manners of reading and estimating interfere with each other, as may naturally be supposed. And a conversation with a friend will only bear good fruit of knowledge when both think only of the matter under consideration and forget that they are friends.

198.

Rhythmical Sacrifice. – Good writers alter the rhythm of many a period merely because they do not credit the general reader with the ability to comprehend the measure followed by the period in its first version; thus they make it easier for the reader, by giving the preference to the better known rhythms. This regard for the rhythmical incapacity of the modern reader has already called forth many a sigh, for much has been sacrificed to it. Does not the same thing happen to good musicians?

199.

The Incomplete as an Artistic Stimulus. – The incomplete is often more effective than perfection, and this is the case with eulogies. To effect their purpose a stimulating incompleteness is necessary, as an irrational element, which calls up a sea before the hearer's imagination, and, like a mist, conceals the opposite coast, i.e. the limits of the object of praise. If the well-known merits of a person are referred to and described at length and in detail, it always gives rise to the suspicion that these are his only merits. The perfect eulogist takes his stand above the person praised, he appears to *overlook* him. Therefore complete praise has a weakening effect.

200.

Precautions in Writing and Teaching. – Whoever has once written and has been seized with the passion for writing learns from almost all that he does and experiences that which is literally communicable. He thinks no longer of himself, but of the author and his public; he desires insight into things; but not for his own use. He who teaches is mostly incapable of doing anything for his own good: he is always thinking of the good of his scholars, and all knowledge delights him only in so far as he is able to teach it. He comes at last to regard himself as a medium of knowledge, and above all as a means thereto, so that he has lost all serious consideration for himself.

201.

The Necessity for Bad Authors. – There will always be a need of bad authors; for they meet the taste of readers of an undeveloped, immature age – these have their requirements as well as mature readers. If human life were of greater length, the number of mature individuals would be greater than that of the immature, or at least equally great; but, as it is, by far the greater number die too young: i.e. there are always many more undeveloped intellects with bad taste. These demand, with the greater impetuosity of youth, the satisfaction of their needs, and they *insist* on having bad authors.

202.

Too Near and too Far. – The reader and the author very often do not understand each other, because the author knows his theme too well and finds it almost slow, so that he omits the examples, of which he knows hundreds; the reader, however, is interested in the subject, and is liable to consider it as badly proved if examples are lacking.

203.

A Vanished Preparation for Art. – Of everything that was practised in public schools, the thing of greatest value was the exercise in Latin style – this was an exercise in art, whilst all other occupations aimed only at the acquirement of knowledge. It is a barbarism to put German composition before it, for there is no typical German style developed by public oratory; but if there is a desire to advance practice in thought by means of German composition, then it is certainly better for the time being to pay no attention to style, to separate the practice in thought, therefore, from the practice in reproduction. The latter should confine itself to the various modes of presenting a given subject, and should not concern itself with the independent finding of a subject. The mere presentment of a given subject was the task of the Latin style, for which the old teachers possessed a long vanished delicacy of ear. Formerly, whoever learned to write well in a modern language had to thank this practice for the acquirement (now we are obliged to go to school to the older French writers). But yet more: he obtained an idea of the loftiness and difficulty of form, and was prepared for art in the only right way: by practice.

204.

Darkness and Over-Brightness Side by Side. – Authors who, in general, do not understand how to express their thoughts clearly are fond of choosing, in detail, the strongest, most exaggerated distinctions and superlatives – thereby is produced an effect of light, which is like torchlight in intricate forest paths.

205.

Literary Painting. – An important object will be best described if the colours for the painting are taken out of the object itself, as a chemist does, and then employed like an artist, so that the drawing develops from the outlines and transitions of the colours. Thus the painting acquires something of the entrancing natural element which gives such importance to the object itself.

206.

Books which Teach how to Dance. – There are authors who, by representing the impossible as possible, and by talking of morality and cleverness as if both were merely moods and humours assumed at will, produce a feeling of exuberant freedom, as if man stood on tiptoe and were compelled to dance from sheer, inward delight.

207.

Unfinished Thoughts. – Just as not only manhood, but also youth and childhood have a value *per se*, and are not to be looked upon merely as passages and bridges, so also unfinished thoughts have their value. For this reason we must not torment a poet with subtle explanations, but must take pleasure in the uncertainty of his horizon, as if the way to further thoughts were still open. We stand on the threshold; we wait as for the digging up of a treasure, it is as if a well of profundity were about to be discovered. The poet anticipates something of the thinker's pleasure in the discovery of a leading thought, and makes us covetous, so that we give chase to it; but it flutters past our head and exhibits the loveliest butterfly-wings – and yet it escapes us.

208.

The Book Grown almost into a Human Being. – Every author is surprised anew at the way in which his book, as soon as he has sent it out, continues to live a life of its own; it seems to him as if one part of an insect had been cut off and now went on its own way. Perhaps he forgets it almost entirely, perhaps he rises above the view expressed therein, perhaps even he understands it no longer, and has lost that impulse upon which he soared at the time he conceived the book; meanwhile it seeks its readers, inflames life, pleases, horrifies, inspires new works, becomes the soul of designs and actions – in short, it lives like a creature endowed with mind and soul, and yet is no human being. The happiest fate is that of the author who, as an old man, is able to say that all there was in him of life-inspiring, strengthening, exalting, enlightening thoughts and feelings still lives on in his writings, and that he himself now only represents the grey ashes, whilst the fire has been kept alive and spread out. And if we consider that every human action, not only a book, is in some way or other the cause of other actions, decisions, and thoughts; that everything that happens is inseparably connected with everything that is going to happen, we recognise the real *immortality*, that of movement – that which has once moved is enclosed and immortalised in the general union of all existence, like an insect within a piece of amber.

209.

Joy in Old Age. – The thinker, as likewise the artist, who has put his best self into his works, feels an almost malicious joy when he sees how mind and body are being slowly damaged and destroyed by time, as if from a dark corner he were spying a thief at his money-chest, knowing all the time that it was empty and his treasures in safety.

210.

Quiet Fruitfulness. – The born aristocrats of the mind are not in too much of a hurry; their creations appear and fall from the tree on some quiet autumn evening, without being rashly desired, instigated, or pushed aside by new matter. The unceasing desire to create is vulgar, and betrays envy, jealousy, and ambition. If a man is something, it is not really necessary for him to do anything – and yet he does a great deal. There is a human species higher even than the 'productive' man.

211.

Achilles and Homer. – It is always like the case of Achilles and Homer – the one *has* the experiences and sensations, the other *describes* them. A genuine author only puts into words the feelings and adventures of others, he is an artist, and divines much from the little he has experienced. Artists are by no means creatures of great passion; but they frequently *represent* themselves as such with the unconscious feeling that their depicted passion will be better believed in if their own life gives credence to their experience in these affairs. They need only let themselves go, not control themselves, and give free play to their anger and their desires, and every one will immediately cry out, 'How passionate he is!' But the deeply stirring passion that consumes and often destroys the individual is another matter: those who have really experienced it do not describe it in dramas, harmonies or romances. Artists are frequently *unbridled* individuals, in so far as they are not artists, but that is a different thing.

212.

Old Doubts about the Effect of Art. – Should pity and fear really be unburdened through tragedy, as Aristotle would have it, so that the hearers return home colder and quieter? Should ghost-stories really make us less fearful and superstitious? In the case of certain physical processes, in the satisfaction of love, for instance, it is true that with the fulfilment of a need there follows an alleviation and temporary decrease in the impulse. But fear and pity are not in this sense the needs of particular organs which require to be relieved. And in time every instinct is even *strengthened* by practice in its satisfaction, in spite of that periodical mitigation. It might be possible that in each single case pity and fear would be soothed and relieved by tragedy; nevertheless, they might, on the whole, be increased by tragic influences, and Plato would be right in saying that tragedy makes us altogether more timid and susceptible. The tragic poet himself would then of necessity acquire a gloomy and fearful view of the world, and a yielding, irritable, tearful soul; it would also agree with Plato's view if the tragic poets, and likewise the entire part of the community that derived particular pleasure from them, degenerated into ever greater licentiousness and intemperance. But what right, indeed, has our age to give an answer to that great question of Plato's as to the moral influence of art? If we even had art – where have we an influence, *any kind* of an art-influence?

213.

Pleasure in Nonsense. – How can we take pleasure in nonsense? But wherever there is laughter in the world this is the case: it may even be said that almost everywhere where there is happiness, there is found pleasure in nonsense. The transformation of experience into its opposite, of the suitable into the unsuitable, the obligatory into the optional (but in such a manner that this process produces no injury and is only imagined in jest), is a pleasure; for it temporarily liberates us from the yoke of the obligatory, suitable and experienced, in which we usually find our pitiless masters; we play and laugh when the expected (which generally causes fear and expectancy) happens without bringing any injury. It is the pleasure felt by slaves in the Saturnalian feasts.

214.

The Ennobling of Reality. – Through the fact that in the aphrodisiac impulse men discerned a godhead and with adoring gratitude felt it working within themselves, this emotion has in the course of time become imbued with higher conceptions, and has thereby been materially ennobled. Thus certain nations, by virtue of this art of idealisation, have created great aids to culture out of diseases – the Greeks, for instance, who in earlier centuries suffered from great nervous epidemics (like epilepsy and St. Vitus' Dance), and developed out of them the splendid type of the Bacchante. The Greeks, however, enjoyed an astonishingly high degree of health – their secret was, to revere even disease as a god, if it only possessed *power*.

215.

Music. – Music by and for itself is not so portentous for our inward nature, so deeply moving, that it ought to be looked upon as the *direct* language of the feelings; but its ancient union with poetry has infused so much symbolism into rhythmical movement, into loudness and softness of tone, that we now *imagine* it speaks directly *to* and comes *from* the inward nature. Dramatic music is only possible when the art of harmony has acquired an immense range of symbolical means, through song, opera, and a hundred attempts at description by sound. 'Absolute music' is either form *per se*, in the rude condition of music, when playing in time and with various degrees of strength gives pleasure, or the symbolism of form which speaks to the understanding even without poetry, after the two arts were joined finally together after long development and the musical form had been woven about with threads of meaning and feeling. People who are backward in musical development can appreciate a piece of harmony merely as execution, whilst those who are advanced will comprehend it symbolically. No music is deep and full of meaning in itself, it does not speak of 'will', of the 'thing-in-itself'; that could be imagined by the intellect only in an age which had conquered for musical symbolism the entire range of inner life. It was the intellect itself that first *gave* this meaning to sound, just as it also gave meaning to the relation between lines and masses in architecture, but which in itself is quite foreign to mechanical laws.

216.

Gesture and Speech. – Older than speech is the imitation of gestures, which is carried on unconsciously and which, in the general repression of the language of gesture and trained control of the muscles, is still so great that we cannot look at a face moved by emotion without feeling an agitation of our own face (it may be remarked that feigned yawning excites real yawning in any one who sees it). The imitated gesture leads the one who imitates back to the sensation it expressed in the face or body of the one imitated. Thus men learned to understand one another, thus the child still learns to understand the mother. Generally speaking, painful sensations may also have been expressed by gestures, and the pain which caused them (for instance, tearing the hair, beating the breast, forcible distortion and straining of the muscles of the face). On the other hand, gestures of joy were themselves joyful and lent themselves easily to the communication of the understanding; (laughter, as the expression of the feeling when being tickled, serves also for the expression of other pleasurable sensations). As soon as men understood each other by gestures, there could be established a *symbolism* of gestures; I mean, an understanding could be arrived at respecting the language of accents, so that first *accent* and gesture (to which it was symbolically added) were produced, and later on the accent alone. In former times there happened very frequently that which now happens in the development of music, especially of dramatic music – while music, without explanatory dance and pantomime (language of gesture), is at first only empty sound, but by long familiarity with that combination of music and movement the ear becomes schooled into instant interpretation of the figures of sound, and finally attains a height of quick understanding, where it has no longer any need of visible movement and *understands* the sound-poet without it. It is then called absolute music, that is music in which, without further help, everything is symbolically understood.

217.

The Spiritualising of Higher Art. – By virtue of extraordinary intellectual exercise through the art-development of the new music, our ears have been growing more intellectual. For this reason we can now endure a much greater volume of sound, much more 'noise', because we are far better practised in listening for the *sense* in it than were our ancestors. As a matter of fact, all our senses have been somewhat blunted, because they immediately look for the sense; that is, they ask what 'it means' and not what 'it is' – such a blunting betrays itself, for instance, in the absolute dominion of the temperature of sounds; for ears which still make the finer distinctions, between *cis* and *des*, for instance, are now amongst the exceptions. In this respect our ear has grown coarser. And then the ugly side of the world, the one originally hostile to the senses, has been conquered for music; its power has been immensely widened, especially in the expression of the noble, the terrible, and the mysterious: our music now gives utterance to things which had formerly no tongue. In the same way certain painters have rendered the eye more intellectual, and have gone far beyond that which was formerly called pleasure in colour and form. Here, too, that side of the world originally considered as ugly has been conquered by the artistic intellect. What results from all this? The more capable of thought that eye and ear become, the more they approach the limit where they become senseless, the seat of pleasure is moved into the brain, the organs of the senses themselves become dulled and weak, the symbolical takes more and more the place of the actual – and thus we arrive at barbarism in this way as surely as in any other. In the meantime we may say: the world is uglier than ever, but it *represents* a more beautiful world than has ever existed. But the more the amber-scent of meaning is dispersed and evaporated, the rarer become those who perceive it, and the remainder halt at what is ugly and endeavour to enjoy it direct, an aim, however, which they never succeed in attaining. Thus, in

Germany there is a twofold direction of musical development, here a throng of ten thousand with ever higher, finer demands, ever listening more and more for the 'it means', and there the immense countless mass which yearly grows more incapable of understanding what is important even in the form of sensual ugliness, and which therefore turns ever more willingly to what in music is ugly and foul in itself, that is, to the basely sensual.

218.

A Stone is More of a Stone than Formerly. – As a general rule we no longer understand architecture, at least by no means in the same way as we understand music. We have outgrown the symbolism of lines and figures, just as we are no longer accustomed to the sound effects of rhetoric, and have not absorbed this kind of mother's milk of culture since our first moment of life. Everything in a Greek or Christian building originally had a meaning, and referred to a higher order of things; this feeling of inexhaustible meaning enveloped the edifice like a mystic veil. Beauty was only a secondary consideration in the system, without in any way materially injuring the fundamental sentiment of the mysteriously-exalted, the divinely and magically consecrated; at the most, beauty *tempered horror* – but this horror was everywhere presupposed. What is the beauty of a building now? The same thing as the beautiful face of a stupid woman, a kind of mask.

219.

The Religious Source of the Newer Music. – Soulful music arose out of the Catholicism re-established after the Council of Trent, through Palestrina, who endowed the newly awakened, earnest, and deeply moved spirit with sound; later on, in Bach, it appeared also in Protestantism, as far as this had been deepened by the Pietists and released from its originally dogmatic character. The supposition and necessary preparation for both origins is the familiarity with music, which existed during and before the Renaissance, namely that learned occupation with music, which was really scientific pleasure in the masterpieces of harmony and voice-training. On the other hand, the opera must have preceded it, wherein the layman made his protest against a music that had grown too learned and cold, and endeavoured to re-endow Polyhymnia with a soul. Without the change to that deeply religious sentiment, without the dying away of the inwardly moved temperament, music would have remained learned or operatic; the spirit of the counter-reformation is the spirit of modern music (for that pietism in Bach's music is also a kind of counter-reformation). So deeply are we indebted to the religious life. Music was the counter-reformation in the field of art; to this belongs also the later painting of the Caracci and Caravaggi, perhaps also the baroque style, in *any* case more than the architecture of the Renaissance or of antiquity. And we might still ask: if our newer music could move stones, would it build them up into antique architecture? I very much doubt it. For that which predominates in this music, affections, pleasure in exalted, highly-strained sentiments, the desire to be alive at any cost, the quick change of feeling, the strong relief-effects of light and shade, the combination of the ecstatic and the naive – all this has already reigned in the plastic arts and created new laws of style: but it was neither in the time of antiquity nor of the Renaissance.

220.

The Beyond in Art. – It is not without deep pain that we acknowledge the fact that in their loftiest soarings, artists of all ages have exalted and divinely transfigured precisely those ideas which we now recognise as false; they are the glorifiers of humanity's religious and philosophical errors, and they could not have been this without belief in the absolute truth of these errors. But if the belief in such truth diminishes at all, if the rainbow colours at the farthest ends of human knowledge and imagination fade, then this kind of art can never re-flourish, for, like the *Divina Commedia*, Raphael's paintings, Michelangelo's frescoes, and Gothic cathedrals, they indicate not only a cosmic but also a metaphysical meaning in the work of art. Out of all this will grow a touching legend that such an art and such an artistic faith once existed.

221.

Revolution in Poetry. – The strict limit which the French dramatists marked out with regard to unity of action, time and place, construction of style, verse and sentence, selection of words and ideas, was a school as important as that of counterpoint and fugue in the development of modern music or that of the Gorgianic figures in Greek oratory. Such a restriction may appear absurd; nevertheless there is no means of getting out of naturalism except by confining ourselves at first to the strongest (perhaps most arbitrary) means. Thus we gradually learn to walk gracefully on the narrow paths that bridge giddy abysses, and acquire great suppleness of movement as a result, as the history of music proves to our living eyes. Here we see how, step by step, the fetters get looser, until at last they may appear to be altogether thrown off; this *appearance* is the highest achievement of a necessary development in art. In the art of modern poetry there existed no such fortunate, gradual emerging from self-imposed fetters. Lessing held up to scorn in Germany the French form, the only modern form of art, and pointed to Shakespeare; and thus the steadiness of that unfettering was lost and a spring was made into naturalism – that is, back into the beginnings of art. From this Goethe endeavoured to save himself, by always trying to limit himself anew in different ways; but even the most gifted only succeeds by continuously experimenting, if the thread of development has once been broken. It is to the unconsciously revered, if also repudiated, model of French tragedy that Schiller owes his comparative sureness of form, and he remained fairly independent of Lessing (whose dramatic attempts he is well known to have rejected). But after Voltaire the French themselves suddenly lacked the great talents which would have led the development of tragedy out of constraint to that apparent freedom; later on they followed the German example and made a spring into a sort of Rousseau-like state of nature and experiments. It is only necessary to read Voltaire's 'Mahomet' from time to time in order to perceive clearly what European culture has lost through that breaking down of tradition. Once for all, Voltaire was the last of the great dramatists who with Greek proportion controlled his manifold soul, equal even to the greatest storms of tragedy – he was able to do what no German could, because the French nature is much nearer akin to the Greek than is the German; he was also the last great writer who in the wielding of prose possessed the Greek ear, Greek artistic conscientiousness, and Greek simplicity and grace; he was, also, one of the last men able to combine in himself the greatest freedom of mind and an absolutely unrevolutionary way of thinking without being inconsistent and cowardly. Since that time the modern spirit, with its restlessness and its hatred of moderation and restrictions, has obtained the mastery on all sides, let loose at first by the fever of revolution, and then once more putting a bridle on itself when it became filled with fear and horror at itself – but it was the bridle of rigid logic, no longer that of artistic moderation. It is true that through that unfettering for a time we are able to enjoy the poetry of all nations, everything that has sprung up in hidden places, original, wild, wonderfully beautiful and gigantically irregular, from folk-songs up to the 'great barbarian' Shakespeare; we taste the joys of local colour and costume, hitherto unknown to all artistic nations; we make liberal use of the 'barbaric advantages' of our time, which Goethe accentuated against Schiller in order to place the formlessness of his *Faust* in the most favourable light. But for how much longer? The encroaching flood of poetry of all styles and all nations *must* gradually sweep away that magic garden upon which a quiet and hidden growth would still have been possible; all poets must become experimenting imitators, daring copyists, however great their primary strength may be. Eventually, the public, which has lost the habit of seeing the actual artistic fact in the *controlling* of depicting power, in the organising mastery over all art-means, *must* come ever more and more to value power for power's sake, colour for colour's sake, idea for idea's sake, inspiration for inspiration's sake; accordingly it will not enjoy the elements and conditions of the work of art, unless *isolated*, and finally will make the very natural demand that the artist *must* deliver it to them isolated. True, the 'senseless 'fetters of Franco-Greek art have been thrown off, but unconsciously we have grown accustomed to consider all fetters, all restrictions as senseless; and so art moves towards its liberation, but, in so doing, it touches – which is certainly highly edifying – upon all the phases of its beginning, its childhood, its incompleteness, its sometime boldness and excesses – in perishing it interprets its origin and growth. One of the great ones, whose instinct may be relied on and whose theory lacked nothing but thirty years *more* of practice, Lord Byron, once said: that with regard to poetry in general, the more he thought about it the more convinced he was that one and all we are entirely on a wrong track, that we are following an inwardly false revolutionary system, and that either our own generation or the next will yet arrive at this same conviction. It is the same Lord Byron who said that he 'looked upon Shakespeare as the very worst model, although the most extraordinary poet'. And does not Goethe's mature artistic insight in the second half of his life say practically the same thing? – that insight by means of which he made such a bound in advance of whole generations that, generally speaking, it may be said that Goethe's influence has not yet begun, that his time has still to come. Just because his nature held him fast for a long time in the path of the poetical revolution, just because he drank to the dregs of whatsoever new sources, views and expedients had been indirectly discovered through that breaking down of tradition, of all that had been unearthed from under the ruins of art, his later transformation and conversion carries so much weight; it shows that he felt the deepest longing to win back the traditions of art, and to give in fancy the ancient perfection and completeness to the abandoned ruins and colonnades of the temple, with the imagination of the eye at least, should the strength of the arm be found too weak to build where such tremendous powers were needed even to destroy. Thus he lived in art as in the remembrance of the true art, his poetry had become an aid to remembrance, to the understanding of old and long-departed ages of art. With respect to the strength of the new age, his demands could not be satisfied; but the pain this occasioned was amply balanced by the joy that they have been satisfied once, and that we ourselves can still participate in this satisfaction. Not individuals, but more or less ideal masks; no reality, but an allegorical generality; topical characters, local colours toned down and rendered mythical almost to the point of invisibility; contemporary feeling and the problems of contemporary society reduced to the simplest forms, stripped of their attractive, interesting pathological qualities, made *ineffective* in every other but the artistic sense; no new materials and characters, but the old, long-accustomed ones in constant new animation and transformation; that is art, as Goethe *understood* it later, as the Greeks and even the French *practised* it.

222.

What Remains of Art. – It is true that art has a much greater value in the case of certain metaphysical hypotheses, for instance when the belief obtains that the character is unchangeable and that the essence of the world manifests itself continually in all character and action; thus the artist's work becomes the symbol of the *eternally constant*, while according to our views the artist can only endow his picture with temporary value, because man on the whole has developed and is mutable, and even the individual man has nothing fixed and constant. The same thing holds good with another metaphysical hypothesis: assuming that our visible world were only a delusion, as metaphysicians declare, then art would come very near to the real world, for there would then be far too much similarity between the world of appearance and the dream-world of the artist; and the remaining difference would place the meaning of art higher even than the meaning of nature, because art would represent the same forms, the types and models of nature. But those suppositions are false; and what position does art retain after this acknowledgement? Above all, for centuries it has taught us to look upon life in every shape with interest and pleasure and to carry our feelings so far that at last we exclaim, 'Whatever it may be, life is good.' This teaching of art, to take pleasure in existence and to regard human life as a piece of nature, without too vigorous movement, as an object of regular development – this teaching has grown into us; it reappears as an all-powerful need of knowledge. We could renounce art, but we should not therewith forfeit the ability it has taught us – just as we have given up religion, but not the exalting and intensifying of temperament acquired through religion. As the plastic arts and music are the standards of that wealth of feeling really acquired and obtained through religion, so also, after a disappearance of art, the intensity and multiplicity of the joys of life which it had implanted in us would still demand satisfaction. The scientific man is the further development of the artistic man.

223.

The After-glow of Art. – Just as in old age we remember our youth and celebrate festivals of memory, so in a short time mankind will stand towards art: its relation will be that of a *touching memory* of the joys of youth. Never, perhaps, in former ages was art dealt with so seriously and thoughtfully as now when it appears to be surrounded by the magic influence of death. We call to mind that Greek city in southern Italy, which once a year still celebrates its Greek feasts, amidst tears and mourning, that foreign barbarism triumphs ever more and more over the customs its people brought with them into the land; and never has Hellenism been so much appreciated, nowhere has this golden nectar been drunk with so great delight, as amongst these fast disappearing Hellenes. The artist will soon come to be regarded as a splendid relic, and to him, as to a wonderful stranger on whose power and beauty depended the happiness of former ages, there will be paid such honour as is not often enjoyed by one of our race. The best in us is perhaps inherited from the sentiments of former times, to which it is hardly possible for us now to return by direct ways; the sun has already disappeared, but the heavens of our life are still glowing and illumined by it, although we can behold it no longer.

FIFTH DIVISION.

THE SIGNS OF HIGHER AND LOWER CULTURE.

224.

Ennoblement through Degeneration. – History teaches that a race of people is best preserved where the greater number hold one common spirit in consequence of the similarity of their accustomed and indisputable principles: in consequence, therefore, of their common faith. Thus strength is afforded by good and thorough customs, thus is learnt the subjection of the individual, and strenuousness of character becomes a birth gift and afterwards is fostered as a habit. The danger to these communities founded on individuals of strong and similar character is that gradually increasing stupidity through transmission, which follows all stability like its shadow. It is on the more unrestricted, more uncertain and morally weaker individuals that depends the *intellectual progress* of such communities, it is they who attempt all that is new and manifold. Numbers of these perish on account of their weakness, without having achieved any specially visible effect; but generally, particularly when they have descendants, they flare up and from time to time inflict a wound on the stable element of the community. Precisely in this sore and weakened place the community is *inoculated* with something new; but its general strength must be great enough to absorb and assimilate this new thing into its blood. Deviating natures are of the utmost importance wherever there is to be progress. Every wholesale progress must be preceded by a partial weakening. The strongest natures *retain* the type, the weaker ones help it to *develop*. Something similar happens in the case of individuals; a deterioration, a mutilation, even a vice and, above all, a physical or moral loss is seldom without its advantage. For instance, a sickly man in the midst of a warlike and restless race will perhaps have more chance of being alone and thereby growing quieter and wiser, the one-eyed man will possess a stronger eye, the blind man will have a deeper inward sight and will certainly have a keener sense of hearing. In so far it appears to me that the famous Struggle for Existence is not the only point of view from which an explanation can be given of the progress or strengthening of an individual or a race. Rather must two different things converge: firstly, the multiplying of stable strength through mental binding in faith and common feeling; secondly, the possibility of attaining to higher aims, through the fact that there are deviating natures and, in consequence, partial weakening and wounding of the stable strength; it is precisely the weaker nature, as the more delicate and free, that makes all progress at all possible. A people that is crumbling and weak in any one part, but as a whole still strong and healthy, is able to absorb the infection of what is new and incorporate it to its advantage. The task of education in a single individual is this: to plant him so firmly and surely that, as a whole, he can no longer be diverted from his path. Then, however, the educator must wound him, or else make use of the wounds which fate inflicts, and when pain and need have thus arisen, something new and noble can be inoculated into the wounded places. With regard to the state, Machiavelli says that, 'the form of Government is of very small importance, although half-educated people think otherwise. The great aim of State-craft should be duration, which outweighs all else, inasmuch as it is more valuable than liberty.' It is only with securely founded and guaranteed duration that continual development and ennobling inoculation are at all possible. As a rule, however, authority, the dangerous companion of all duration, will rise in opposition to this.

225.

Free-Thinker a Relative Term. – We call that man a free-thinker who thinks otherwise than is expected of him in consideration of his origin, surroundings, position, and office, or by reason of the prevailing contemporary views. He is the exception, fettered minds are the rule; these latter reproach him, saying that his free principles either have their origin in a desire to be remarkable or else cause free actions to be inferred – that is to say, actions which are not compatible with fettered morality. Sometimes it is also said that the cause of such and such free principles may be traced to mental perversity and extravagance; but only malice speaks thus, nor does it believe what it says, but wishes thereby to do an injury, for the free-thinker usually bears the proof of his greater goodness and keenness of intellect written in his face so plainly that the fettered spirits understand it well enough. But the two other derivations of free-thought are honestly intended; as a matter of fact, many free-thinkers are created in one or other of these ways. For this reason, however, the tenets to which they attain in this manner might be truer and more reliable than those of the fettered spirits. In the knowledge of truth, what really matters is the *possession* of it, not the impulse under which it was sought, the way in which it was found. If the free-thinkers are right then the fettered spirits are wrong, and it is a matter of indifference whether the former have reached truth through immorality or the latter hitherto retained hold of untruths through morality. Moreover, it is not essential to the free-thinker that he should hold more correct views, but that he should have liberated himself from what was customary, be it successfully or disastrously. As a rule, however, he will have truth, or at least the spirit of truth-investigation, on his side; he demands reasons, the others demand faith.

226.

The Origin of Faith. – The fettered spirit does not take up his position from conviction, but from habit; he is a Christian, for instance, not because he had a comprehension of different creeds and could take his choice; he is an Englishman, not because he decided for England, but he found Christianity and England ready-made and accepted them without any reason, just as one who is born in a wine-country becomes a wine-drinker. Later on, perhaps, as he was a Christian and an Englishman, he discovered a few reasons in favour of his habit; these reasons may be upset, but he is not therefore upset in his whole position. For instance, let a fettered spirit be obliged to bring forward his reasons against bigamy and then it will be seen whether his holy zeal in favour of monogamy is based upon reason or upon custom. The adoption of guiding principles without reasons is called *faith*.

227.

Conclusions drawn from the Consequences and traced back to Reason and Un-reason. – All states and orders of society, professions, matrimony, education, law: all these find strength and duration only in the faith which the fettered spirits repose in them – that is, in the absence of reasons, or at least in the averting of inquiries as to reasons. The restricted spirits do not willingly acknowledge this, and feel that it is a *pudendum*. Christianity, however, which was very simple in its intellectual ideas, remarked nothing of this *pudendum*, required faith and nothing but faith, and passionately repulsed the demand for reasons; it pointed to the success of faith: 'You will soon feel the advantages of faith,' it suggested, 'and through faith shall ye be saved.' As an actual fact, the State pursues the same course, and every father brings up his son in the same way: 'Only believe this,' he says, 'and you will soon feel the good it does.' This implies, however, that the truth of an opinion is proved by its personal usefulness; the wholesomeness of a doctrine must be a guarantee for its intellectual surety and solidity. It is exactly as if an accused person in a court of law were to say, 'My counsel speaks the whole truth, for only see what is the result of his speech: I shall be acquitted.' Because the fettered spirits retain their principles on account of their usefulness, they suppose that the free spirit also seeks his own advantage in his views and only holds that to be true which is profitable to him. But as he appears to find profitable just the contrary of that which his compatriots or equals find profitable, these latter assume that his principles are dangerous to them; they say or feel, 'He must not be right, for he is injurious to us.'

228.

The Strong, Good Character. – The restriction of views, which habit has made instinct, leads to what is called strength of character. When any one acts from few but always from the same motives, his actions acquire great energy; if these actions accord with the principles of the fettered spirits they are recognised, and they produce, moreover, in those who perform them the sensation of a good conscience. Few motives, energetic action, and a good conscience compose what is called strength of character. The man of strong character lacks a knowledge of the many possibilities and directions of action; his intellect is fettered and restricted, because in a given case it shows him, perhaps, only two possibilities; between these two he must now of necessity choose, in accordance with his whole nature, and he does this easily and quickly because he has not to choose between fifty possibilities. The educating surroundings aim at fettering every individual, by always placing before him the smallest number of possibilities. The individual is always treated by his educators as if he were, indeed, something new, but should become a *duplicate*. If he makes his first appearance as something unknown, unprecedented, he must be turned into something known and precedented. In a child, the familiar manifestation of restriction is called a good character; in placing itself on the side of the fettered spirits the child first discloses its awakening common feeling; with this foundation of common sentiment, he will eventually become useful to his State or rank.

229.

The Standards and Values of the Fettered Spirits. – There are four species of things concerning which the restricted spirits say they are in the right. Firstly: all things that last are right; secondly: all things that are not burdens to us are right; thirdly: all things that are advantageous for us are right; fourthly: all things for which we have made sacrifices are right. The last sentence, for instance, explains why a war that was begun in opposition to popular feeling is carried on with enthusiasm directly a sacrifice has been made for it. The free spirits, who bring their case before the forum of the fettered spirits, must prove that free spirits always existed, that free-spiritism is therefore enduring, that it will not become a burden, and, finally, that on the whole they are an advantage to the fettered spirits. It is because they cannot convince the restricted spirits on this last point that they profit nothing by having proved the first and second propositions.

230.

Esprit Fort. – Compared with him who has tradition on his side and requires no reasons for his actions, the free spirit is always weak, especially in action; for he is acquainted with too many motives and points of view, and has, therefore, an uncertain and unpractised hand. What means exist of making him *strong in spite of this* so that he will, at least, manage to survive, and will not perish ineffectually? What is the source of the strong spirit (*esprit fort*)? This is especially the question as to the production of genius. Whence comes the energy, the unbending strength, the endurance with which the one, in opposition to accepted ideas, endeavours to obtain an entirely individual knowledge of the world?

231.

The Rise of Genius. – The ingenuity with which a prisoner seeks the means of freedom, the most cold-blooded and patient employment of every smallest advantage, can teach us of what tools Nature sometimes makes use in order to produce Genius – a word which I beg will be understood without any mythological and religious flavour; she, Nature, begins it in a dungeon and excites to the utmost its desire to free itself. Or to give another picture: some one who has completely *lost his way* in a wood, but who with unusual energy strives to reach the open in one direction or another, will sometimes discover a new path which nobody knew previously, thus arise geniuses, who are credited with originality. It has already been said that mutilation, crippling, or the loss of some important organ, is frequently the cause of the unusual development of another organ, because this one has to fulfil its own and also another function. This explains the source of many a brilliant talent. These general remarks on the origin of genius may be applied to the special case, the origin of the perfect free spirit.

232.

Conjecture as to the Origin of Free Spiritism. – Just as the glaciers increase when in equatorial regions the sun shines upon the seas with greater force than hitherto, so may a very strong and spreading free-spiritism be a proof that somewhere or other the force of feeling has grown extraordinarily.

233.

The Voice of History. – In general, history *appears* to teach the following about the production of genius: it ill-treats and torments mankind – calls to the passions of envy, hatred, and rivalry – drives them to desperation, people against people, throughout whole centuries! Then, perhaps, like a stray spark from the terrible energy thereby aroused, there flames up suddenly the light of genius; the will, like a horse maddened by the rider's spur, thereupon breaks out and leaps over into another domain. He who could attain to a comprehension of the production of genius, and desires to carry out practically the manner in which Nature usually goes to work, would have to be just as evil and regardless as Nature itself. But perhaps we have not heard rightly.

234.

The Value of the Middle of the Road. – It is possible that the production of genius is reserved to a limited period of mankind's history. For we must not expect from the future everything that very defined conditions were able to produce; for instance, not the astounding effects of religious feeling. This has had its day, and much that is very good can never grow again, because it could grow out of that alone. There will never again be a horizon of life and culture that is bounded by religion. Perhaps even the type of the saint is only possible with that certain narrowness of intellect, which apparently has completely disappeared. And thus the greatest height of intelligence has perhaps been reserved for a single age; it appeared – and appears, for we are still in that age – when an extraordinary, long-accumulated energy of will concentrates itself, as an exceptional case, upon *intellectual* aims. That height will no longer exist when this wildness and energy cease to be cultivated. Mankind probably approaches nearer to its actual aim in the middle of its road, in the middle time of its existence than at the end. It may be that powers with which, for instance, art is a condition, die out altogether; the pleasure in lying, in the undefined, the symbolical, in intoxication, in ecstasy might fall into disrepute. For certainly, when life is ordered in the perfect State, the present will provide no more motive for poetry, and it would only be those persons who had remained behind who would ask for poetical unreality. These, then, would assuredly look longingly backwards to the times of the imperfect State, of half-barbaric society, to our times.

235.

Genius and the Ideal State in Conflict. – The Socialists demand a comfortable life for the greatest possible number. If the lasting house of this life of comfort, the perfect State, had really been attained, then this life of comfort would have destroyed the ground out of which grow the great intellect and the mighty individual generally, I mean powerful energy. Were this State reached, mankind would have grown too weary to be still capable of producing genius. Must we not hence wish that life should retain its forcible character, and that wild forces and energies should continue to be called forth afresh? But warm and sympathetic hearts desire precisely the *removal* of that wild and forcible character, and the warmest hearts we can imagine desire it the most passionately of all, whilst all the time its passion derived its fire, its warmth, its very existence precisely from that wild and forcible character; the warmest heart, therefore, desires the removal of its own foundation, the destruction of itself – that is, it desires something illogical, it is not intelligent. The highest intelligence and the warmest heart cannot exist together in one person, and the wise man who passes judgement upon life looks beyond goodness and only regards it as something which is not without value in the general summing-up of life. The wise man must *oppose* those digressive wishes of unintelligent goodness, because he has an interest in the continuance of his type and in the eventual appearance of the highest intellect; at least, he will not advance the founding of the 'perfect State', inasmuch as there is only room in it for wearied individuals. Christ, on the contrary, he whom we may consider to have had the warmest heart, advanced the process of making man stupid, placed himself on the side of the intellectually poor, and retarded the production of the greatest intellect, and this was consistent. His opposite, the man of perfect wisdom – this may be safely prophesied – will just as necessarily hinder the production of a Christ. The State is a wise arrangement for the protection of one individual against another; if its ennobling is exaggerated the individual will at last be weakened by it, even effaced – thus the original purpose of the State will be most completely frustrated.

236.

The Zones of Culture. – It may be figuratively said that the ages of culture correspond to the zones of the various climates, only that they lie one behind another and not beside each other like the geographical zones. In comparison with the temperate zone of culture, which it is our object to enter, the past, speaking generally, gives the impression of a *tropical* climate. Violent contrasts, sudden changes between day and night, heat and colour-splendour, the reverence of all that was sudden, mysterious, terrible, the rapidity with which storms broke: everywhere that lavish abundance of the provisions of nature; and opposed to this, in our culture, a clear but by no means bright sky, pure but fairly unchanging air, sharpness, even cold at times; thus the two zones are contrasts to each other. When we see how in that former zone the most raging passions are suppressed and broken down with mysterious force by metaphysical representations, we feel as if wild tigers were being crushed before our very eyes in the coils of mighty serpents; our mental climate lacks such episodes, our imagination is temperate, even in dreams there does not happen to us what former peoples saw waking. But should we not rejoice at this change, even granted that artists are essentially spoiled by the disappearance of the tropical culture and find us non-artists a little too timid? In so far artists are certainly right to deny 'progress', for indeed it is doubtful whether the last three thousand years show an advance in the arts. In the same way, a metaphysical philosopher like Schopenhauer would have no cause to acknowledge progress with a regard to metaphysical philosophy and religion if he glanced back over the last four thousand years. For us, however, the *existence* even of the temperate zones of culture is progress.

237.

Renaissance and Reformation. – The Italian Renaissance contained within itself all the positive forces to which we owe modern culture. Such were the liberation of thought, the disregard of authorities, the triumph of education over the darkness of tradition, enthusiasm for science and the scientific past of mankind, the unfettering of the Individual, an ardour for truthfulness and a dislike of delusion and mere effect (which ardour blazed forth in an entire company of artistic characters, who with the greatest moral purity required from themselves perfection in their works, and nothing but perfection); yes, the Renaissance had positive forces, which have, *as yet*, never become so mighty again in our modern culture. It was the

Golden Age of the last thousand years, in spite of all its blemishes and vices. On the other hand, the German Reformation stands out as an energetic protest of antiquated spirits, who were by no means tired of mediaeval views of life, and who received the signs of its dissolution, the extraordinary flatness and alienation of the religious life, with deep dejection instead of with the rejoicing that would have been seemly. With their northern strength and stiff-neckedness they threw mankind back again, brought about the counter-reformation, that is, a Catholic Christianity of self-defence, with all the violences of a state of siege, and delayed for two or three centuries the complete awakening and mastery of the sciences; just as they probably made for ever impossible the complete inter-growth of the antique and the modern spirit. The great task of the Renaissance could not be brought to a termination, this was prevented by the protest of the contemporary backward German spirit (which, for its salvation, had had sufficient sense in the Middle Ages to cross the Alps again and again). It was the chance of an extraordinary constellation of politics that Luther was preserved, and that his protest gained strength, for the Emperor protected him in order to employ him as a weapon against the Pope, and in the same way he was secretly favoured by the Pope in order to use the Protestant princes as a counter-weight against the Emperor. Without this curious counter-play of intentions, Luther would have been burnt like Huss – and the morning sun of enlightenment would probably have risen somewhat earlier, and with a splendour more beauteous than we can now imagine.

238.

Justice against the Becoming God. – When the entire history of culture unfolds itself to our gaze, as a confusion of evil and noble, of true and false ideas, and we feel almost seasick at the sight of these tumultuous waves, we then understand what comfort resides in the conception of a *becoming God*. This Deity is unveiled ever more and more throughout the changes and fortunes of mankind; it is not all blind mechanism, a senseless and aimless confusion of forces. The deification of the process of being is a metaphysical outlook, seen as from a lighthouse overlooking the sea of history, in which a far-too historical generation of scholars found their comfort. This must not arouse anger, however erroneous the view may be. Only those who, like Schopenhauer, deny development also feel none of the misery of this historical wave, and therefore, because they know nothing of that becoming God and the need of His supposition, they should in justice withhold their scorn.

239.

The Fruits According to their Seasons. – Every better future that is desired for mankind is necessarily in many respects also a worse future, for it is foolishness to suppose that a new, higher grade of humanity will combine in itself all the good points of former grades, and must produce, for instance, the highest form of art. Rather has every season its own advantages and charms, which exclude those of the other seasons. That which has grown out of religion and in its neighbourhood cannot grow again if this has been destroyed; at the most, straggling and belated off-shoots may lead to deception on that point, like the occasional outbreaks of remembrance of the old art, a condition that probably betrays the feeling of loss and deprivation, but which is no proof of the power from which a new art might be born.

240.

The Increasing Severity of the World. – The higher culture an individual attains, the less field there is left for mockery and scorn. Voltaire thanked Heaven from his heart for the invention of marriage and the Church, by which it had so well provided for our cheer. But he and his time, and before him the sixteenth century, had exhausted their ridicule on this theme; everything that is now made fun of on this theme is out of date, and above all too cheap to tempt a purchaser. Causes are now inquired after; ours is an age of seriousness. Who cares now to discern, laughingly, the difference between reality and pretentious sham, between that which man is and that which he wishes to represent; the feeling of this contrast has quite a different effect if we seek reasons. The more thoroughly any one understands life, the less he will mock, though finally, perhaps, he will mock at the 'thoroughness of his understanding'.

241.

The Genius of Culture. – If any one wished to imagine a genius of culture, what would it be like? It handles as its tools falsehood, force, and thoughtless selfishness so surely that it could only be called an evil, demoniacal being; but its aims, which are occasionally transparent, are great and good. It is a centaur, half-beast, half-man, and, in addition, has angel's wings upon its head.

242.

The Miracle-Education. – Interest in Education will acquire great strength only from the moment when belief in a God and His care is renounced, just as the art of healing could only flourish when the belief in miracle-cures ceased. So far, however, there is universal belief in the miracle-education; out of the greatest disorder and confusion of aims and unfavourableness of conditions, the most fertile and mighty men have been seen to grow; could this happen naturally? Soon these cases will be more closely looked into, more carefully examined; but miracles will never be discovered. In similar circumstances countless persons perish constantly; the few saved have, therefore, usually grown stronger, because they endured these bad conditions by virtue of an inexhaustible inborn strength, and this strength they had also exercised and increased by fighting against these circumstances; thus the miracle is explained. An education that no longer believes in miracles must pay attention to three things: first, how much energy is inherited? Secondly, by what means can new energy be aroused? Thirdly, how can the individual be adapted to so many and manifold claims of culture without being disquieted and destroying his personality – in short, how can the individual be initiated into the counterpoint of private and public culture, how can he lead the melody and at the same time accompany it?

243.

The Future of the Physician. – There is now no profession which would admit of such an enhancement as that of the physician; that is, after the spiritual physicians the so-called pastors, are no longer allowed to practise their conjuring tricks to public applause, and a cultured person gets out of their way. The highest mental development of a physician has not yet been reached, even if he understands the best and newest methods, is practised in them, and knows how to draw those rapid conclusions from effects to causes for which the diagnostics are celebrated; besides this, he must possess a gift of eloquence that adapts itself to every individual and draws his heart out of his body; a manliness, the sight of which alone drives away all despondency (the canker of all sick people), the tact and suppleness of a diplomatist in negotiations between such as have need of joy for their recovery and such as, for reasons of health, must (and can) give joy; the acuteness of a detective and an attorney to divine the secrets of a soul without betraying them – in short, a good physician now has need of all the artifices and artistic privileges of every other professional class. Thus equipped, he is then ready to be a benefactor to the whole of society, by increasing good works, mental joys and fertility, by preventing evil thoughts, projects and villainies (the evil source of which is so often the belly), by the restoration of a mental and physical aristocracy (as a maker and hinderer of marriages), by judiciously checking all so-called soul-torments and pricks of conscience. Thus from a 'medicine man' he becomes saviour, and yet need work no miracle, neither is he obliged to let himself be crucified.

244.

In the Neighbourhood of Insanity. – The sum of sensations, knowledge and experiences, the whole burden of culture, therefore, has become so great that an overstraining of nerves and powers of thought is a common danger, indeed the cultivated classes of European countries are throughout neurotic, and almost every one of their great families is on the verge of insanity in one of their branches. True, health is now sought in every possible way; but in the main a diminution of that tension of feeling, of that oppressive burden of culture, is needful, which, even though it might be bought at a heavy sacrifice, would at least give us room for the great hope of a *new Renaissance*. To Christianity, to the philosophers, poets, and musicians we owe an abundance of deeply emotional sensations; in order that these may not get beyond our control we must invoke the spirit of science, which on the whole makes us somewhat colder and more sceptical, and in particular cools the faith in final and absolute truths; it is chiefly through Christianity that it has grown so wild.

245.

The Bell-founding of Culture. – Culture has been made like a bell, within a covering of coarser, commoner material, falsehood, violence, the boundless extension of every individual 'I', of every separate people – this was the covering. Is it time to take it off? Has the liquid set, have the good and useful impulses, the habits of the nobler nature become so certain and so general that they no longer require to lean on metaphysics and the errors of religion, no longer have need of hardnesses and violence as powerful all bonds between man and man, people and people? No sign from any God can any longer help us to answer this question; our own insight must decide. The earthly rule of man must be taken in hand by man himself, his 'omniscience' must watch over the further fate of culture with a sharp eye.

246.

The Cyclopes of Culture. – Whoever has seen those furrowed basins which once contained glaciers, will hardly deem it possible that a time will come when the same spot will be a valley of woods and meadows and streams. It is the same in the history of mankind; the wildest forces break the way, destructively at first, but their activity was nevertheless necessary in order that later on a milder civilisation might build up its house. These terrible energies – that which is called Evil – are the cyclopic architects and road-makers of humanity.

247.

The Circulation of Humanity. – It is possible that all humanity is only a phase of development of a certain species of animal of limited duration. Man may have grown out of the ape and will return to the ape again,[11] without anybody taking an interest in the ending of this curious comedy. Just as with the decline of Roman civilisation and its most important cause, the spread of Christianity, there was a general uglification of man within the Roman Empire, so, through the

11 This may remind one of Gobineau's more jocular saying: *'Nous ne descendons pas du singe, mats nous y allons.'*– J. M. K.

eventual decline of general culture, there might result a far greater uglification and finally an animalising of man till he reached the ape. But just because we are able to face this prospect, we shall perhaps be able to avert such an end.

248.

The Consoling Speech of a Desperate Advance. – Our age gives the impression of an intermediate condition; the old ways of regarding the world, the old cultures still partially exist, the new are not yet sure and customary and hence are without decision and consistency. It appears as if everything would become chaotic, as if the old were being lost, the new worthless and ever becoming weaker. But this is what the soldier feels who is learning to march; for a time he is more uncertain and awkward, because his muscles are moved sometimes according to the old system and sometimes according to the new, and neither gains a decisive victory. We waver, but it is necessary not to lose courage and give up what we have newly gained. Moreover, we *cannot* go back to the old, we *have* burnt our boats; there remains nothing but to be brave whatever happens. *March ahead*, only get forward! Perhaps our behaviour looks like *progress*; but if not, then the words of Frederick the Great may also be applied to us, and indeed as a consolation: '*Ah, mon cher Sulzer, vous ne connaissez pas assez cette race Maudite, à laquelle nous appartenons.*'

249.

Suffering from Past Culture. – Whoever has solved the problem of culture suffers from a feeling similar to that of one who has inherited unjustly-gotten riches, or of a prince who reigns thanks to the violence of his ancestors. He thinks of their origin with grief and is often ashamed, often irritable. The whole sum of strength, joy, vigour, which he devotes to his possessions, is often balanced by a deep weariness, he cannot forget their origin. He looks despondingly at the future; he knows well that his successors will suffer from the past as he does.

250.

Manners. – Good manners disappear in proportion as the influence of a Court and an exclusive aristocracy lessens; this decrease can be plainly observed from decade to decade by those who have an eye for public behaviour, which grows visibly more vulgar. No one any longer knows how to court and flatter intelligently; hence arises the ludicrous fact that in cases where we *must* render actual homage (to a great statesman or artist, for instance), the words of deepest feeling, of simple, peasant-like honesty, have to be borrowed, owing to the embarrassment resulting from the lack of grace and wit. Thus the public ceremonious meeting of men appears ever more clumsy, but more full of feeling and honesty without really being so. But must there always be a decline in manners? It appears to me, rather, that manners take a deep curve and that we are approaching their lowest point. When society has become sure of its intentions and principles, so that they have a moulding effect (the manners we have learnt from former moulding conditions are now inherited and always more weakly learnt), there will then be company manners, gestures and social expressions, which must appear as necessary and simply natural because they are intentions and principles. The better division of time and work, the gymnastic exercise transformed into the accompaniment of all beautiful leisure, increased and severer meditation, which brings wisdom and suppleness even to the body, will bring all this in its train. Here, indeed, we might think with a smile of our scholars, and consider whether, as a matter of fact, they who wish to be regarded as the forerunners of that new culture are distinguished by their better manners? This is hardly the case; although their spirit may be willing enough their flesh is weak. The past of culture is still too powerful in their muscles, they still stand in a fettered position, and are half worldly priests and half dependent educators of the upper classes, and besides this they have been rendered crippled and lifeless by the pedantry of science and by antiquated, spiritless methods. In any case, therefore, they are physically, and often three-fourths mentally, still the courtiers of an old, even antiquated culture, and as such are themselves antiquated; the new spirit that occasionally inhabits these old dwellings often serves only to make them more uncertain and frightened. In them there dwell the ghosts of the past as well as the ghosts of the future; what wonder if they do not wear the best expression or show the most pleasing behaviour?

251.

The Future of Science. – To him who works and seeks in her, Science gives much pleasure – to him who *learns* her facts, very little. But as all important truths of science must gradually become commonplace and everyday matters, even this small amount of pleasure ceases, just as we have long ceased to take pleasure in learning the admirable multiplication table. Now if Science goes on giving less pleasure in herself, and always takes more pleasure in throwing suspicion on the consolations of metaphysics, religion and art, that greatest of all sources of pleasure, to which mankind owes almost its whole humanity, becomes impoverished. Therefore a higher culture must have man a double brain, two brain-chambers, so to speak, one to feel science and the other to feel non-science, which can lie side by side, without confusion, divisible, exclusive; this is a necessity of health. In one part lies the source of strength, in the other lies the regulator; it must be heated with illusions, onesidednesses, passions; and the malicious and dangerous consequences of overheating must be averted by the help of conscious Science. If this necessity of the higher culture is not satisfied, the further course of human development can almost certainly be foretold: the interest in what is true ceases as it guarantees less pleasure; illusion, error, and imagination reconquer step by step the ancient territory, because they are united to pleasure; the ruin of science: the relapse into barbarism is the next result; mankind must begin to weave its web afresh after having, like Penelope, destroyed it during the night. But who will assure us that it will always find the necessary strength for this?

252.

The Pleasure in Discernment. – Why is discernment, that essence of the searcher and the philosopher, connected with pleasure? Firstly, and above all, because thereby we become conscious of our strength, for the same reason that gymnastic exercises, even without spectators, are enjoyable. Secondly, because in the course of knowledge we surpass older ideas and their representatives, and become, or believe ourselves to be, conquerors. Thirdly, because even a very little new knowledge exalts us above *every one*, and makes us feel we are the only ones who know the subject aright. These are the three most important reasons of the pleasure, but there are many others, according to the nature of the discerner. A not inconsiderable index of such is given, where no one would look for it, in a passage of my parenetic work on Schopenhauer,[12] with the arrangement of which every experienced servant of knowledge may be satisfied, even though he might wish to dispense with the ironical touch that seems to pervade those pages. For if it be true that for the making of a scholar 'a number of very human impulses and desires must be thrown together', that the scholar is indeed a very noble but not a pure metal, and 'consists of a confused blending of very different impulses and attractions', the same thing may be said equally of the making and nature of the artist, the philosopher and the moral genius – and whatever glorified great names there may be in that list. *Everything* human deserves ironical consideration with respect to its *origin* – therefore irony is so *superfluous* in the world.

253.

Fidelity as a Proof of Validity. – It is a perfect sign of a sound theory if during *forty years* its originator does not mistrust it; but I maintain that there has never yet been a philosopher who has not eventually deprecated the philosophy of his youth. Perhaps, however, he has not spoken publicly of this change of opinion, for reasons of ambition, or, what is more probable in noble natures, out of delicate consideration for his adherents.

254.

The Increase of what is Interesting. – In the course of higher education everything becomes interesting to man, he knows how to find the instructive side of a thing quickly and to put his finger on the place where it can fill up a gap in his ideas, or where it may verify a thought. Through this boredom disappears more and more, and so does excessive excitability of temperament. Finally he moves among men like a botanist among plants, and looks upon himself as a phenomenon, which only greatly excites his discerning instinct.

---

12 This refers to his essay, 'Schopenhauer as Educator', in *Thoughts Out of Season*, vol. ii. of the English edition. – J. M. K.

255.

The Superstition of the Simultaneous. – Simultaneous things hold together, it is said. A relative dies far away, and at the same time we dream about him – Consequently! But countless relatives die and we do not dream about them. It is like shipwrecked people who make vows; afterwards, in the temples, we do not see the votive tablets of those who perished. A man dies, an owl hoots, a clock stops, all at one hour of the night – must there not be some connection? Such an intimacy with nature as this supposition implies is flattering to mankind. This species of superstition is found again in a refined form in historians and delineators of culture, who usually have a kind of hydrophobic horror of all that senseless mixture, in which individual and national life is so rich.

256.

Action and not Knowledge Exercised by Science. – The value of strictly pursuing science for a time does not lie precisely in its results, for these, in proportion to the ocean of what is worth knowing, are but an infinitesimally small drop. But it gives an additional energy, decisiveness, and toughness of endurance; it teaches how to attain an *aim suitably*. In so far it is very valuable, with a view to all that is done later on, to have once been a scientific man.

257.

The Youthful Charm of Science. – The search for truth still retains the charm of being in strong contrast to grey and now tiresome error; but this charm is gradually disappearing. It is true we still live in the youthful age of science and are accustomed to follow truth as a lovely girl; but how will it be when one day she becomes an elderly, ill-tempered looking woman? In almost all sciences the fundamental knowledge is either found in earliest times or is still being sought; what a different attraction this exerts compared to that time when everything essential has been found and there only remains for the seeker a scanty gleaning (which sensation may be learnt in several historical disciplines).

258.

The Statue of Humanity. – The genius of culture fares as did Cellini when his statue of Perseus was being cast; the molten mass threatened to run short, but it *had* to suffice, so he flung in his plates and dishes, and whatever else his hands fell upon. In the same way genius flings in errors, vices, hopes, ravings, and other things of baser as well as of nobler metal, for the statue of humanity must emerge and be finished; what does it matter if commoner material is used here and there?

259.

A Male Culture. – The Greek culture of the classic age is a male culture. As far as women are concerned, Pericles expresses everything in the funeral speech: 'They are best when they are as little spoken of as possible amongst men.' The erotic relation of men to youths was the necessary and sole preparation, to a degree unattainable to our comprehension, of all manly education (pretty much as for a long time all higher education of women was only attainable through love and marriage). All idealism of the strength of the Greek nature threw itself into that relation, and it is probable that never since have young men been treated so attentively, so lovingly, SO entirely with a view to their welfare (*virtus*) as in the fifth and sixth centuries BC – according to the beautiful saying of Holderlin: '*denn liebend giebt der Sterbliche vom Besten*'.[13] The higher the light in which this relation was regarded, the lower sank intercourse with woman; nothing else was taken into consideration than the production of children and lust; there was no intellectual intercourse, not even real love-making. If it be further remembered that women were even excluded from contests and spectacles of every description, there only remain the religious cults as their sole higher occupation. For although in the tragedies Electra and Antigone were represented, this was only *tolerated* in art, but not liked in real life – just as now we cannot endure anything pathetic in *life* but like it in art. The women had no other mission than to produce beautiful, strong bodies, in which the father's character lived on as unbrokenly as possible, and therewith to counteract the increasing nerve-tension of such a highly developed culture. This kept the Greek culture young for a relatively long time; for in the Greek mothers the Greek genius always returned to nature.

---

13 For it is when loving that mortal man gives of his best. – J. M. K.

260.

The Prejudice in Favour of Greatness. – It is clear that men overvalue everything great and prominent. This arises from the conscious or unconscious idea that they deem it very useful when one person throws all his strength into one thing and makes himself into a monstrous organ. Assuredly, an *equal* development of all his powers is more useful and happier for man; for every talent is a vampire which sucks blood and strength from other powers, and an exaggerated production can drive the most gifted almost to madness. Within the circle of the arts, too, extreme natures excite far too much attention; but a much lower culture is necessary to be captivated by them. Men submit from habit to everything that seeks power.

261.

The Tyrants of the Mind. – It is only where the ray of myth falls that the life of the Greeks shines; otherwise it is gloomy. The Greek philosophers are now robbing themselves of this myth; is it not as if they wished to quit the sunshine for shadow and gloom? Yet no plant avoids the light; and, as a matter of fact, those philosophers were only seeking a *brighter* sun; the myths not pure enough, not shining enough for them. They found this light in their knowledge, in that which each of them called his 'truth'. But in those times knowledge shone with a greater glory; it was still young and knew but little of all the difficulties and dangers of its path; it could still hope to reach in one single bound the central point of all being, and from thence to solve the riddle of the world. These philosophers had a firm belief in themselves and their 'truth', and with it they overthrew all their neighbours and predecessors; each one was a warlike, violent *tyrant*. The happiness in believing themselves the possessors of truth was perhaps never greater in the world, but neither were the hardness, the arrogance, and the tyranny and evil of such a belief. They were tyrants, they were that, therefore, which every Greek wanted to be, and which every one was if he *was able*. Perhaps Solon alone is an exception; he tells in his poems how he disdained personal tyranny. But he did it for love of his works, of his law-giving; and to be a law-giver is a sublimated form of tyranny. Parmenides also made laws. Pythagoras and Empedocles probably did the same; Anaximander founded a city. Plato was the incarnate wish to become the greatest philosophic law-giver and founder of States; he appears to have suffered terribly over the non-fulfilment of his nature, and towards his end his soul was filled with the bitterest gall. The more the Greek philosophers lost in power the more they suffered inwardly from this bitterness and malice; when the various sects fought for their truths in the street, then first were the souls of these wooers of truth completely clogged through envy and spleen; the tyrannical element then raged like poison within their bodies. These many petty tyrants would have liked to devour each other; there survived not a single spark of love and very little joy in their own knowledge. The saying that tyrants are generally murdered and that their descendants are short-lived, is true also of the tyrants of the mind. Their history is short and violent, and their after-effects break off suddenly. It may be said of almost all great Hellenes that they appear to have come too late: it was thus with Aeschylus, with Pindar, with Demosthenes, with Thucydides: one generation – and then it is passed for ever. That is the stormy and dismal element in Greek history. We now, it is true, admire the gospel of the tortoises. To think historically is almost the same thing now as if in all ages history had been made according to the theory 'The smallest possible amount in the longest possible time!' Oh! how quickly Greek history runs on! Since then life has never been so extravagant – so unbounded. I cannot persuade myself that the history of the Greeks followed that *natural* course for which it is so celebrated. They were much too variously gifted to be *gradual* in the orderly manner of the tortoise when running a race with Achilles, and that is called natural development. The Greeks went rapidly forward, but equally rapidly downwards; the movement of the whole machine is so intensified that a single stone thrown amid its wheels was sufficient to break it. Such a stone for instance, was Socrates; the hitherto so wonderfully regular, although certainly too rapid, development of the philosophical science was destroyed in one night. It is no idle question whether Plato, had he remained free from the Socratic charm', would not have discovered a still higher type of the philosophic man, which type is for ever lost to us. We look into the ages before him as into a sculptor's workshop of such types. The fifth and sixth centuries BC seemed to promise something more and higher even than they produced; they stopped short at promising and announcing. And yet there is hardly a greater loss than the loss of a type, of a new, hitherto undiscovered highest *possibility of the philosophic life*. Even of the older type the greater number are badly transmitted; it seems to me that all philosophers, from Thales to Democritus, are remarkably difficult to recognise, but whoever succeeds in imitating these figures walks amongst specimens of the mightiest and purest type. This ability is certainly rare, it was even absent in those later Greeks, who occupied themselves with the knowledge of the older philosophy; Aristotle, especially, hardly seems to have had eyes in his head when he stands before these great ones. And thus it appears as if these splendid philosophers had lived in vain, or as if they had only been intended to prepare the quarrelsome and talkative followers of the Socratic schools. As I have said, here is a gap, a break in development; some great misfortune must have happened, and the only statue which might have revealed the meaning and purpose of that great artistic training was either broken or unsuccessful; what actually happened has remained for ever a secret of the workshop.

That which happened amongst the Greeks – namely, that every great thinker who believed himself to be in possession of the absolute truth became a tyrant, so that even the mental history of the Greeks acquired that violent, hasty and dangerous character shown by their political history – this type of event was not therewith exhausted, much that is similar has happened even in more modern times, although gradually becoming rarer and now but seldom showing the pure, naive conscience of the Greek philosophers. For on the whole, opposition doctrines and scepticism now speak too powerfully, too loudly. The period of mental tyranny is past. It is true that in the spheres of higher culture there must always be a supremacy, but henceforth this supremacy lies in the hands of the *oligarchs of the mind*. In spite of local and political separation they form a cohesive society, whose members *recognise and acknowledge* each other, whatever public opinion and the verdicts of review and newspaper writers who influence the masses may circulate in favour of or against them. Mental superiority, which formerly divided and embittered, nowadays generally *unites*; how could the separate individuals assert themselves and swim through life on their own course, against all currents, if they did not see others like them living here and there under similar conditions, and grasped their hands, in the struggle as much against the ochlocratic character of the half mind and half culture as against the occasional attempts to establish a tyranny with the help of the masses? Oligarchs are necessary to each other, they are each other's best joy, they understand their signs, but each is nevertheless free, he fights and conquers in *his* place and perishes rather than submit.

262.

Homer. – The greatest fact in Greek culture remains this, that Homer became so early Pan-Hellenic. All mental and human freedom to which the Greeks attained is traceable to this fact. At the same time it has actually been fatal to Greek culture; for Homer levelled, inasmuch as he centralised, and dissolved the more serious instincts of independence. From time to time there arose from the depths of Hellenism an opposition to Homer; but he always remained victorious. All great mental powers have an oppressing effect as well as a liberating one; but it certainly makes a difference whether it is Homer or the Bible or Science that tyrannises over mankind.

263.

Talents. – In such a highly developed humanity as the present, each individual naturally has access to many talents. Each has an *inborn* talent, but only in a few is that degree of toughness, endurance, and energy born and trained that he really becomes a talent, *becomes* what he *is* – that is, that he discharges it in works and actions.

264.

The Witty Person either Overvalued or Undervalued. – Unscientific but talented people value every mark of intelligence, whether it be on a true or a false track; above all, they want the person with whom they have intercourse to entertain them with his wit, to spur them on, to inflame them, to carry them away in seriousness and play, and in any case to be a powerful amulet to protect them against boredom. Scientific natures, on the other hand, know that the gift of possessing all manner of notions should be strictly controlled by the scientific spirit: it is not that which shines, deludes and excites, but the often insignificant truth that is the fruit which he knows how to shake down from the tree of knowledge. Like Aristotle, he is not permitted to make any distinction between the 'bores', and the 'wits', his *daemon* leads him through the desert as well as through tropical vegetation, in order that he may only take pleasure in the really actual, tangible, true. In insignificant scholars this produces a general disdain and suspicion of cleverness, and, on the other hand, clever people frequently have an aversion to science, as have, for instance, almost all artists.

265.

Sense in School. – School has no task more important than to teach strict thought, cautious judgement, and logical conclusions, hence it must pay no attention to what hinders these operations, such as religion, for instance. It can count on the fact that human vagueness, custom, and need will later on unstring the bow of all-too-severe thought. But so long as its influence lasts it should enforce that which is the essential and distinguishing point in man: 'Sense and Science, the *very highest* power of man' – as Goethe judges. The great natural philosopher, Von Baer, thinks that the superiority of all Europeans, when compared to Asiatics, lies in the trained capability of giving reasons for that which they believe, of which the latter are utterly incapable. Europe went to the school of logical and critical thought, Asia still fails to know how to distinguish between truth and fiction, and is not conscious whether its convictions spring from individual observation and systematic thought or from imagination. Sense in the school has made Europe what it is; in the Middle Ages it was on the road to become once more a part and dependent of Asia – forfeiting, therefore, the scientific mind which it owed to the Greeks.

266.

The Undervalued Effect of Public School Teaching. – The value of a public school is seldom sought in those things which are really learnt there and are carried away never to be lost, but in those things which are learnt and which the pupil only acquires against his will, in order to get rid of them again as soon as possible. Every educated person acknowledges that the reading of the classics, as now practised, is a monstrous proceeding carried on before young people are ripe enough for it by teachers who with every word, often by their appearance alone, throw a mildew on a good author. But therein lies the value, generally unrecognised, of these teachers who *speak the abstract language of the higher culture*, which, though dry and difficult to understand, is yet a sort of higher gymnastics of the brain; and there is value in the constant recurrence in their language of ideas, artistic expressions, methods and allusions which the young people hardly ever hear in the conversations of their relatives and in the street. Even if the pupils only *hear*, their intellect is involuntarily trained to a scientific mode of regarding things. It is not possible to emerge from this discipline entirely untouched by its abstract character, and to remain a simple child of nature.

267.

Learning many Languages. – The learning of many languages fills the memory with words instead of with facts and thoughts, and this is a vessel which, with every person, can only contain a certain limited amount of contents. Therefore the learning of many languages is injurious, inasmuch as it arouses a belief in possessing dexterity and, as a matter of fact, it lends a kind of delusive importance to social intercourse. It is also indirectly injurious in that it opposes the acquirement of solid knowledge and the intention to win the respect of men in an honest way. Finally, it is the axe which is laid to the root of a delicate sense of language in our mother-tongue, which thereby is incurably injured and destroyed. The two nations which produced the greatest stylists, the Greeks and the French, learned no foreign languages. But as human intercourse must always grow more cosmopolitan, and as, for instance, a good merchant in London must now be able to read and write eight languages, the learning of many tongues has certainly become a necessary evil; but which, when finally carried to an extreme, will compel mankind to find a remedy, and in some far-off future there will be a new language, used at first as a language of commerce, then as a language of intellectual intercourse generally, then for all, as surely as some time or other there will be aviation. Why else should philology have studied the laws of languages for a whole century, and have estimated the necessary, the valuable, and the successful portion of each separate language?

268.

The War History of the Individual. – In a single human life that passes through many styles of culture we find that struggle condensed which would otherwise have been played out between two generations, between father and son; the closeness of the relationship *sharpens* this struggle, because each party ruthlessly drags in the familiar inward nature of the other party; and thus this struggle in the single individual becomes most *embittered*; here every new phase disregards the earlier ones with cruel injustice and misunderstanding of their means and aims.

269.

A Quarter of an Hour Earlier. – A man is found occasionally whose views are beyond his time, but only to such an extent that he anticipates the common views of the next decade. He possesses public opinion before it is public; that is, he has fallen into the arms of a view that deserves to be trivial a quarter of an hour sooner than other people. But his fame is usually far noisier than the fame of those who are really great and prominent.

270.

The Art of Reading. – Every strong tendency is one-sided; it approaches the aim of the straight line and, like this, is exclusive, that is, it does not touch many other aims, as do weak parties and natures in their wave-like rolling to-and-fro; it must also be forgiven to philologists that they are one-sided. The restoration and keeping pure of texts, besides their explanation, carried on in common for hundreds of years, has finally enabled the right methods to be found; the whole of the Middle Ages was absolutely incapable of a strictly philological explanation, that is, of the simple desire to comprehend what an author says – it *was* an achievement, finding these methods, let it not be undervalued! Through this all science first acquired continuity and steadiness, so that the art of reading rightly, which is called philology, attained its summit.

271.

The Art of Reasoning. – The greatest advance that men have made lies in their acquisition of the art to *reason rightly*. It is not so very natural, as Schopenhauer supposes when he says, 'All are capable of reasoning, but few of judging,' it is learnt late and has not yet attained supremacy. False conclusions are the rule in older ages; and the mythologies of all peoples, their magic and their superstition, their religious cult and their law are the inexhaustible sources of proof of this theory.

272.

Phases of Individual Culture. – The strength and weakness of mental productiveness depend far less on inherited talents than on the accompanying amount of *elasticity*. Most educated young people of thirty turn round at this solstice of their lives and are afterwards disinclined for new mental turnings. Therefore, for the salvation of a constantly increasing culture, a new generation is immediately necessary, which will not do very much either, for in order to come up with the father's culture the son must exhaust almost all the inherited energy which the father himself possessed at that stage of life when his son was born; with the little addition he gets further on (for as here the road is being traversed for the second time progress is a little quicker; in order to learn that which the father knew, the son does not consume quite so much strength). Men of great elasticity, like Goethe, for instance, get through almost more than four generations in succession would be capable of; but then they advance too quickly, so that the rest of mankind only comes up with them in the next century, and even then perhaps not completely, because the exclusiveness of culture and the consecutiveness of development have been weakened by the frequent interruptions. Men catch up more quickly with the ordinary phases of intellectual culture which has been acquired in the course of history. Nowadays they begin to acquire culture as religiously inclined children, and perhaps about their tenth year these sentiments attain to their highest point, and are then changed into weakened forms (pantheism), whilst they draw near to science; they entirely pass by God, immortality, and such-like things, but are overcome by the witchcraft of a metaphysical philosophy. Eventually they find even this unworthy of belief; art, on the contrary, seems to vouchsafe more and more, so that for a time metaphysics is metamorphosed and continues to exist either as a transition to art or as an artistically transfiguring temperament. But the scientific sense grows more imperious and conducts man to natural sciences and history, and particularly to the severest methods of knowledge, whilst art has always a milder and less exacting meaning. All this usually happens within the first thirty years of a man's life. It is the recapitulation of a *pensum*, for which humanity had laboured perhaps thirty thousand years.

273.

Retrograded, not Left Behind. – Whoever, in the present day, still derives his development from religious sentiments, and perhaps lives for some length of time afterwards in metaphysics and art, has assuredly gone back a considerable distance and begins his race with other modern men under unfavourable conditions; he apparently loses time and space. But because he stays in those domains where ardour and energy are liberated and force flows continuously as a volcanic stream out of an inexhaustible source, he goes forward all the more quickly as soon as he has freed himself at the right moment from those dominators; his feet are winged, his breast has learned quieter, longer, and more enduring breathing. He has only retreated in order to have sufficient room to leap; thus something terrible and threatening may lie in this retrograde movement.

274.

A Portion of our Ego as an Artistic Object. – It is a sign of superior culture consciously to retain and present a true picture of certain phases of development which commoner men live through almost thoughtlessly and then efface from the tablets of their souls: this is a higher species of the painter's art which only the few understand. For this it is necessary to isolate those phases artificially. Historical studies form the qualification for this painting, for they constantly incite us in regard to a portion of history, a people, or a human life, to imagine for ourselves a quite distinct horizon of thoughts, a certain strength of feelings, the prominence of this or the obscurity of that. Herein consists the historic sense, that out of given instances we can quickly reconstruct such systems of thoughts and feelings, just as we can mentally reconstruct a temple out of a few pillars and remains of walls accidentally left standing. The next result is that we understand our fellow-men as belonging to distinct systems and representatives of different cultures – that is, as necessary, but as changeable; and, again, that we can separate portions of our own development and put them down independently.

275.

Cynics and Epicureans. – The cynic recognises the connection between the multiplied and stronger pains of the more highly cultivated man and the abundance of requirements; he comprehends, therefore, that the multitude of opinions about what is beautiful, suitable, seemly and pleasing, must also produce very rich sources of enjoyment, but also of displeasure. In accordance with this view he educates himself backwards, by giving up many of these opinions and withdrawing from certain demands of culture; he thereby gains a feeling of freedom and strength; and gradually, when habit has made his manner of life endurable, his sensations of displeasure are, as a matter of fact, rarer and weaker than those of cultivated people, and approach those of the domestic animal; moreover, he experiences everything with the charm of contrast, and – he can also scold to his heart's content; so that thereby he again rises high above the sensation-range of the animal. The Epicurean has the same point of view as the cynic; there is usually only a difference of temperament between them. Then the Epicurean makes use of his higher culture to render himself independent of prevailing opinions, he raises himself above them, whilst the cynic only remains negative. He walks, as it were, in wind-protected, well-sheltered, half-dark paths, whilst over him, in the wind, the tops of the trees rustle and show him how violently agitated is the world out there. The cynic, on the contrary, goes, as it were, naked into the rushing of the wind and hardens himself to the point of insensibility.

276.

Microcosm and Macrocosm of Culture. – The best discoveries about culture man makes within himself when he finds two heterogeneous powers ruling therein. Supposing some one were living as much in love for the plastic arts or for music as he was carried away by the spirit of science, and that he were to regard it as impossible for him to end this contradiction by the destruction of one and complete liberation of the other power, there would therefore remain nothing for him to do but to erect around himself such a large edifice of culture that those two powers might both dwell within it, although at different ends, whilst between them there dwelt reconciling, intermediary powers, with predominant strength to quell, in case of need, the rising conflict. But such an edifice of culture in the single individual will bear a great resemblance to the culture of entire periods, and will afford consecutive analogical teaching concerning it. For wherever the great architecture of culture manifested itself it was its mission to compel opposing powers to agree, by means of an overwhelming accumulation of other less unbearable powers, without thereby oppressing and fettering them.

277.

Happiness and Culture. – We are moved at the sight of our childhood's surroundings – the arbour, the church with its graves, the pond and the wood – all this we see again with pain. We are seized with pity for ourselves; for what have we not passed through since then! And everything here is so silent, so eternal, only we are so changed, so moved; we even find a few human beings, on whom Time has sharpened his teeth no more than on an oak tree – peasants, fishermen, woodmen – they are unchanged. Emotion and self-pity at the sight of lower culture is the sign of higher culture; from which the conclusion may be drawn that happiness has certainly not been increased by it. Whoever wishes to reap happiness and comfort in life should always avoid higher culture.

278.

The Simile of the Dance. – It must now be regarded as a decisive sign of great culture if some one possesses sufficient strength and flexibility to be as pure and strict in discernment as, in other moments, to be capable of giving poetry, religion, and metaphysics a hundred paces' start and then feeling their force and beauty. Such a position amid two such different demands is very difficult, for science urges the absolute supremacy of its methods, and if this insistence is not yielded to, there arises the other danger of a weak wavering between different impulses. Meanwhile, to cast a glance, in simile at least, on a solution of this difficulty, it may be remembered that *dancing* is not the same as a dull reeling to and fro between different impulses. High culture will resemble a bold dance – wherefore, as has been said, there is need of much strength and suppleness.

279.

Of the Relieving of Life. – A primary way of lightening life is the idealisation of all its occurrences; and with the help of painting we should make it quite clear to ourselves what idealising means. The painter requires that the spectator should not observe too closely or too sharply, he forces him back to a certain distance from whence to make his observations; he is obliged to take for granted a fixed distance of the spectator from the picture – he must even suppose an equally certain amount of sharpness of eye in his spectator; in such things he must on no account waver. Every one, therefore, who desires to idealise his life must not look at it too closely, and must always keep his gaze at a certain distance. This was a trick that Goethe, for instance, understood.

280.

Aggravation as Relief, and *Vice Versa*. – Much that makes life more difficult in certain grades of mankind serves to lighten it in a higher grade, because such people have become familiar with greater aggravations of life. The contrary also happens; for instance, religion has a double face, according to whether a man looks up to it to relieve him of his burden and need, or looks down upon it as upon fetters laid on him to prevent him from soaring too high into the air.

281.

The Higher Culture is Necessarily Misunderstood. – He who has strung his instrument with only two strings, like the scholars (who, besides the *instinct of knowledge* possess only an acquired *religious* instinct), does not understand people who can play upon more strings. It lies in the nature of the higher, *many-stringed* culture that it should always be falsely interpreted by the lower; an example of this is when art appears as a disguised form of the religious. People who are only religious understand even science as a searching after the religious sentiment, just as deaf mutes do not know what music is, unless it be visible movement.

282.

Lamentation. – It is, perhaps, the advantages of our epoch that bring with them a backward movement and an occasional undervaluing of the *vita contemplativa*. But it must be acknowledged that our time is poor in the matter of great moralists, that Pascal, Epictetus, Seneca, and Plutarch are now but little read, that work and industry – formerly in the following of the great goddess Health – sometimes appear to rage like a disease. Because time to think and tranquillity in thought are lacking, we no longer ponder over different views, but content ourselves with hating them. With the enormous acceleration of life, mind and eye grow accustomed to a partial and false sight and judgement, and all people are like travellers whose only acquaintance with countries and nations is derived from the railway. An independent and cautious attitude of knowledge is looked upon almost as a kind of madness; the free spirit is brought into disrepute, chiefly through scholars, who miss their thoroughness and ant-like industry in his art of regarding things and would gladly banish him into one single corner of science, while it has the different and higher mission of commanding the battalion rear-guard of scientific and learned men from an isolated position, and showing them the ways and aims of culture. A song of lamentation such as that which has just been sung will probably have its own period, and will cease of its own accord on a forcible return of the genius of meditation.

283.

The Chief Deficiency of Active People. – Active people are usually deficient in the higher activity, I mean individual activity. They are active as officials, merchants, scholars, that is as a species, but not as quite distinct separate and *single* individuals; in this respect they are idle. It is the misfortune of the active that their activity is almost always a little senseless. For instance, we must not ask the money-making banker the reason of his restless activity, it is foolish. The active roll as the stone rolls, according to the stupidity of mechanics. All mankind is divided, as it was at all times and is still, into slaves and freemen; for whoever has not two-thirds of his day for himself is a slave, be he otherwise whatever he likes, statesman, merchant, official, or scholar.

284.

In Favour of the Idle. – As a sign that the value of a contemplative life has decreased, scholars now vie with active people in a sort of hurried enjoyment, so that they appear to value this mode of enjoying more than that which really pertains to them, and which, as a matter of fact, is a far greater enjoyment. Scholars are ashamed of *otium*. But there is one noble thing about idleness and idlers. If idleness is really the *beginning* of all vice, it finds itself, therefore, at least in near neighbourhood of all the virtues; the idle man is still a better man than the active. You do not suppose that in speaking of idleness and idlers I am alluding to you, you sluggards?

285.

Modern Unrest. – Modern restlessness increases towards the west, so that Americans look upon the inhabitants of Europe as altogether peace-loving and enjoying beings, whilst in reality they swarm about like wasps and bees. This restlessness is so great that the higher culture cannot mature its fruits, it is as if the seasons followed each other too quickly. For lack of rest our civilisation is turning into a new barbarism. At no period have the active, that is, the restless, been of more importance. One of the necessary corrections, therefore, which must be undertaken in the character of humanity is to strengthen the contemplative element on a large scale. But every individual who is quiet and steady in heart and head already has the right to believe that he possesses not only a good temperament, but also a generally useful virtue, and even fulfils a higher mission by the preservation of this virtue.

286.

To what Extent the Active Man is Lazy. – I believe that every one must have his own opinion about everything concerning which opinions are possible, because he himself is a peculiar, unique thing, which assumes towards all other things a new and never hitherto existing attitude. But idleness, which lies at the bottom of the active man's soul, prevents him from drawing water out of his own well. Freedom of opinion is like health; both are individual, and no good general conception can be set up of either of them. That which is necessary for the health of one individual is the cause of disease in another, and many means and ways to the freedom of the spirit are for more highly developed natures the ways and means to confinement.

287.

Censor Vitae. – Alternations of love and hatred for a long period distinguish the inward condition of a man who desires to be free in his judgement of life; he does not forget, and bears everything a grudge, for good and evil. At last, when the whole tablet of his soul is written full of experiences, he will not hate and despise existence, neither will he love it, but will regard it sometimes with a joyful, sometimes with a sorrowful eye, and, like nature, will be now in a summer and now in an autumn mood.

288.

The Secondary Result. – Whoever earnestly desires to be free will therewith and without any compulsion lose all inclination for faults and vices; he will also be more rarely overcome by anger and vexation. His will desires nothing more urgently than to discern, and the means to do this – that is, the permanent condition in which he is best able to discern.

289.

The Value of Disease. – The man who is bed-ridden often perceives that he is usually ill of his position, business, or society, and through them has lost all self-possession. He gains this piece of knowledge from the idleness to which his illness condemns him.

290.

Sensitiveness in the Country. – If there are no firm, quiet lines on the horizon of his life, a species of mountain and forest line, man's inmost will itself becomes restless, inattentive, and covetous, as is the nature of a dweller in towns; he has no happiness and confers no happiness.

291.

Prudence of the Free Spirits. – Free-thinkers, those who live by knowledge alone, will soon attain the supreme aim of their life and their ultimate position towards society and State, and will gladly content themselves, for instance, with a small post or an income that is just sufficient to enable them to live; for they will arrange to live in such a manner that a great change of outward prosperity, even an overthrow of the political order, would not cause an overthrow of their life. To all these things they devote as little energy as possible in order that with their whole accumulated strength, and with a long breath, they may dive into the element of knowledge. Thus they can hope to dive deep and be able to see the bottom. Such a spirit seizes only the point of an event, he does not care for things in the whole breadth and prolixity of their folds, for he does not wish to entangle himself in them. He, too, knows the weekdays of restraint, of dependence and servitude. But from time to time there must dawn for him a Sunday of liberty, otherwise he could not endure life. It is probable that even his love for humanity will be prudent and somewhat short-winded, for he desires to meddle with the world of inclinations and of blindness only as far as is necessary for the purpose of knowledge. He must trust that the genius of justice will say something for its disciple and protege if accusing voices were to call him poor in love. In his mode of life and thought there is a *refined heroism*, which scorns to offer itself to the great mob-reverence, as its coarser brother does, and passes quietly through and out of the world. Whatever labyrinths it traverses, beneath whatever rocks its stream has occasionally worked its way – when it reaches the light it goes clearly, easily, and almost noiselessly on its way, and lets the sunshine strike down to its very bottom.

292.

Forward. – And thus forward upon the path of wisdom, with a firm step and good confidence! However you may be situated, serve yourself as a source of experience! Throw off the displeasure at your nature, forgive yourself your own individuality, for in any case you have in yourself a ladder with a hundred steps upon which you can mount to knowledge. The age into which with grief you feel yourself thrown thinks you happy because of this good fortune; it calls out to you that you shall still have experiences which men of later ages will perhaps be obliged to forego. Do not despise the fact of having been religious; consider fully how you have had a genuine access to art. Can you not, with the help of these experiences, follow immense stretches of former humanity with a clearer understanding? Is not that ground which sometimes displeases you so greatly, that ground of clouded thought, precisely the one upon which have grown many of the most glorious fruits of older civilisations? You must have loved religion and art as you loved mother and nurse – otherwise you cannot be wise. But you must be able to see beyond them, to outgrow them; if you remain under their ban you do not understand them. You must also be familiar with history and that cautious play with the balances: 'On the one hand – on the other hand.' Go back, treading in the footsteps made by mankind in its great and painful journey through the desert of the past, and you will learn most surely whither it is that all later humanity never can or may go again. And inasmuch as you wish with all your strength to see in advance how the knots of the future are tied, your own life acquires the value of an instrument and means of knowledge. It is within your power to see that all you have experienced, trials, errors, faults, deceptions, passions, your love and your hope, shall be merged wholly in your aim. This aim is to become a necessary chain of culture-links yourself, and from this necessity to draw a conclusion as to the necessity in the progress of general culture. When your sight has become strong enough to see to the bottom of the dark well of your nature and your knowledge, it is possible that in its mirror you may also behold the far-away visions of future civilisations. Do you think that such a life with such an aim is too wearisome, too empty of all that is agreeable? Then you have still to learn that no honey is sweeter than that of knowledge, and that the overhanging clouds of trouble must be to you as an udder from which you shall draw milk for your refreshment. And only when old age approaches will you rightly perceive how you listened to the voice of nature, that nature which rules the whole world through pleasure; the same life which has its zenith in age has also its zenith in wisdom, in that mild sunshine of a constant mental joyfulness; you meet them both, old age and wisdom, upon one ridge of life – it was thus intended by Nature. Then it is time, and no cause for anger, that the mists of death approach. Towards the light is your last movement; a joyful cry of knowledge is your last sound.

SIXTH DIVISION. MAN IN SOCIETY.

293.

Well-Meant Dissimulation. – In intercourse with men a well-meant dissimulation is often necessary, as if we did not see through the motives of their actions.

294.

Copies. – We not unfrequently meet with copies of prominent persons; and as in the case of pictures, so also here, the copies please more than the originals.

295.

The Public Speaker. – One may speak with the greatest appropriateness, and yet so that everybody cries out to the contrary – that is to say, when one does not speak to everybody.

296.

Want of Confidence. – Want of confidence among friends is a fault that cannot be censured without becoming incurable.

297.

The Art of Giving. – To have to refuse a gift, merely because it has not been offered in the right way, provokes animosity against the giver.

298.

The most Dangerous Partisan. – In every party there is one who, by his far too dogmatic expression of the party-principles, excites defection among the others.

299.

Advisers of the Sick. – Whoever gives advice to a sick person acquires a feeling of superiority over him, whether the advice be accepted or rejected. Hence proud and sensitive sick persons hate advisers more than their sickness.

300.

Double Nature of Equality. – The rage for equality may so manifest itself that we seek either to draw all others down to ourselves (by belittling, disregarding, and tripping up), or ourselves and all others upwards (by recognition, assistance, and congratulation).

301.

Against Embarrassment. – The best way to relieve and calm very embarrassed people is to give them decided praise.

302.

Preference for Certain Virtues. – We set no special value on the possession of a virtue until we perceive that it is entirely lacking in our adversary.

303.

Why we Contradict. – We often contradict an opinion when it is really only the tone in which it is expressed that is unsympathetic to us.

304.

Confidence and Intimacy. – Whoever proposes to command the intimacy of a person is usually uncertain of possessing his confidence. Whoever is sure of a person's confidence attaches little value to intimacy with him.

305.

The Equilibrium of Friendship. – The right equilibrium of friendship in our relation to other men is sometimes restored when we put a few grains of wrong on our own side of the scales.

306.

The most Dangerous Physicians. – The most dangerous physicians are those who, like born actors, imitate the born physician with the perfect art of imposture.

307.

When Paradoxes are Permissible. – In order to interest clever persons in a theory, it is sometimes only necessary to put it before them in the form of a prodigious paradox.

308.

How Courageous People are Won Over. – Courageous people are persuaded to a course of action by representing it as more dangerous than it really is.

309.

Courtesies. – We regard the courtesies shown us by unpopular persons as offences.

310.

Keeping People Waiting. – A sure way of exasperating people and of putting bad thoughts into their heads is to keep them waiting long. That makes them immoral.

311.

Against the Confidential. – Persons who give us their full confidence think they have thereby a right to ours. That is a mistake; people acquire no rights through gifts.

312.

A Mode of Settlement. – It often suffices to give a person whom we have injured an opportunity to make a joke about us to give his personal satisfaction, and even to make him favourably disposed to us.

313.

The Vanity of the Tongue. – Whether man conceals his bad qualities and vices, or frankly acknowledges them, his vanity in either case seeks its advantage thereby – only let it be observed how nicely he distinguishes those from whom he conceals such qualities from those with whom he is frank and honest.

314.

Considerate. – To have no wish to offend or injure any one may as well be the sign of a just as of a timid nature.

315.

Requisite for Disputation. – He who cannot put his thoughts on ice should not enter into the heat of dispute.

316.

Intercourse and Pretension. – We forget our pretensions when we are always conscious of being amongst meritorious people; being alone implants presumption in us. The young are pretentious, for they associate with their equals, who are all ciphers but would fain have a great significance.

317.

Motives of an Attack. – One does not attack a person merely to hurt and conquer him, but perhaps merely to become conscious of one's own strength.

318.

Flattery. – Persons who try by means of flattery to put us off our guard in intercourse with them, employ a dangerous expedient, like a sleeping-draught, which, when it does not send the patient to sleep, keeps him all the wider awake.

319.

A Good Letter-Writer. – A person who does not write books, thinks much, and lives in unsatisfying society, will usually be a good letter writer.

320.

The Ugliest of All. – It may be doubted whether a person who has travelled much has found anywhere in the world uglier places than those to be met with in the human face.

321.
The Sympathetic Ones. – Sympathetic natures, ever ready to help in misfortune, are seldom those that participate in joy; in the happiness of others they have nothing to occupy them, they are superfluous, they do not feel themselves in possession of their superiority, and hence readily show their displeasure.

322.
The Relatives of a Suicide. – The relatives of a suicide take it in ill part that he did not remain alive out of consideration for their reputation.

323.
Ingratitude Foreseen. – He who makes a large gift gets no gratitude; for the recipient is already overburdened by the acceptance of the gift.

324.
In Dull Society. – Nobody thanks a witty man for politeness when he puts himself on a par with a society in which it would not be polite to show one's wit.

325.
The Presence of Witnesses. – We are doubly willing to jump into the water after some one who has fallen in, if there are people present who have not the courage to do so.

326.
Being Silent. – For both parties in a controversy, the most disagreeable way of retaliating is to be vexed and silent; for the aggressor usually regards the silence as a sign of contempt.

327.
Friends' Secrets. – Few people will not expose the private affairs of their friends when at a loss for a subject of conversation.

328.
Humanity. – The humanity of intellectual celebrities consists in courteously submitting to unfairness in intercourse with those who are not celebrated.

329.

The Embarrassed. – People who do not feel sure of themselves in society seize every opportunity of publicly showing their superiority to close friends, for instance by teasing them.

330.

Thanks. – A refined nature is vexed by knowing that some one owes it thanks, a coarse nature by knowing that it owes thanks to some one.

331.

A Sign of Estrangement. – The surest sign of the estrangement of the opinions of two persons is when they both say something ironical to each other and neither of them feels the irony.

332.

Presumption in Connection with Merit. – Presumption in connection with merit offends us even more than presumption in persons devoid of merit, for merit in itself offends us.

333.

Danger in the Voice. – In conversation we are sometimes confused by the tone of our own voice, and misled to make assertions that do not at all correspond to our opinions.

334.

In Conversation. – Whether in conversation with others we mostly agree or mostly disagree with them is a matter of habit; there is sense in both cases.

335.

Fear of Our Neighbour. – We are afraid of the animosity of our neighbour, because we are apprehensive that he may thereby discover our secrets.

336.

Distinguishing by Blaming. – Highly respected persons distribute even their blame in such fashion that they try to distinguish us therewith. It is intended to remind us of their serious interest in us. We misunderstand them entirely when we take their blame literally and protest against it; we thereby offend them and estrange ourselves from them.

337.

Indignation at the Goodwill of Others. – We are mistaken as to the extent to which we think we are hated or feared; because, though we ourselves know very well the extent of our divergence from a person, tendency, or party, those others know us only superficially, and can, therefore, only hate us superficially. We often meet with goodwill which is inexplicable to us; but when we comprehend it, it shocks us, because it shows that we are not considered with sufficient seriousness or importance.

338.

Thwarting Vanities. – When two persons meet whose vanity is equally great, they have afterwards a bad impression of each other; because each has been so occupied with the impression he wished to produce on the other that the other has made no impression upon him; at last it becomes clear to them both that their efforts have been in vain, and each puts the blame on the other.

339.

Improper Behaviour as a Good Sign. – A superior mind takes pleasure in the tactlessness, pretentiousness, and even hostility of ambitious youths; it is the vicious habit of fiery horses which have not yet carried a rider, but, in a short time, will be so proud to carry one.

340.

When it is Advisable to Suffer Wrong. – It is well to put up with accusations without refutation, even when they injure us, when the accuser would see a still greater fault on our part if we contradicted and perhaps even refuted him. In this way, certainly, a person may always be wronged and always have right on his side, and may eventually, with the best conscience in the world, become the most intolerable tyrant and tormentor; and what happens in the individual may also take place in whole classes of society.

341.

Too Little Honoured. – Very conceited persons, who have received less consideration than they expected, attempt for a long time to deceive themselves and others with regard to it, and become subtle psychologists in order to make out that they have been amply honoured. Should they not attain their aim, should the veil of deception be torn, they give way to all the greater fury.

342.

Primitive Conditions Re-echoing in Speech. – By the manner in which people make assertions in their intercourse we often recognise an echo of the times when they were more conversant with weapons than anything else; sometimes they handle their assertions like sharpshooters using their arms, sometimes we think we hear the whizz and clash of swords, and with some men an assertion crashes down like a stout cudgel. Women, on the contrary, speak like beings who for thousands of years have sat at the loom, plied the needle, or played the child with children.

343.

The Narrator. – He who gives an account of something readily betrays whether it is because the fact interests him, or because he wishes to excite interest by the narration. In the latter case he will exaggerate, employ superlatives, and such like. He then does not usually tell his story SO well, because he does not think so much about his subject as about himself.

344.

The Reciter. – He who recites dramatic works makes discoveries about his own character; he finds his voice more natural in certain moods and scenes than in others, say in the pathetic or in the scurrilous, while in ordinary life, perhaps, he has not had the opportunity to exhibit pathos or scurrility.

345.

A Comedy Scene in Real Life. – Some one conceives an ingenious idea on a theme in order to express it in society. Now in a comedy we should hear and see how he sets all sail for that point, and tries to land the company at the place where he can make his remark, how he continuously pushes the conversation towards the one goal, sometimes losing the way, finding it again, and finally arriving at the moment: he is almost breathless – and then one of the company takes the remark itself out of his mouth! What will he do? Oppose his own opinion?

346.

Unintentionally Discourteous. – When a person treats another with unintentional discourtesy – for instance, not greeting him because not recognising him – he is vexed by it, although he cannot reproach his own sentiments; he is hurt by the bad opinion which he has produced in the other person, or fears the consequences of his bad humour, or is pained by the thought of having injured him – vanity, fear, or pity may therefore be aroused; perhaps all three together.

347.

A Masterpiece of Treachery. – To express a tantalising distrust of a fellow-conspirator, lest he should betray one, and this at the very moment when one is practising treachery one's self, is a masterpiece of wickedness; because it absorbs the other's attention and compels him for a time to act very unsuspiciously and openly, so that the real traitor has thus acquired a free hand.

348.

To Injure and to be Injured. – It is far pleasanter to injure and afterwards beg for forgiveness than to be injured and grant forgiveness. He who does the former gives evidence of power and afterwards of kindness of character. The person injured, however, if he does not wish to be considered inhuman, *must* forgive; his enjoyment of the other's humiliation is insignificant on account of this constraint.

349.

In a Dispute. – When we contradict another's opinion and at the same time develop our own, the constant consideration of the other opinion usually disturbs the natural attitude of our own which appears more intentional, more distinct, and perhaps somewhat exaggerated.

350.

An Artifice. – He who wants to get another to do something difficult must on no account treat the matter as a problem, but must set forth his plan plainly as the only one possible; and when the adversary's eye betrays objection and opposition he must understand how to break off quickly, and allow him no time to put in a word.

351.

Pricks of Conscience after Social Gatherings. – Why does our conscience prick us after ordinary social gatherings? Because we have treated serious things lightly, because in talking of persons we have not spoken quite justly or have been silent when we should have spoken, because, sometimes, we have not jumped up and run away – in short, because we have behaved in society as if we belonged to it.

352.

We are Misjudged. – He who always listens to hear how he is judged is always vexed. For we are misjudged even by those who are nearest to us ('who know us best'). Even good friends sometimes vent their ill-humour in a spiteful word; and would they be our friends if they knew us rightly? The judgements of the indifferent wound us deeply, because they sound so impartial, so objective almost. But when we see that some one hostile to us knows us in a concealed point as well as we know ourselves, how great is then our vexation!

353.

The Tyranny of the Portrait. – Artists and statesmen, who out of particular features quickly construct the whole picture of a man or an event, are mostly unjust in demanding that the event or person should afterwards be actually as they have painted it; they demand straightway that a man should be just as gifted, cunning, and unjust as he is in their representation of him.

354.

Relatives as the Best Friends. – The Greeks, who knew so well what a friend was, they alone of all peoples have a profound and largely philosophical discussion of friendship; so that it is by them firstly (and as yet lastly) that the problem of the friend has been recognised as worthy of solution – these same Greeks have designated *relatives* by an expression which is the superlative of the word 'friend'. This is inexplicable to me.

355.

Misunderstood Honesty. – When any one quotes himself in conversation ('I then said,' 'I am accustomed to say'), it gives the impression of presumption; whereas it often proceeds from quite an opposite source; or at least from honesty, which does not wish to deck and adorn the present moment with wit which belongs to an earlier moment.

356.

The Parasite. – It denotes entire absence of a noble disposition when a person prefers to live in dependence at the expense of others, usually with a secret bitterness against them, in order only that he may not be obliged to work. Such a disposition is far more frequent in women than in men, also far more pardonable (for historical reasons).

357.

On the Altar of Reconciliation. – There are circumstances under which one can only gain a point from a person by wounding him and becoming hostile; the feeling of having a foe torments him so much that he gladly seizes the first indication of a milder disposition to effect a reconciliation, and offers on the altar of this reconciliation what was formerly of such importance to him that he would not give it up at any price.

358.

Presumption in Demanding Pity. – There are people who, when they have been in a rage and have insulted others, demand, firstly, that it shall all be taken in good part; and, secondly, that they shall be pitied because they are subject to such violent paroxysms. So far does human presumption extend.

359.

Bait. – 'Every man has his price' – that is not true. But perhaps every one can be found a bait of one kind or other at which he will snap. Thus, in order to gain some supporters for a cause, it is only necessary to give it the glamour of being philanthropic, noble, charitable, and self-denying – and to what cause could this glamour not be given! It is the sweetmeat and dainty of *their* soul; others have different ones.

360.

The Attitude in Praising. – When good friends praise a gifted person he often appears to be delighted with them out of politeness and goodwill, but in reality he feels indifferent. His real nature is quite unmoved towards them, and will not budge a step on that account out of the sun or shade in which it lies; but people wish to please by praise, and it would grieve them if one did not rejoice when they praise a person.

361.

The Experience of Socrates. – If one has become a master in one thing, one has generally remained, precisely thereby, a complete dunce in most other things; but one forms the very reverse opinion, as was already experienced by Socrates. This is the annoyance which makes association with masters disagreeable.

362.

A Means of Defence. – In warring against stupidity, the most just and gentle of men at last become brutal. They are thereby, perhaps, taking the proper course for defence; for the most appropriate argument for a stupid brain is the clenched fist. But because, as has been said, their character is just and gentle, they suffer more by this means of protection than they injure their opponents by it.

363.

Curiosity. – If curiosity did not exist, very little would be done for the good of our neighbour. But curiosity creeps into the houses of the unfortunate and the needy under the name of duty or of pity. Perhaps there is a good deal of curiosity even in the much-vaunted maternal love.

364.

Disappointment in Society. – One man wishes to be interesting for his opinions, another for his likes and dislikes, a third for his acquaintances, and a fourth for his solitariness – and they all meet with disappointment. For he before whom the play is performed thinks himself the only play that is to be taken into account.

365.

The Duel. – It may be said in favour of duels and all affairs of honour that if a man has such susceptible feelings that he does not care to live when So-and-so says or thinks this or that about him; he has a right to make it a question of the death of the one or the other. With regard to the fact that he is so susceptible, it is not at all to be remonstrated with, in that matter we are the heirs of the past, of its greatness as well as of its exaggerations, without which no greatness ever existed. So when there exists a code of honour which lets blood stand in place of death, so that the mind is relieved after a regular duel it is a great blessing, because otherwise many human lives would be in danger. Such an institution, moreover, teaches men to be cautious in their utterances and makes intercourse with them possible.

366.

Nobleness and Gratitude. – A noble soul will be pleased to owe gratitude, and will not anxiously avoid opportunities of coming under obligation; it will also be moderate afterwards in the expression of its gratitude; baser souls, on the other hand, are unwilling to be under any obligation, or are afterwards immoderate in their expressions of thanks and altogether too devoted. The latter is, moreover, also the case with persons of mean origin or depressed circumstances; to show them a favour seems to them a miracle of grace.

367.

Occasions of Eloquence. – In order to talk well one man needs a person who is decidedly and avowedly his superior to talk to, while another can only find absolute freedom of speech and happy turns of eloquence before one who is his inferior. In both cases the cause is the same; each of them talks well only when he talks *sans gêne* – the one because in the presence of something higher he does not feel the impulse of rivalry and competition, the other because he also lacks the same impulse in the presence of something lower. Now there is quite another type of men, who talk well only when debating, with the intention of conquering. Which of the two types is the more aspiring: the one that talks well from excited ambition, or the one that talks badly or not at all from precisely the same motive?

368.

The Talent for Friendship. – Two types are distinguished amongst people who have a special faculty for friendship. The one is ever on the ascent, and for every phase of his development he finds a friend exactly suited to him. The series of friends which he thus acquires is seldom a consistent one, and is sometimes at variance and in contradiction, entirely in accordance with the fact that the later phases of his development neutralise or prejudice the earlier phases. Such a man may jestingly be called a *ladder*. The other type is represented by him who exercises an attractive influence on very different characters and endowments, so that he wins a whole circle of friends; these, however, are thereby brought voluntarily into friendly relations with one another in spite of all differences. Such a man may be called a *circle*, for this homogeneousness of such different temperaments and natures must somehow be typified in him. Furthermore, the faculty for having good friends is greater in many people than the faculty for being a good friend.

369.

Tactics in Conversation. – After a conversation with a person one is best pleased with him when one has had an opportunity of exhibiting one's intelligence and amiability in all its glory. Shrewd people who wish to impress a person favourably make use of this circumstance, they provide him with the best opportunities for making a good joke, and so on in conversation. An amusing conversation might be imagined between two very shrewd persons, each wishing to impress the other favourably, and therefore each throwing to the other the finest chances in conversation, which neither of them accepted, so that the conversation on the whole might turn out spiritless and unattractive because each assigned to the other the opportunity of being witty and charming.

370.

Discharge of Indignation. – The man who meets with a failure attributes this failure rather to the ill-will of another than to fate. His irritated feelings are alleviated by thinking that a person and not a thing is the cause of his failure; for he can revenge himself on persons, but is obliged to swallow down the injuries of fate. Therefore when anything has miscarried with a prince, those about him are accustomed to point out some individual as the ostensible cause, who is sacrificed in the interests of all the courtiers; for otherwise the prince's indignation would vent itself on them all, as he can take no revenge on the Goddess of Destiny herself.

371.

Assuming the Colours of the Environment. – Why are likes and dislikes so contagious that we can hardly live near a very sensitive person without being filled, like a hogshead, with his *fors* and *againsts*? In the first place, complete forbearance of judgement is very difficult, and sometimes absolutely intolerable to our vanity; it has the same appearance as poverty of thought and sentiment, or as timidity and unmanliness; and so we are, at least, driven on to take a side, perhaps contrary to our environment, if this attitude gives greater pleasure to our pride. As a rule, however – and this is the second point – we are not conscious of the transition from indifference to liking or disliking, but we gradually accustom ourselves to the sentiments of our environment, and because sympathetic agreement and acquiescence are so agreeable, we soon wear all the signs and party-colours of our surroundings.

372.

Irony. – Irony is only permissible as a pedagogic expedient, on the part of a teacher when dealing with his pupils; its purpose is to humble and to shame, but in the wholesome way that causes good resolutions to spring up and teaches people to show honour and gratitude, as they would to a doctor, to him who has so treated them. The ironical man pretends to be ignorant, and does it so well that the pupils conversing with him are deceived, and in their firm belief in their own superior knowledge they grow bold and expose all their weak points; they lose their cautiousness and reveal themselves as they are – until all of a sudden the light which they have held up to the teacher's face casts its rays back very humiliatingly upon themselves. Where such a relation, as that between teacher and pupil, does not exist, irony is a rudeness and a vulgar conceit. All ironical writers count on the silly species of human beings, who like to feel themselves superior to all others in common with the author himself, whom they look upon as the mouthpiece of their arrogance. Moreover, the habit of irony, like that of sarcasm, spoils the character; it gradually fosters the quality of a malicious superiority; one finally grows like a snappy dog, that has learnt to laugh as well as to bite.

373.

Arrogance. – There is nothing one should so guard against as the growth of the weed called arrogance, which spoils all one's good harvest; for there is arrogance in cordiality, in showing honour, in kindly familiarity, in caressing, in friendly counsel, in acknowledgment of faults, in sympathy for others – and all these fine things arouse aversion when the weed in question grows up among them. The arrogant man – that is to say, he who desires to appear more than he is *or passes for* – always miscalculates. It is true that he obtains a momentary success, inasmuch as those with whom he is arrogant generally give him the amount of honour that he demands, owing to fear or for the sake of convenience; but they take a bad revenge for it, inasmuch as they subtract from the value which they hitherto attached to him just as much as he demands above that amount. There is nothing for which men ask to be paid dearer than for humiliation. The arrogant man can make his really great merit so suspicious and small in the eyes of others that they tread on it with dusty feet. If at all, we should only allow ourselves a *proud* manner where we are quite sure of not being misunderstood and considered as arrogant; as, for instance, with friends and wives. For in social intercourse there is no greater folly than to acquire a reputation for arrogance; it is still worse than not having learnt to deceive politely.

374.

Tête-à-Tête – Private conversation is the perfect conversation, because everything the one person says receives its particular colouring, its tone, and its accompanying gestures *out of strict consideration for the other person* engaged in the conversation, it therefore corresponds to what takes place in intercourse by letter, viz., that one and the same person exhibits ten kinds of psychical expression, according as he writes now to this individual and now to that one. In duologue there is only a single refraction of thought; the person conversed with produces it, as the mirror in whom we want to behold our thoughts anew in their finest form. But how is it when there are two or three, or even more persons conversing with one? Conversation then necessarily loses something of its individualising subtlety, different considerations thwart and neutralise each other; the style which pleases one does not suit the taste of another. In intercourse with several individuals a person is therefore to withdraw within himself and represent facts as they are; but he has also to remove from the subjects the pulsating ether of humanity which makes conversation one of the pleasantest things in the world. Listen only to the tone in which those who mingle with whole groups of men are in the habit of speaking; it is as if the fundamental base of all speech were, 'It is *myself*; I say this, so make what you will of it!' That is the reason why clever ladies usually leave a singular, painful, and forbidding impression on those who have met them in society; it is the talking to many people, before many people, that robs them of all intellectual amiability and shows only their conscious dependence on themselves, their tactics, and their intention of gaining a public victory in full light; whilst in a private conversation the same ladies become womanly again, and recover their intellectual grace and charm.

375.

Posthumous Fame. – There is sense in hoping for recognition in a distant future only when we take it for granted that mankind will remain essentially unchanged, and that whatever is great is not for one age only but will be looked upon as great for all time. But this is an error. In all their sentiments and judgements concerning what is good and beautiful mankind have greatly changed; it is mere fantasy to imagine one's self to be a mile ahead, and that the whole of mankind is coming *our* way. Besides, a scholar who is misjudged may at present reckon with certainty that his discovery will be made by others, and that, at best, it will be allowed to him later on by some historian that he also already knew this or that but was not in a position to secure the recognition of his knowledge. Not to be recognised is always interpreted by posterity as lack of power. In short, one should not so readily speak in favour of haughty solitude. There are, however, exceptional cases; but it is chiefly our faults, weakness, and follies that hinder the recognition of our great qualities.

376.

Of Friends. – Just consider with thyself how different are the feelings, how divided are the opinions of even the nearest acquaintances; how even the same opinions in thy friend's mind have quite a different aspect and strength from what they have in thine own; and how manifold are the occasions which arise for misunderstanding and hostile severance. After all this thou wilt say to thyself, 'How insecure is the ground upon which all our alliances and friendships rest, how liable to cold downpours and bad weather, how lonely is every creature!' When a person recognises this fact, and, in addition, that all opinions and the nature and strength of them in his fellow-men are just as necessary and irresponsible as their actions; when his eye learns to see this internal necessity of opinions, owing to the indissoluble interweaving of character, occupation, talent, and environment – he will perhaps get rid of the bitterness and sharpness of the feeling with which the sage exclaimed, 'Friends, there are no friends!' Much rather will he make the confession to himself: Yes, there are friends, but they were drawn towards thee by error and deception concerning thy character; and they must have learnt to be silent in order to remain thy friends; for such human relationships almost always rest on the fact that some few things are never said, are never, indeed, alluded to; but if these pebbles are set rolling friendship follows afterwards and is broken. Are there any who would not be mortally injured if they were to learn what their most intimate friends really knew about them? By getting a knowledge of ourselves, and by looking upon our nature as a changing sphere of opinions and moods, and thereby learning to despise ourselves a little, we recover once more our equilibrium with the rest of mankind. It is true that we have good reason to despise each of our acquaintances, even the greatest of them; but just as good reason to turn this feeling against ourselves. And so we will bear with each other, since we bear with ourselves; and perhaps there will come to each a happier hour, when he will exclaim:

> 'Friends, there are really no friends!' thus cried th' expiring old sophist;
>
> 'Foes, there is really no foe!' – thus shout I, the incarnate fool.

SEVENTH DIVISION.
WIFE AND CHILD.

377.

The Perfect Woman. – The perfect woman is a higher type of humanity than the perfect man, and also something much rarer. The natural history of animals furnishes grounds in support of this theory.

378.

Friendship and Marriage. – The best friend will probably get the best wife, because a good marriage is based on talent for friendship.

379.

The Survival of the Parents. – The undissolved dissonances in the relation of the character and sentiments of the parents survive in the nature of the child and make up the history of its inner sufferings.

380.

Inherited from the Mother. – Every one bears within him an image of woman, inherited from his mother: it determines his attitude towards women as a whole, whether to honour, despise, or remain generally indifferent to them.

381.

Correcting Nature. – Whoever has not got a good father should procure one.

382.

Fathers and Sons. – Fathers have much to do to make amends for having sons.

383.

The Error of Gentlewomen. – Gentlewomen think that a thing does not really exist when it is not possible to talk of it in society.

384.

A Male Disease. – The surest remedy for the male disease of self-contempt is to be loved by a sensible woman.

385.

A Species of Jealousy. – Mothers are readily jealous of the friends of sons who are particularly successful. As a rule a mother loves *herself* in her son more than the son.

386.

Rational Irrationality. – In the maturity of life and intelligence the feeling comes over a man that his father did wrong in begetting him.

387.

Maternal Excellence. – Some mothers need happy and honoured children, some need unhappy ones – otherwise they cannot exhibit their maternal excellence.

388.

Different Sighs. – Some husbands have sighed over the elopement of their wives, the greater number, however, have sighed because nobody would elope with theirs.

389.

Love Matches. – Marriages which are contracted for love (so-called love-matches) have error for their father and need (necessity) for their mother.

390.

Women's Friendships. – Women can enter into friendship with a man perfectly well; but in order to maintain it the aid of a little physical antipathy is perhaps required.

391.

Ennui. – Many people, especially women, never feel ennui because they have never learnt to work properly.

392.

An Element of Love. – In all feminine love something of maternal love also comes to light.

393.

Unity of Place and Drama. – If married couples did not live together, happy marriages would be more frequent.

394.

The Usual Consequences of Marriage. – All intercourse which does not elevate a person, debases him, and *vice versa*; hence men usually sink a little when they marry, while women are somewhat elevated. Over-intellectual men require marriage in proportion as they are opposed to it as to a repugnant medicine.

395.

Learning to Command. – Children of unpretentious families must be taught to command, just as much as other children must be taught to obey.

396.

Wanting to be in Love. – Betrothed couples who have been matched by convenience often exert themselves *to fall in love*, to avoid the reproach of cold, calculating expediency. In the same manner those who become converts to Christianity for their advantage exert themselves to become genuinely pious; because the religious cast of countenance then becomes easier to them.

397.

No Standing Still in Love. – A musician who *loves* the slow *tempo* will play the same pieces ever more slowly. There is thus no standing still in any love.

398.

Modesty. – Women's modesty usually increases with their beauty.[14]

---

14 The opposite of this aphorism also holds good. – J. M. K.

399.

Marriage on a Good Basis. – A marriage in which each wishes to realise an individual aim by means of the other will stand well; for instance, when the woman wishes to become famous through the man and the man beloved through the woman.

400.

Proteus-Nature. – Through love women actually become what they appear to be in the imagination of their lovers.

401.

To Love and to Possess. – As a rule women love a distinguished man to the extent that they wish to possess him exclusively. They would gladly keep him under lock and key, if their vanity did not forbid, but vanity demands that he should also appear distinguished before others.

402.

The Test of a Good Marriage. – The goodness of a marriage is proved by the fact that it can stand an 'exception'.

403.

Bringing Anyone Round to Anything. – One may make any person so weak and weary by disquietude, anxiety, and excess of work or thought that he no longer resists anything that appears complicated, but gives way to it – diplomatists and women know this.

404.

Propriety and Honesty. – Those girls who mean to trust exclusively to their youthful charms for their provision in life, and whose cunning is further prompted by worldly mothers, have just the same aims as courtesans, only they are wiser and less honest.

405.

Masks. – There are women who, wherever one examines them, have no inside, but are mere masks. A man is to be pitied who has connection with such almost spectre-like and necessarily unsatisfactory creatures, but it is precisely such women who know how to excite a man's desire most strongly; he seeks for their soul, and seeks evermore.

406.

Marriage as a Long Talk. – In entering on a marriage one should ask one's self the question, 'Do you think you will pass your time well with this woman till your old age?' All else in marriage is transitory; talk, however, occupies most of the time of the association.

407.

Girlish Dreams. – Inexperienced girls flatter themselves with the notion that it is in their power to make a man happy; later on they learn that it is equivalent to underrating a man to suppose that he needs only a girl to make him happy. Women's vanity requires a man to be something more than merely a happy husband.

408.

The Dying-out of Faust and Marguerite. – According to the very intelligent remark of a scholar, the educated men of modern Germany resemble somewhat a mixture of Mephistopheles and Wagner, but are not at all like Faust, whom our grandfathers (in their youth at least) felt agitating within them. To them, therefore – to continue the remark – Marguerites are not suited, for two reasons. And because the latter are no longer desired they seem to be dying out.

409.

Classical Education for Girls. – For goodness' sake let us not give our classical education to girls! An education which, out of ingenious, inquisitive, ardent youths, so frequently makes – copies of their teacher!

410.

Without Rivals. – Women readily perceive in a man whether his soul has already been taken possession of; they wish to be loved without rivals, and find fault with the objects of his ambition, his political tasks, his sciences and arts, if he have a passion for such things. Unless he be distinguished thereby – then, in the case of a love-relationship between them, women look at the same time for an increase of *their own* distinction; under such circumstances, they favour the lover.

411.

The Feminine Intellect. – The intellect of women manifests itself as perfect mastery, presence of mind, and utilisation of all advantages. They transmit it as a fundamental quality to their children, and the father adds thereto the darker background of the will. His influence determines as it were the rhythm and harmony with which the new life is to be performed; but its melody is derived from the mother. For those who know how to put a thing properly: women have intelligence, men have character and passion. This does not contradict the fact that men actually achieve so much more with their intelligence: they have deeper and more powerful impulses; and it is these which carry their understanding (in itself something passive) to such an extent. Women are often silently surprised at the great respect men pay to their character. When, therefore, in the choice of a partner men seek specially for a being of deep and strong character, and women for a being of intelligence, brilliancy, and presence of mind, it is plain that at bottom men seek for the ideal man, and women for the ideal woman – consequently not for the complement but for the completion of their own excellence.

412.

Hesiod's Opinion Confirmed. – It is a sign of women's wisdom that they have almost always known how to get themselves supported, like drones in a bee-hive. Let us just consider what this meant originally, and why men do not depend upon women for their support. Of a truth it is because masculine vanity and reverence are greater than feminine wisdom; for women have known how to secure for themselves by their subordination the greatest advantage, in fact, the upper hand. Even the care of children may originally have been used by the wisdom of women as an excuse for withdrawing themselves as much as possible from work. And at present they still understand when they are really active (as housekeepers, for instance) how to make a bewildering fuss about it, so that the merit of their activity is usually ten times over-estimated by men.

413.

Lovers as Short-sighted People. – A pair of powerful spectacles has sometimes sufficed to cure a person in love; and whoever has had sufficient imagination to represent a face or form twenty years older, has probably gone through life not much disturbed.

414.

Women in Hatred. – In a state of hatred women are more dangerous than men; for one thing, because they are hampered by no regard for fairness when their hostile feelings have been aroused; but let their hatred develop unchecked to its utmost consequences; then also, because they are expert in finding sore spots (which every man and every party possess), and pouncing upon them: for which purpose their dagger-pointed intelligence is of good service (whilst men, hesitating at the sight of wounds, are often generously and conciliatorily inclined).

415.

Love. – The love idolatry which women practise is fundamentally and originally an intelligent device, inasmuch as they increase their power by all the idealisings of love and exhibit themselves as so much the more desirable in the eyes of men. But by being accustomed for centuries to this exaggerated appreciation of love, it has come to pass that they have been caught in their own net and have forgotten the origin of the device. They themselves are now still more deceived than the men, and on that account also suffer more from the disillusionment which, almost necessarily, enters into the life of every woman – so far, at any rate, as she has sufficient imagination and intelligence to be able to be deceived and undeceived.

416.

The Emancipation of Women. – Can women be at all just, when they are so accustomed to love and to be immediately biased for or against? For that reason they are also less interested in things and more in individuals: but when they are interested in things they immediately become their partisans, and thereby spoil their pure, innocent effect. Thus there arises a danger, by no means small, in entrusting politics and certain portions of science to them (history, for instance). For what is rarer than a woman who really knows what science is? Indeed the best of them cherish in their breasts a secret scorn for science, as if they were somehow superior to it. Perhaps all this can be changed in time; but meanwhile it is so.

417.

The Inspiration in Women's Judgements. – The sudden decisions, for or against, which women are in the habit of making, the flashing illumination of personal relations caused by their spasmodic inclinations and aversions – in short, the proofs of feminine injustice have been invested with a lustre by men who are in love, as if all women had inspirations of wisdom, even without the Delphic cauldron and the laurel wreaths; and their utterances are interpreted and duly set forth as Sibylline oracles for long afterwards. When one considers, however, that for every person and for every cause something can be said in favour of it but equally also something against it, that things are not only two-sided, but also three- and four-sided, it is almost difficult to be entirely at fault in such sudden decisions; indeed, it might be said that the nature of things has been so arranged that women should always carry their point.[15]

418.

Being Loved. – As one of every two persons in love is usually the one who loves, the other the one who is loved, the belief has arisen that in every love-affair there is a constant amount of love; and that the more of it the one person monopolises the less is left for the other.

---

15 It may be remarked that Nietzsche changed his view on this subject later on, and ascribed more importance to woman's intuition. Cf. also Disraeli's reference to the 'High Priestesses of predestination.' – J. M. K.

Exceptionally it happens that the vanity of each of the parties persuades him or her that it is he or she who must be loved; so that both of them wish to be loved: from which cause many half funny, half absurd scenes take place, especially in married life.

419.

Contradictions in Feminine Minds. – Owing to the fact that women are so much more personal than objective, there are tendencies included in the range of their ideas which are logically in contradiction to one another; they are accustomed in turn to become enthusiastically fond just of the representatives of these tendencies and accept their systems in the lump; but in such wise that a dead place originates wherever a new personality afterwards gets the ascendancy. It may happen that the whole philosophy in the mind of an old lady consists of nothing but such dead places.

420.

Who Suffers the More? – After a personal dissension and quarrel between a woman and a man the latter party suffers chiefly from the idea of having wounded the other, whilst the former suffers chiefly from the idea of not having wounded the other sufficiently; so she subsequently endeavours by tears, sobs, and discomposed mien, to make his heart heavier.

421.

An Opportunity for Feminine Magnanimity. – If we could disregard the claims of custom in our thinking we might consider whether nature and reason do not suggest several marriages for men, one after another: perhaps that, at the age of twenty-two, he should first marry an older girl who is mentally and morally his superior, and can be his leader through all the dangers of the twenties (ambition, hatred, self-contempt, and passions of all kinds). This woman's affection would subsequently change entirely into maternal love, and she would not only submit to it but would encourage the man in the most salutary manner, if in his thirties he contracted an alliance with quite a young girl whose education he himself should take in hand. Marriage is a necessary institution for the twenties; a useful, but not necessary, institution for the thirties; for later life it is often harmful, and promotes the mental deterioration of the man.

422.

The Tragedy of Childhood. – Perhaps it not infrequently happens that noble men with lofty aims have to fight their hardest battle in childhood; by having perchance to carry out their principles in opposition to a base-minded father addicted to feigning and falsehood, or living, like Lord Byron, in constant warfare with a childish and passionate mother. He who has had such an experience will never be able to forget all his life who has been his greatest and most dangerous enemy.

423.

Parental Folly. – The grossest mistakes in judging a man are made by his parents – this is a fact, but how is it to be explained? Have the parents too much experience of the child and cannot any longer arrange this experience into a unity? It has been noticed that it is only in the earlier period of their sojourn in foreign countries that travellers rightly grasp the general distinguishing features of a people; the better they come to know it, they are the less able to see what is typical and distinguishing in a people. As soon as they grow short-sighted their eyes cease to be long-sighted. Do parents, therefore, judge their children falsely because they have never stood far enough away from them? The following is quite another explanation: people are no longer accustomed to reflect on what is close at hand and surrounds them, but just accept it. Perhaps the usual thoughtlessness of parents is the reason why they judge so wrongly when once they are compelled to judge their children.

424.

The Future of Marriage. – The noble and liberal-minded women who take as their mission the education and elevation of the female sex, should not overlook one point of view: 'Marriage regarded in its highest aspect, as the spiritual friendship of two persons of opposite sexes, and accordingly such as is hoped for in future, contracted for the purpose of producing and educating a new generation – such marriage, which only makes use of the sensual, so to speak, as a rare and occasional means to a higher purpose, will, it is to be feared, probably need a natural auxiliary, namely, *concubinage*. For if, on the grounds of his health, the wife is also to serve for the sole satisfaction of the man's sexual needs, a wrong perspective, opposed to the aims indicated, will have most influence in the choice of a wife. The aims referred to: the production of descendants, will be accidental, and their successful education highly improbable. A good wife, who has to be friend, helper, child-bearer, mother, family-head and manager, and has even perhaps to conduct her own business and affairs separately from those of the husband, cannot at the same time be a concubine; it would, in general, be asking too much of her. In the future, therefore, a state of things might take place the opposite of what existed at Athens in the time of Pericles; the men, whose wives were then little more to them than concubines, turned besides to the Aspasias, because they longed for the charms of a companionship gratifying both to head and heart, such as the grace and intellectual suppleness of women could alone provide. All human institutions, just like marriage, allow only a moderate amount of practical idealising, failing which coarse remedies immediately become necessary.

425.

The 'Storm and Stress' Period of Women. – In the three or four civilised countries of Europe, it is possible, by several centuries of education, to make out of women anything we like – even men, not in a sexual sense, of course, but in every other. Under such influences they will acquire all the masculine virtues and forces, at the same time, of course, they must also have taken all the masculine weaknesses and vices into the bargain: so much, as has been said, we can command. But how shall we endure the intermediate state thereby induced, which may even last two or three centuries, during which feminine follies and injustices, woman's original birthday endowment, will still maintain the ascendancy over all that has been otherwise gained and acquired? This will be the time when indignation will be the peculiar masculine passion; indignation, because all arts and sciences have been overflowed and choked by an unprecedented dilettanteism, philosophy talked to death by brain-bewildering chatter, politics more fantastic and partisan than ever, and society in complete disorganisation, because the conservatrices of ancient customs have become ridiculous to themselves, and have endeavoured in every way to place themselves outside the pale of custom. If indeed women had their greatest power in custom, where will they have to look in order to reacquire a similar plenitude of power after having renounced custom?

426.

Free-Spirit and Marriage. – Will free-thinkers live with women? In general, I think that, like the prophesying birds of old, like the truth-thinkers and truth-speakers of the present, they must prefer to *fly alone*.

427.

The Happiness of Marriage. – Everything to which we are accustomed draws an ever-tightening cobweb-net around us; and presently we notice that the threads have become cords, and that we ourselves sit in the middle like a spider that has here got itself caught and must feed on its own blood. Hence the free spirit hates all rules and customs, all that is permanent and definitive, hence he painfully tears asunder again and again the net around him, though in consequence thereof he will suffer from numerous wounds, slight and severe; for he must break off every thread *from himself*, from his body and soul. He must learn to love where he has hitherto hated, and *vice versa*. Indeed, it must not be a thing impossible for him to sow dragon's teeth in the same field in which he formerly scattered the abundance of his bounty. From this it can be inferred whether he is suited for the happiness of marriage.

428.

Too Intimate. – When we live on too intimate terms with a person it is as if we were again and again handling a good engraving with our fingers; the time comes when we have soiled and damaged paper in our hands, and nothing more. A man's soul also gets worn out by constant handling; at least, it eventually *appears* so to us – never again do we see its original design and beauty. We always lose through too familiar association with women and friends; and sometimes we lose the pearl of our life thereby.

429.

The Golden Cradle. – The free spirit will always feel relieved when he has finally resolved to shake off the motherly care and guardianship with which women surround him. What harm will a rough wind, from which he has been so anxiously protected, do him? Of what consequence is a genuine disadvantage, loss, misfortune, sickness, illness, fault, or folly more or less in his life, compared with the bondage of the golden cradle, the peacock's-feather fan, and the oppressive feeling that he must, in addition, be grateful because he is waited on and spoiled like a baby? Hence it is that the milk which is offered him by the motherly disposition of the women about him can so readily turn into gall.

430.

A Voluntary Victim. – There is nothing by which able women can so alleviate the lives of their husbands, should these be great and famous, as by becoming, so to speak, the receptacle for the general disfavour and occasional ill-humour of the rest of mankind. Contemporaries are usually accustomed to overlook many mistakes, follies, and even flagrant injustices in their great men if only they can find some one to maltreat and kill, as a proper victim for the relief of their feelings. A wife not infrequently has the ambition to present herself for this sacrifice, and then the husband may indeed feel satisfied – he being enough of an egoist to have such a voluntary storm, rain, and lightning-conductor beside him.

431.

Agreeable Adversaries. – The natural inclination of women towards quiet, regular, happily tuned existences and intercourse, the oil-like and calming effect of their influence upon the sea of life, operates unconsciously against the heroic inner impulse of the free spirit. Without knowing it, women act as if they were taking away the stones from the path of the wandering mineralogist in order that he might not strike his foot against them – when he has gone out for the very purpose of striking against them.

432.

The Discord of Two Concords. – Woman wants to serve, and finds her happiness therein; the free spirit does not want to be served, and therein finds his happiness.

433.

Xantippe. – Socrates found a wife such as he required – but he would not have sought her had he known her sufficiently well; even the heroism of his free spirit would not have gone so far. As a matter of fact, Xantippe forced him more and more into his peculiar profession, inasmuch as she made house and home doleful and dismal to him; she taught him to live in the streets and wherever gossiping and idling went on, and thereby made him the greatest Athenian street-dialectician, who had, at last, to compare himself to a gad-fly which a god had set on the neck of the beautiful horse Athens to prevent it from resting.

434.

Blind to the Future. – Just as mothers have senses and eye only for those pains of their children that are evident to the senses and eye, so the wives of men of high aspirations cannot accustom themselves to see their husbands suffering, starving, or slighted – although all this is, perhaps, not only the proof that they have rightly chosen their attitude in life, but even the guarantee that their great aims *must* be achieved some time. Women always intrigue privately against the higher souls of their husbands; they want to cheat them out of their future for the sake of a painless and comfortable present.

435.

Authority and Freedom. – However highly women may honour their husbands, they honour still more the powers and ideas recognised by society; they have been accustomed for millennia to go along with their hands folded on their breasts, and their heads bent before everything dominant, disapproving of all resistance to public authority. They therefore unintentionally, and as if from instinct, hang themselves as a drag on the wheels of free-spirited, independent endeavour, and in certain circumstances make their husbands highly impatient, especially when the latter persuade themselves that it is really love which prompts the action of their wives. To disapprove of women's methods and generously to honour the motives that prompt them – that is man's nature and often enough his despair.

436.

Ceterum Censeo. – It is laughable when a company of paupers decree the abolition of the right of inheritance, and it is not less laughable when childless persons labour for the practical lawgiving of a country: they have not enough ballast in their ship to sail safely over the ocean of the future. But it seems equally senseless if a man who has chosen for his mission the widest knowledge and estimation of universal existence, burdens himself with personal considerations for a family, with the support, protection, and care of wife and child, and in front of his telescope hangs that gloomy veil through which hardly a ray from the distant firmament can penetrate. Thus I, too, agree with the opinion that in matters of the highest philosophy all married men are to be suspected.

437.

Finally. – There are many kinds of hemlock, and fate generally finds an opportunity to put a cup of this poison to the lips of the free spirit – in order to 'punish' him, as every one then says. What do the women do about him then? They cry and lament, and perhaps disturb the sunset calm of the thinker, as they did in the prison at Athens. 'Oh Crito, bid some one take those women away!' said Socrates at last.

EIGHTH DIVISION. A GLANCE AT THE STATE.

438.

Asking to be Heard. – The demagogic disposition and the intention of working upon the masses is at present common to all political parties; on this account they are all obliged to change their principles into great *al fresco* follies and thus make a show of them. In this matter there is no further alteration to be made: indeed, it is superfluous even to raise a finger against it; for here Voltaire's saying applies: '*Quand la populace se mile de raisonner, tout est perdu.*' Since this has happened we have to accommodate ourselves to the new conditions, as we have to accommodate ourselves when an earthquake has displaced the old boundaries and the contour of the land and altered the value of property. Moreover, when it is once for all a question in the politics of all parties to make life endurable to the greatest possible majority, this majority may always decide what they understand by an endurable life; if they believe their intellect capable of finding the right means to this end why should we doubt about it? They *want*, once for all, to be the architects of their own good or ill fortune; and if their feeling of free choice and their pride in the five or six ideas that their brain conceals and brings to light, really makes life so agreeable to them that they gladly put up with the fatal consequences of their narrow-mindedness, there is little to object to, provided that their narrow-mindedness does not go so far as to demand that everything shall become politics in this sense, that all shall live and act according to this standard. For, in the first place, it must be more than ever permissible for some people to keep aloof from politics and to stand somewhat aside. To this they are also impelled by the pleasure of free choice, and connected with this there may even be some little pride in keeping silence when too many, and only the many, are speaking. Then this small group must be excused if they do not attach such great importance to the happiness of the majority (nations or strata of population may be understood thereby), and are occasionally guilty of an ironical grimace; for their seriousness lies elsewhere, their conception of happiness is quite different, and their aim cannot be encompassed by every clumsy hand that has just five fingers. Finally, there comes from time to time – what is certainly most difficult to concede to them, but must also be conceded – a moment when they emerge from their silent solitariness and try once more the strength of their lungs; they then call to each other like people lost in a wood, to make themselves known and for mutual encouragement; whereby, to be sure, much becomes audible that sounds evil to ears for which it is not intended. Soon, however, silence again prevails in the wood, such silence that the buzzing, humming, and fluttering of the countless insects that live in, above, and beneath it, are again plainly heard.

439.

Culture and Caste. – A higher culture can only originate where there are two distinct castes of society: that of the working class, and that of the leisured class who are capable of true leisure; or, more strongly expressed, the caste of compulsory labour and the caste of free labour. The point of view of the division of happiness is not essential when it is a question of the production of a higher culture; in any case, however, the leisured caste is more susceptible to suffering and suffer more, their pleasure in existence is less and their task is greater. Now supposing there should be quite an interchange between the two castes, so that on the one hand the duller and less intelligent families and individuals are lowered from the higher caste into the lower, and, on the other hand, the freer men of the lower caste obtain access to the higher, a condition of things would be attained beyond which one can only perceive the open sea of vague wishes. Thus speaks to us the vanishing voice of the olden time; but where are there still ears to hear it?

440.

Of Good Blood. – That which men and women of good blood possess much more than others, and which gives them an undoubted right to be more highly appreciated, are two arts which are always increased by inheritance: the art of being able to command, and the art of proud obedience. Now wherever commanding is the business of the day (as in the great world of commerce and industry), there results something similar to these families of good blood, only the noble bearing in obedience is lacking which is an inheritance from feudal conditions and hardly grows any longer in the climate of our culture.

441.

Subordination. – The subordination which is so highly valued in military and official ranks will soon become as incredible to us as the secret tactics of the Jesuits have already become; and when this subordination is no longer possible a multitude of astonishing results will no longer be attained, and the world will be all the poorer. It must disappear, for its foundation is disappearing, the belief in unconditional authority, in ultimate truth; even in military ranks physical compulsion is not sufficient to produce it, but only the inherited adoration of the princely as of something superhuman. In *freer* circumstances people subordinate themselves only on conditions, in compliance with a mutual contract, consequently with all the provisos of self-interest.

442.

The National Army. – The greatest disadvantage of the national army, now so much glorified, lies in the squandering of men of the highest civilisation; it is only by the favourableness of all circumstances that there are such men at all; how carefully and anxiously should we deal with them, since long periods are required to create the chance conditions for the production of such delicately organised brains! But as the Greeks wallowed in the blood of Greeks, so do Europeans now in the blood of Europeans: and indeed, taken relatively, it is mostly the highly cultivated who are sacrificed, those who promise an abundant and excellent posterity; for such stand in the front of the battle as commanders, and also expose themselves to most danger, by reason of their higher ambition. At present, when quite other and higher tasks are assigned than *patria* and *honour*, the rough Roman patriotism is either something dishonourable or a sign of being behind the times.

443.

Hope as Presumption. – Our social order will slowly melt away, as all former orders have done, as soon as the suns of new opinions have shone upon mankind with a new glow. We can only *wish* this melting away in the hope thereof, and we are only reasonably entitled to hope when we believe that we and our equals have more strength in heart and head than the representatives of the existing state of things. As a rule, therefore, this hope will be a presumption, an *over-estimation*.

444.

War. – Against war it may be said that it makes the victor stupid and the vanquished revengeful. In favour of war it may be said that it barbarises in both its above-named results, and thereby makes more natural; it is the sleep or the winter period of culture; man emerges from it with greater strength for good and for evil.

445.

In the Prince's Service. – To be able to act quite regardlessly it is best for a statesman to carry out his work not for himself but for a prince. The eye of the spectator is dazzled by the splendour of this general disinterestedness, so that it does not see the malignancy and severity which the work of a statesman brings with it.[16]

446.

A Question of Power, not of Right. – As regards Socialism, in the eyes of those who always consider higher utility, if it is *really* a rising against their oppressors of those who for centuries have been oppressed and downtrodden, there is no problem of *right* involved (notwithstanding the ridiculous, effeminate question, 'How far *ought* we to grant its demands?') but only a problem of *power* ('How far *can* we make use of its demands?'); the same, therefore, as in the case of a natural force – steam, for instance – which is either forced by man into his service, as a machine-god, or which, in case of defects of the machine, that is to say, defects of human calculation in its construction, destroys it and man together. In order to solve this question of power we must know how strong Socialism is, in what modification it may yet be employed as a powerful lever in the present

16 This aphorism may have been suggested by Nietzsche's observing the behaviour of his great contemporary, Bismarck, towards the dynasty. – J. M. K.

mechanism of political forces; under certain circumstances we should do all we can to strengthen it. With every great force – be it the most dangerous – men have to think how they can make of it an instrument for their purposes. Socialism acquires a *right* only if war seems to have taken place between the two powers, the representatives of the old and the new, when, however, a wise calculation of the greatest possible preservation and advantageousness to both sides gives rise to a desire for a treaty. Without treaty no right. So far, however, there is neither war nor treaty on the ground in question, therefore no rights, no 'ought'.

447.

Utilising the most Trivial Dishonesty. – The power of the press consists in the fact that every individual who ministers to it only feels himself bound and constrained to a very small extent. He usually expresses *his* opinion, but sometimes also does *not* express it in order to serve his party or the politics of his country, or even himself. Such little faults of dishonesty, or perhaps only of a dishonest silence, are not hard to bear by the individual, but the consequences are extraordinary, because these little faults are committed by many at the same time. Each one says to himself: 'For such small concessions I live better and can make my income; by the want of such little compliances I make myself impossible.' Because it seems almost morally indifferent to write a line more (perhaps even without signature), or not to write it, a person who has money and influence can make any opinion a public one. He who knows that most people are weak in trifles, and wishes to attain his own ends thereby, is always dangerous.

448.

Too Loud a Tone in Grievances. – Through the fact that an account of a bad state of things (for instance, the crimes of an administration, bribery and arbitrary favour in political or learned bodies) is greatly exaggerated, it fails in its effect on intelligent people, but has all the greater effect on the unintelligent (who would have remained indifferent to an accurate and moderate account). But as these latter are considerably in the majority, and harbour in themselves stronger will-power and more impatient desire for action, the exaggeration becomes the cause of investigations, punishments, promises, and reorganisations. In so far it is useful to exaggerate the accounts of bad states of things.

449.

The Apparent Weather Makers of Politics. – Just as people tacitly assume that he who understands the weather, and foretells it about a day in advance, makes the weather, so even the educated and learned, with a display of superstitious faith, ascribe to great statesmen as their most special work all the important changes and conjunctures that have taken place during their administration, when it is only evident that they knew something thereof a little earlier than other people and made their calculations accordingly – thus they are also looked upon as weather-makers – and this belief is not the least important instrument of their power.

450.

New and Old Conceptions of Government. – To draw such a distinction between Government and people as if two separate spheres of power, a stronger and higher, and a weaker and lower, negotiated and came to terms with each other, is a remnant of transmitted political sentiment, which still accurately represents the historic establishment of the conditions of power in *most* States. When Bismarck, for instance, describes the constitutional system as a compromise between Government and people, he speaks in accordance with a principle which has its reason in history (from whence, to be sure, it also derives its admixture of folly, without which nothing human can exist). On the other hand, we must now learn – in accordance with a principle which has originated only in the *brain* and has still to *make* history – that Government is nothing but an organ of the people – not an attentive, honourable 'higher' in relation to a 'lower' accustomed to modesty. Before we accept this hitherto unhistorical and arbitrary, although logical, formulation of the conception of Government, let us but consider its consequences, for the relation between people and Government is the strongest typical relation, after the pattern of which the relationship between teacher and pupil, master and servants, father and family, leader and soldier, master and apprentice, is unconsciously formed. At present, under the influence of the prevailing constitutional system of government, all these relationships are changing a little – they are becoming compromises. But how they will have to be reversed and shifted, and change name and nature, when that newest of all conceptions has got the upper hand everywhere in people's minds! To achieve which, however, a century may yet be required. In this matter there is nothing *further* to be wished for except caution and slow development.

451.

Justice as the Decoy-Cry of Parties. – Well may noble (if not exactly very intelligent) representatives of the governing classes asseverate: 'We will treat men equally and grant them equal rights'; so far a socialistic mode of thought which is based on *justice* is possible; but, as has been said, only within the ranks of the governing class, which in this case *practises* justice with sacrifices and abnegations. On the other hand, to *demand* equality of rights, as do the Socialists of the subject caste, is by no means the outcome of justice, but of covetousness. If you expose bloody pieces of flesh to a beast, and withdraw them again, until it finally begins to roar, do you think that roaring implies justice?

452.

Possession and Justice. – When the Socialists point out that the division of property at the present day is the consequence of countless deeds of injustice and violence, and, *in summa*, repudiate obligation to anything with so unrighteous a basis, they only perceive something isolated. The entire past of ancient civilisation is built up on violence, slavery, deception, and error; we, however, cannot annul ourselves, the heirs of all these conditions, nay, the concrescences of all this past, and are not entitled to demand the withdrawal of a single fragment thereof. The unjust disposition lurks also in the souls of non-possessors; they are not better than the possessors and have no moral prerogative; for at one time or another their ancestors have been possessors. Not forcible new distributions, but gradual transformations of opinion are necessary; justice in all matters must become greater, the instinct of violence weaker.

453.

The Helmsman of the Passions. – The statesman excites public passions in order to have the advantage of the counter-passions thereby aroused. To give an example: a German statesman knows quite well that the Catholic Church will never have the same plans as Russia; indeed, that it would far rather be allied with the Turks than with the former country; he likewise knows that Germany is threatened with great danger from an alliance between France and Russia. If he can succeed, therefore, in making France the focus and fortress of the Catholic Church, he has averted this danger for a lengthy period. He has, accordingly, an interest in showing hatred against the Catholics in transforming, by all kinds of hostility, the supporters of the Pope's authority into an impassioned political power which is opposed to German politics, and must, as a matter of course, coalesce with France as the adversary of Germany; his aim is the catholicising of France, just as necessarily as Mirabeau saw the salvation of his native land in de-catholicising it. The one State, therefore, desires to muddle millions of minds of another State in order to gain advantage thereby. It is the same disposition which supports the republican form of government of a neighbouring State – *le désordre organisé*, as Mérimée says for the sole reason that it assumes that this form of government makes the nation weaker, more distracted, less fit for war.

454.

The Dangerous Revolutionary Spirits. – Those who are bent on revolutionising society may be divided into those who seek something for themselves thereby and those who seek something for their children and grandchildren. The latter are the more dangerous, for they have the belief and the good conscience of disinterestedness. The others can be appeased by favours: those in power are still sufficiently rich and wise to adopt that expedient. The danger begins as soon as the aims become impersonal; revolutionists seeking impersonal interests may consider all defenders of the present state of things as personally interested, and may therefore feel themselves superior to their opponents.

455.

The Political Value of Paternity. – When a man has no sons he has not a full right to join in a discussion concerning the needs of a particular community. A person must himself have staked his dearest object along with the others: that alone binds him fast to the State; he must have in view the well-being of his descendants, and must, therefore, above all, have descendants in order to take a right and natural share in all institutions and the changes thereof. The development of higher morality depends on a person's having sons; it disposes him to be unegoistic, or, more correctly, it extends his egoism in its duration and permits him earnestly to strive after goals which lie beyond his individual lifetime.

456.

Pride of Descent. – A man may be justly proud of an unbroken line of *good* ancestors down to his father – not however of the line itself, for every one has that. Descent from good ancestors constitutes the real nobility of birth; a single break in the chain, one bad ancestor, therefore, destroys the nobility of birth. Every one who talks about his nobility should be asked: 'Have you no violent, avaricious, dissolute, wicked, cruel man amongst your ancestors?' If with good cognisance and conscience he can answer No, then let his friendship be sought.

457.

Slaves and Labourers. – The fact that we regard the gratification of vanity as of more account than all other forms of well-being (security, position, and pleasures of all sorts), is shown to a ludicrous extent by every one wishing for the abolition of slavery and utterly abhorring to put any one into this position (apart altogether from political reasons), while every one must acknowledge to himself that in all respects slaves live more securely and more happily than modern labourers, and that slave labour is very easy labour compared with that of the 'labourer'. We protest in the name of the 'dignity of man'; but, expressed more simply, that is just our darling vanity which feels non-equality, and inferiority in public estimation, to be the hardest lot of all. The cynic thinks differently concerning the matter, because he despises honour: and so Diogenes was for some time a slave and tutor.

458.

Leading Minds and their Instruments. – We see that great statesmen, and in general all who have to employ many people to carry out their plans, sometimes proceed one way and sometimes another; they either choose with great skill and care the people suitable for their plans, and then leave them a comparatively large amount of liberty, because they know that the nature of the persons selected impels them precisely to the point where they themselves would have them go; or else they choose badly, in fact take whatever comes to hand, but out of every piece of clay they form something useful for their purpose. These latter minds are the more high-handed; they also desire more submissive instruments; their knowledge of mankind is usually much smaller, their contempt of mankind greater than in the case of the first mentioned class, but the machines they construct generally work better than the machines from the workshops of the former.

459.

Arbitrary Law Necessary. – Jurists dispute whether the most perfectly thought-out law or that which is most easily understood should prevail in a nation. The former, the best model of which is Roman Law, seems incomprehensible to the layman, and is therefore not the expression of his sense of justice. Popular laws, the Germanic, for instance, have been rude, superstitious, illogical, and in part idiotic, but they represented very definite, inherited national morals and sentiments. But where, as with us, law is no longer custom, it can only *command* and be compulsion; none of us any longer possesses a traditional sense of justice; we must therefore content ourselves with *arbitrary laws*, which are the expressions of the necessity that there *must be* law. The most logical is then in any case the most acceptable, because it is the most *impartial*, granting even that in every case the smallest unit of measure in the relation of crime and punishment is arbitrarily fixed.

460.

The Great Man of the Masses. – The recipe for what the masses call a great man is easily given. In all circumstances let a person provide them with something very pleasant, or first let him put it into their heads that this or that would be very pleasant, and then let him give it to them. On no account give it *immediately*, however: but let him acquire it by the greatest exertions, or seem thus to acquire it. The masses must have the impression that there is a powerful, nay indomitable strength of will operating; at least it must seem to be there operating. Everybody admires a strong will, because nobody possesses it, and everybody says to himself that if he did possess it there would no longer be any bounds for him and his egoism. If, then, it becomes evident that such a strong will effects something very agreeable to the masses, instead of hearkening to the wishes of covetousness, people admire once more, and wish good luck to themselves. Moreover, if he has all the qualities of the masses, they are the less ashamed before him, and he is all the more popular. Consequently, he may be violent, envious, rapacious, intriguing, flattering, fawning, inflated, and, according to circumstances, anything whatsoever.

461.

Prince and God. – People frequently commune with their princes in the same way as with their God, as indeed the prince himself was frequently the Deity's representative, or at least His high priest. This almost uncanny disposition of veneration, disquiet, and shame, grew, and has grown, much weaker, but occasionally it flares up again, and fastens upon powerful persons generally. The cult of genius is an echo of this veneration of Gods and Princes. Wherever an effort is made to exalt particular men to the superhuman, there is also a tendency to regard whole grades of the population as coarser and baser than they really are.

462.

My Utopia. – In a better arranged society the heavy work and trouble of life will be assigned to those who suffer least through it, to the most obtuse, therefore; and so step by step up to those who are most sensitive to the highest and sublimest kinds of suffering, and who therefore still suffer notwithstanding the greatest alleviations of life.

463.

A Delusion in Subversive Doctrines. – There are political and social dreamers who ardently and eloquently call for the overthrow of all order, in the belief that the proudest fane of beautiful humanity will then rear itself immediately, almost of its own accord. In these dangerous dreams there is still an echo of Rousseau's superstition, which believes in a marvellous primordial goodness of human nature, buried up, as it were; and lays all the blame of that burying-up on the institutions of civilisation, on society, State, and education. Unfortunately, it is well known by historical experiences that every such overthrow reawakens into new life the wildest energies, the long-buried horrors and extravagances of remotest ages; that an overthrow, therefore, may possibly be a source of strength to a deteriorated humanity, but never a regulator, architect, artist, or perfecter of human nature. It was not *Voltaire's* moderate nature, inclined towards regulating, purifying, and reconstructing, but *Rousseau's* passionate follies and half-lies that aroused the optimistic spirit of the Revolution, against which I cry, '*Ecrasez l'infâme*!' Owing to this *the Spirit of enlightenment* and *progressive development* has been long scared away; let us see – each of us individually – if it is not possible to recall it!

464.

Moderation. – When perfect resoluteness in thinking and investigating, that is to say, freedom of spirit, has become a feature of character, it produces moderation of conduct; for it weakens avidity, attracts much extant energy for the furtherance of intellectual aims, and shows the semi-usefulness, or uselessness and danger, of all sudden changes.

465.

The Resurrection of the Spirit. – A nation usually renews its youth on a political sick-bed, and there finds again the spirit which it had gradually lost in seeking and maintaining power. Culture is indebted most of all to politically weakened periods.

466.

New Opinions in the Old Home. – The overthrow of opinions is not immediately followed by the overthrow of institutions; on the contrary, the new opinions dwell for a long time in the desolate and haunted house of their predecessors, and conserve it even for want of a habitation.

467.

Public Education. – In large States public education will always be extremely mediocre, for the same reason that in large kitchens the cooking is at best only mediocre.

468.

Innocent Corruption. – In all institutions into which the sharp breeze of public criticism does not penetrate an innocent corruption grows up like a fungus (for instance, in learned bodies and senates).

469.

Scholars as Politicians. – To scholars who become politicians the comic role is usually assigned; they have to be the good conscience of a state policy.

470.

The Wolf hidden behind the Sheep. – Almost every politician, in certain circumstances, has such need of an honest man that he breaks into the sheep-fold like a famished wolf; not, however, to devour a stolen sheep, but to hide himself behind its woolly back.

471.

Happy Times. – A happy age is no longer possible, because men only wish for it but do not desire to have it; and each individual, when good days come for him, learns positively to pray for disquiet and misery. The destiny of mankind is arranged for *happy moments* – every life has such – but not for happy times. Nevertheless, such times will continue to exist in man's imagination as 'over the hills and far away', an heirloom of his earliest ancestors; for the idea of the happy age, from the earliest times to the present, has no doubt been derived from the state in which man, after violent exertions in hunting and warfare, gives himself over to repose, stretches out his limbs, and hears the wings of sleep rustle around him. It is a false conclusion when, in accordance with that old habit, man imagines that after *whole periods* of distress and trouble he will be able also to enjoy the state of happiness in *proportionate increase and duration*.

472.

Religion and Government. – So long as the State, or, more properly, the Government, regards itself as the appointed guardian of a number of minors, and on their account considers the question whether religion should be preserved or abolished, it is highly probable that it will always decide for the preservation thereof. For religion satisfies the nature of the individual in times of loss, destitution, terror, and distrust, in cases, therefore, where the Government feels itself incapable of doing anything directly for the mitigation of the spiritual sufferings of the individual; indeed, even in general unavoidable and next to inevitable evils (famines, financial crises, and wars) religion gives to the masses an attitude of tranquillity and confiding expectancy. Whenever the necessary or accidental deficiencies of the State Government, or the dangerous consequences of dynastic interests, strike the eyes of the intelligent and make them refractory, the unintelligent will only think they see the finger of God therein and will submit with patience to the dispensations from *on high* (a conception in which divine and human modes of government usually coalesce); thus internal civil peace and continuity of development will be preserved. The power, which lies in the unity of popular feeling, in the existence of the same opinions and aims for all, is protected and confirmed by religion – the rare cases excepted in which a priesthood cannot agree with the State about the price, and therefore comes into conflict with it. As a rule the State will know how to win over the priests, because it needs their most private and secret system for educating souls, and knows how to value servants who apparently, and outwardly, represent quite other interests. Even at present no power can become 'legitimate' without the assistance of the priests; a fact which Napoleon understood. Thus, absolutely paternal government and the careful preservation of religion necessarily go hand-in-hand. In this connection it must be taken for granted that the rulers and governing classes are enlightened concerning the advantages which religion affords, and consequently feel themselves to a certain extent superior to it, inasmuch as they use it as a means; thus freedom of spirit has its origin here. But how will it be when the totally different interpretation of the idea of Government, such as is taught in *democratic* States, begins to prevail? When one sees in it nothing but the instrument of the popular will, no 'upper' in contrast to an 'under', but merely a function of the sole sovereign, the people? Here also only the same attitude which the people assume towards religion can be assumed by the Government; every diffusion of enlightenment will have to find an echo even in the representatives, and the utilising and exploiting of religious impulses and consolations for State purposes will not be so easy (unless powerful party leaders occasionally exercise an influence resembling that of enlightened despotism). When, however, the State is not permitted to derive any further advantage from religion, or when people think far too variously on religious matters to allow the State to adopt a consistent and uniform procedure with respect to them, the way out of the difficulty will necessarily present itself, namely to treat religion as a private affair and leave it to the conscience and custom of each single individual. The first result of all is that religious feeling seems to be strengthened, inasmuch as hidden and suppressed impulses thereof, which the State had unintentionally or intentionally stifled, now break forth and rush to extremes; later on, however, it is found that religion is overgrown with sects, and that an abundance of dragon's teeth were sown as soon as religion was made a private affair. The spectacle of strife, and the hostile laying bare of all the weaknesses of religious confessions, admit finally of no other expedient except that every better and more talented person should make irreligiousness his private affair, a sentiment which now obtains the upper hand even in the minds of the governing classes, and, almost against their will, gives an anti-religious character to their pleasures. As soon as this happens, the sentiment of persons still religiously disposed, who formerly adored the State as something half sacred or wholly sacred, changes into decided *hostility to the State*; they lie in wait for governmental measures, seeking to hinder, thwart, and disturb as much as they can, and, by the fury of their contradiction, drive the opposing parties, the irreligious ones, into an almost fanatical enthusiasm *for* the State; in connection with which there is also the silently co-operating influence, that since their separation from religion the hearts of persons in these circles are conscious of a void, and seek by devotion to the State to provide themselves provisionally with a substitute for religion, a kind of stuffing for the void. After these perhaps lengthy transitional struggles, it is finally decided whether the religious parties are still strong enough to revive an old condition of things, and turn the wheel backwards: in which case enlightened despotism (perhaps less enlightened and more timorous than formerly), inevitably gets the State into its hands – or whether the non-religious parties achieve their purpose, and, possibly through schools and education, check the increase of their opponents during several generations, and finally make them no longer possible. Then, however, their enthusiasm for the State also abates: it always becomes more obvious that along with the religious adoration which regards the State as a mystery and a supernatural institution, the reverent and pious relation to it has also been convulsed. Henceforth individuals see only that side of the State which may be useful or injurious to them, and press forward by all means to obtain an influence over it. But this rivalry soon becomes too great; men and parties change too rapidly, and throw each other down again too furiously from the mountain when they have only just succeeded in getting aloft. All the measures which such a Government carries out lack the guarantee of permanence; people then fight shy of undertakings which would require the silent growth of future decades or centuries to produce ripe fruit. Nobody henceforth feels any other obligation to a law than to submit for the moment to the power which introduced the law; people immediately set to work, however, to undermine it by a new power, a newly-formed majority. Finally – it may be confidently asserted – the distrust of all government, the insight into the useless and harassing nature of these short-winded struggles, must drive men to an entirely new resolution: to the abrogation of the conception of the State and the abolition of the contrast of 'private and public'. Private concerns gradually absorb the business of the State; even the toughest residue which is left over from the old work of governing (the business, for instance, which is meant to protect private persons from private persons) will at last some day be managed by private enterprise. The neglect, decline, and *death of the State*, the liberation of the private person (I am careful not to say the individual), are the consequences of the democratic conception of the State; that is its mission. When it has accomplished its task – which, like everything human, involves much rationality and irrationality – and when all relapses into the old malady have been overcome, then a new leaf in the story-book of humanity will be unrolled, on which readers will find all kinds of strange tales and perhaps also some amount of good. To repeat shortly what has been said: the interests of the tutelary Government and the interests of religion go hand-in-hand, so that when the latter begins to decay the foundations of the State are also shaken. The belief in a divine regulation of political affairs, in a mystery in the existence of the State, is of religious origin: if religion disappears, the State will inevitably lose its old veil of Isis, and will no longer arouse veneration. The sovereignty of the people, looked at closely, serves also to dispel the final fascination and superstition in the realm of these sentiments; modern democracy is the historical form of the *decay of the State*. The outlook which results from this certain decay is not, however, unfortunate in every respect; the wisdom and the selfishness of men are the best developed of all their qualities; when the State no longer meets the demands of these impulses, chaos will least of all result, but a still more appropriate expedient than the State will get the mastery over the State. How many organising forces have already been seen to die out! For example, that of the *gens* or clan which for millennia was far mightier than the power of the family, and indeed already ruled and regulated long before the latter existed. We ourselves see the important notions of the right and might of the family, which once possessed the supremacy as far as the Roman system extended, always becoming paler and feebler. In the same way a later generation will also see the State become meaningless in certain parts of the world – an idea which many contemporaries can hardly contemplate without alarm and horror. To *labour* for the propagation and realisation of this idea is, certainly, another thing; one must think very presumptuously of one's reason, and only half understand history, to set one's hand to the plough at present – when as yet no one can show us the seeds that are afterwards to be sown upon the broken soil. Let us, therefore, trust to the 'wisdom and selfishness of men' that the State may *yet* exist a good while longer, and that the destructive attempts of over-zealous, too hasty sciolists may be in vain!

473.

Socialism, with Regard to its Means. – Socialism is the fantastic younger brother of almost decrepit despotism, which it wants to succeed; its efforts are, therefore, in the deepest sense reactionary. For it desires such an amount of State power as only despotism has possessed, indeed, it outdoes all the past, in that it aims at the complete annihilation of the individual, whom it deems an unauthorised luxury of nature, which is to be improved by it into an appropriate *organ of the general community.* Owing to its relationship, it always appears in proximity to excessive developments of power, like the old typical socialist, Plato, at the court of the Sicilian tyrant; it desires (and under certain circumstances furthers) the Caesarian despotism of this century, because, as has been said, it would like to become its heir. But even this inheritance would not suffice for its objects, it requires the most submissive prostration of all citizens before the absolute State, such as has never yet been realised; and as it can no longer even count upon the old religious piety towards the State, but must rather strive involuntarily and continuously for the abolition thereof – because it strives for the abolition of all existing *States* – it can only hope for existence occasionally, here and there for short periods, by means of the extremest terrorism. It is therefore silently preparing itself for reigns of terror, and drives the word 'justice' like a nail into the heads of the half-cultured masses in order to deprive them completely of their understanding (after they had already suffered seriously from the half-culture), and to provide them with a good conscience for the bad game they are to play. Socialism may serve to teach, very brutally and impressively, the danger of all accumulations of State power, and may serve so far to inspire distrust of the State itself. When its rough voice strikes up the way-cry 'as much State as possible' the shout at first becomes louder than ever – but soon the opposition cry also breaks forth, with so much greater force: 'as little State as possible'.

474.

The Development of the Mind Feared by the State. – The Greek *polis* was, like every organising political power, exclusive and distrustful of the growth of culture; its powerful fundamental impulse seemed almost solely to have a paralysing and obstructive effect thereon. It did not want to let any history or any becoming have a place in culture; the education laid down in the State laws was meant to be obligatory on all generations to keep them at *one* stage of development. Plato also, later on, did not desire it to be otherwise in his ideal State. *In spite of* the polis culture developed itself in this manner; indirectly to be sure, and against its will, the polis furnished assistance because the ambition of individuals therein was stimulated to the utmost, so that, having once found the path of intellectual development, they followed it to its farthest extremity. On the other hand, appeal should not be made to the panegyric of Pericles, for it is only a great optimistic dream about the alleged necessary connection between the Polis and Athenian culture; immediately before the night fell over Athens (the plague and the breakdown of tradition), Thucydides makes this culture flash up once more like a transfiguring afterglow, to efface the remembrance of the evil day that had preceded.

475.

European Man and the Destruction of Nationalities. – Commerce and industry, interchange of books and letters, the universality of all higher culture, the rapid changing of locality and landscape, and the present nomadic life of all who are not landowners – these circumstances necessarily bring with them a weakening, and finally a destruction of nationalities, at least of European nationalities; so that, in consequence of perpetual crossings, there must arise out of them all a mixed race, that of the European man. At present the isolation of nations, through the rise of *national* enmities, consciously or unconsciously counteracts this tendency; but nevertheless the process of fusing advances slowly, in spite of those occasional counter-currents. This artificial nationalism is, however, as dangerous as was artificial Catholicism, for it is essentially an unnatural condition of extremity and martial law, which has been proclaimed by the few over the many, and requires artifice, lying, and force to maintain its reputation. It is not the interests of the many (of the peoples), as they probably say, but it is first of all the interests of certain princely dynasties, and then of certain commercial and social classes, which impel to this nationalism; once we have recognised this fact, we should just fearlessly style ourselves *good Europeans* and labour actively for the amalgamation of nations; in which efforts Germans may assist by virtue of their hereditary position as *interpreters and intermediaries between nations*. By the way, the great problem of the *Jews* only exists within the national States, inasmuch as their energy and higher intelligence, their intellectual and volitional capital, accumulated from generation to generation in tedious schools of suffering, must necessarily attain to universal supremacy here to an extent provocative of envy and hatred; so that the literary misconduct is becoming prevalent in almost all modern nations – and all the more so as they again set up to be national – of sacrificing the Jews as the scapegoats of all possible public and private abuses. So soon as it is no longer a question of the preservation or establishment of nations, but of the production and training of a European mixed-race of the greatest possible strength, the Jew is just as useful and desirable an ingredient as any other national remnant. Every nation, every individual, has unpleasant and even dangerous qualities – it is cruel to require that the Jew should be an exception. Those qualities may even be dangerous and frightful in a special degree in his case; and perhaps the young Stock-Exchange Jew is in general the most repulsive invention of the human species. Nevertheless, in a general summing up, I should like to know how much must be excused in a nation which, not without blame on the part of all of us, has had the most mournful history of all nations, and to which we owe the most loving of men (Christ), the most upright of sages (Spinoza), the mightiest book, and the most effective moral law in the world? Moreover, in the darkest times of the Middle Ages, when Asiatic clouds had gathered darkly over Europe, it was Jewish free-thinkers, scholars, and physicians who upheld the banner of enlightenment and of intellectual independence under the severest personal sufferings, and defended Europe against Asia; we owe it not least to their efforts that a more natural, more reasonable, at all events un-mythical, explanation of the world was finally able to get the upper hand once more, and that the link of culture which now unites us with the enlightenment of Greco-Roman antiquity has remained unbroken. If Christianity has done everything to orientalise the Occident, Judaism has assisted essentially in occidentalising it anew; which, in a certain sense, is equivalent to making Europe's mission and history a *continuation of that of Greece.*

476.

Apparent Superiority of the Middle Ages. – The Middle Ages present in the Church an institution with an absolutely universal aim, involving the whole of humanity – an aim, moreover, which – presumedly – concerned man's highest interests; in comparison therewith the aims of the States and nations which modern history exhibits make a painful impression; they seem petty, base, material, and restricted in extent. But this different impression on our imagination should certainly not determine our judgement; for that universal institution corresponded to feigned and fictitiously fostered needs, such as the need of salvation, which, wherever they did not already exist, it had first of all to create: the new institutions, however, relieve actual distresses; and the time is coming when institutions will arise to minister to the common, genuine needs of all men, and to cast that fantastic prototype, the Catholic Church, into shade and oblivion.

477.

War Indispensable. – It is nothing but fanaticism and beautiful soulism to expect very much (or even, much only) from humanity when it has forgotten how to wage war. For the present we know of no other means whereby the rough energy of the camp, the deep impersonal hatred, the cold-bloodedness of murder with a good conscience, the general ardour of the system in the destruction of the enemy, the proud indifference to great losses, to one's own existence and that of one's friends, the hollow, earthquake-like convulsion of the soul, can be as forcibly and certainly communicated to enervated nations as is done by every great war: owing to the brooks and streams that here break forth, which, certainly, sweep stones and rubbish of all sorts along with them and destroy the meadows of delicate cultures, the mechanism in the workshops of the mind is afterwards, in favourable circumstances, rotated by new power. Culture can by no means dispense with passions, vices, and malignities. When the Romans, after having become Imperial, had grown rather tired of war, they attempted to gain new strength by beast-baitings, gladiatoral combats, and Christian persecutions. The English of today, who appear on the whole to have also renounced war, adopt other means in order to generate anew those vanishing forces; namely, the dangerous exploring expeditions, sea voyages and mountaineerings, nominally undertaken for scientific purposes, but in reality to bring home surplus strength from adventures and dangers of all kinds. Many other such substitutes for war will be discovered, but perhaps precisely thereby it will become more and more obvious that such a highly cultivated and therefore necessarily enfeebled humanity as that of modern Europe not only needs wars, but the greatest and most terrible wars – consequently occasional relapses into barbarism – lest, by the means of culture, it should lose its culture and its very existence.

478.

Industry in the South and the North. – Industry arises in two entirely different ways. The artisans of the South are not industrious because of acquisitiveness but because of the constant needs of others. The smith is industrious because some one is always coming who wants a horse shod or a carriage mended. If nobody came he would loiter about in the market-place. In a fruitful land he has little trouble in supporting himself, for that purpose he requires only a very small amount of work, certainly no industry; eventually he would beg and be contented. The industry of English workmen, on the contrary, has acquisitiveness behind it; it is conscious of itself and its aims; with property it wants power, and with power the greatest possible liberty and individual distinction.

479.

Wealth as the Origin of a Nobility of Race. – Wealth necessarily creates an aristocracy of race, for it permits the choice of the most beautiful women and the engagement of the best teachers; it allows a man cleanliness, time for physical exercises, and, above all, immunity from dulling physical labour. So far it provides all the conditions for making man, after a few generations, move and even act nobly and handsomely: greater freedom of character and absence of niggardliness, of wretchedly petty matters, and of abasement before bread-givers. It is precisely these negative qualities which are the most profitable birthday gift, that of happiness, for the young man; a person who is quite poor usually comes to grief through nobility of disposition, he does not get on, and acquires nothing, his race is not capable of living. In this connection, however, it must be remembered that wealth produces almost the same effects whether one have three hundred or thirty thousand thalers a year; there is no further essential progression of the favourable conditions afterwards. But to have less, to beg in boyhood and to abase one's self is terrible, although it may be the proper starting-point for such as seek their happiness in the splendour of courts, in subordination to the mighty and influential, or for such as wish to be heads of the Church. (It teaches how to slink crouching into the underground passages to favour.)

480.

Envy and Inertia in Different Courses. – The two opposing parties, the socialist and the national – or whatever they may be called in the different countries of Europe – are worthy of each other; envy and laziness are the motive powers in each of them. In the one camp they desire to work as little as possible with their hands, in the other as little as possible with their heads; in the latter they hate and envy prominent, self-evolving individuals, who do not willingly allow themselves to be drawn up in rank and file for the purpose of a collective effect; in the former they hate and envy the better social caste, which is more favourably circumstanced outwardly, whose peculiar mission, the production of the highest blessings of culture, makes life inwardly all the harder and more painful. Certainly, if it be possible to make the spirit of the collective effect the spirit of the higher classes of society, the socialist crowds are quite right, when they also seek outward equalisation between themselves and these classes, since they are certainly internally equalised with one another already in head and heart. Live as higher men, and always do the deeds of higher culture – thus everything that lives will acknowledge your right, and the order of society, whose summit ye are, will be safe from every evil glance and attack!

481.

High Politics and their Detriments. – Just as a nation does not suffer the greatest losses that war and readiness for war involve through the expenses of the war, or the stoppage of trade and traffic, or through the maintenance of a standing army – however great these losses may now be, when eight European States expend yearly the sum of five milliards of marks thereon – but owing to the fact that year after year its ablest, strongest, and most industrious men are withdrawn in extraordinary numbers from their proper occupations and callings to be turned into soldiers: in the same way, a nation that sets about practising high politics and securing a decisive voice among the great Powers does not suffer its greatest losses where they are usually supposed to be. In fact, from this time onward it constantly sacrifices a number of its most conspicuous talents upon the 'Altar of the Fatherland' or of national ambition, whilst formerly other spheres of activity were open to those talents which are now swallowed up by politics. But apart from these public hecatombs, and in reality much more horrible, there is a drama which is constantly being performed simultaneously in a hundred thousand acts; every able, industrious, intellectually striving man of a nation that thus covets political laurels, is swayed by this covetousness, and no longer belongs entirely to himself alone as he did formerly; the new daily questions and cares of the public welfare devour a daily tribute of the intellectual and emotional capital of every citizen; the sum of all these sacrifices and losses of individual energy and labour is so enormous, that the political growth of a nation almost necessarily entails an intellectual impoverishment and lassitude, a diminished capacity for the performance of works that require great concentration and specialisation. The question may finally be asked: Does it then *pay*, all this bloom and magnificence of the total (which indeed only manifests itself as the fear of the new Colossus in other nations, and as the compulsory favouring by them of national trade and commerce) when all the nobler, finer, and more intellectual plants and products, in which its soil was hitherto so rich, must be sacrificed to this coarse and opalescent flower of the nation?[17]

482.

Repeated Once More. – Public opinion – private laziness.

17 This is once more an allusion to modem Germany. – J. M. K.

NINTH DIVISION.
MAN ALONE BY HIMSELF.

483.

The Enemies of Truth. – Convictions are more dangerous enemies of truth than lies.

484.

A Topsy-Turvy World. – We criticise a thinker more severely when he puts an unpleasant statement before us; and yet it would be more reasonable to do so when we find his statement pleasant.

485.

Decided Character. – A man far oftener appears to have a decided character from persistently following his temperament than from persistently following his principles.

486.

The One Thing Needful. – One thing a man must have: either a naturally light disposition or a disposition *lightened* by art and knowledge.

487.

The Passion for Things. – Whoever sets his passion on things (sciences, arts, the common weal, the interests of culture) withdraws much fervour from his passion for persons (even when they are the representatives of those things; as statesmen, philosophers, and artists are the representatives of their creations).

488.

Calmness in Action. – As a cascade in its descent becomes more deliberate and suspended, so the great man of action usually acts with *more* calmness than his strong passions previous to action would lead one to expect.

489.

Not too Deep. – Persons who grasp a matter in all its depth seldom remain permanently true to it. They have just brought the depth up into the light, and there is always much evil to be seen there.

490.

The Illusion of Idealists. – All idealists imagine that the cause which they serve is essentially better than all other causes, and will not believe that if their cause is really to flourish it requires precisely the same evil-smelling manure which all other human undertakings have need of.

491.

Self-Observation. – Man is exceedingly well protected from himself and guarded against his self-exploring and self-besieging; as a rule he can perceive nothing of himself but his outworks. The actual fortress is inaccessible, and even invisible, to him, unless friends and enemies become traitors and lead him inside by secret paths.

492.

The Right Calling. – Men can seldom hold on to a calling unless they believe or persuade themselves that it is really more important than any other. Women are the same with their lovers.

493.

Nobility of Disposition. – Nobility of disposition consists largely in good-nature and absence of distrust, and therefore contains precisely that upon which money-grabbing and successful men take a pleasure in walking with superiority and scorn.

494.

Goal and Path. – Many are obstinate with regard to the once-chosen path, few with regard to the goal.

495.

The Offensiveness in an Individual Way of Life. – All specially individual lines of conduct excite irritation against him who adopts them; people feel themselves reduced to the level of commonplace creatures by the extraordinary treatment he bestows on himself.

496.

The Privilege of Greatness. – It is the privilege of greatness to confer intense happiness with insignificant gifts.

497.

Unintentionally Noble. – A person behaves with unintentional nobleness when he has accustomed himself to seek naught from others and always to give to them.

498.

A Condition of Heroism. – When a person wishes to become a hero, the serpent must previously have become a dragon, otherwise he lacks his proper enemy.

499.

Friends. – Fellowship in joy, and not sympathy in sorrow, makes people friends.

500.

Making Use of Ebb and Flow. – For the purpose of knowledge we must know how to make use of the inward current which draws us towards a thing, and also of the current which after a time draws us away from it.

501.

Joy in Itself. – 'Joy in the Thing' people say; but in reality it is joy in itself by means of the thing.

502.

The Unassuming Man. – He who is unassuming towards persons manifests his presumption all the more with regard to things (town, State, society, time, humanity). That is his revenge.

503.

Envy and Jealousy. – Envy and jealousy are the pudenda of the human soul. The comparison may perhaps be carried further.

504.

The Noblest Hypocrite. – It is a very noble hypocrisy not to talk of one's self at all.

505.

Vexation. – Vexation is a physical disease, which is not by any means cured when its cause is subsequently removed.

506.

The Champions of Truth. – Truth does not find fewest champions when it is dangerous to speak it, but when it is dull.

507.

More Troublesome even than Enemies. – Persons of whose sympathetic attitude we are not, in all circumstances, convinced, while for some reason or other (gratitude, for instance) we are obliged to maintain the appearance of unqualified sympathy with them, trouble our imagination far more than our enemies do.

508.

Free Nature. – We are so fond of being out among Nature, because it has no opinions about us.

509.

Each Superior in one Thing. – In civilised intercourse every one feels himself superior to all others in at least one thing; kindly feelings generally are based thereon, inasmuch as every one can, in certain circumstances, render help, and is therefore entitled to accept help without shame.

510.

Consolatory Arguments. – In the case of a death we mostly use consolatory arguments not so much to alleviate the grief as to make excuses for feeling so easily consoled.

511.

Persons Loyal to their Convictions. – Whoever is very busy retains his general views and opinions almost unchanged. So also does every one who labours in the service of an idea; he will nevermore examine the idea itself, he no longer has any time to do so; indeed, it is against his interests to consider it as still admitting of discussion.

512.

Morality and Quantity. – The higher morality of one man as compared with that of another, often lies merely in the fact that his aims are quantitively greater. The other, living in a circumscribed sphere, is dragged down by petty occupations.

513.

'The Life' as the Proceeds of Life. – A man may stretch himself out ever so far with his knowledge; he may seem to himself ever so objective, but eventually he realises nothing therefrom but his own biography.

514.

Iron Necessity. – Iron necessity is a thing which has been found, in the course of history, to be neither iron nor necessary.

515.

From Experience. – The unreasonableness of a thing is no argument against its existence, but rather a condition thereof.

516.

Truth. – Nobody dies nowadays of fatal truths, there are too many antidotes to them.

517.

A Fundamental Insight. – There is no pre-established harmony between the promotion of truth and the welfare of mankind.

518.

Man's Lot. – He who thinks most deeply knows that he is always in the wrong, however he may act and decide.

519.

Truth as Circe. – Error has made animals into men; is truth perhaps capable of making man into an animal again?

520.

The Danger of Our Culture. – We belong to a period of which the culture is in danger of being destroyed by the appliances of culture.

521.

Greatness Means Leading the Way. – No stream is large and copious of itself, but becomes great by receiving and leading on so many tributary streams. It is so, also, with all intellectual greatnesses. It is only a question of some one indicating the direction to be followed by so many affluents; not whether he was richly or poorly gifted originally.

522.

A Feeble Conscience. – People who talk about their importance to mankind have a feeble conscience for common bourgeois rectitude, keeping of contracts, promises, etc.

523.

Desiring to be Loved. – The demand to be loved is the greatest of presumptions.

524.

Contempt for Men. – The most unequivocal sign of contempt for man is to regard everybody merely as a means to *one's own* ends, or of no account whatever.

525.

Partisans through Contradiction. – Whoever has driven men to fury against himself has also gained a party in his favour.

526.

Forgetting Experiences. – Whoever thinks much and to good purpose easily forgets his own experiences, but not the thoughts which these experiences have called forth.

527.

Sticking to an Opinion. – One person sticks to an opinion because he takes pride in having acquired it himself – another sticks to it because he has learnt it with difficulty and is proud of having understood it; both of them, therefore, out of vanity.

528.

Avoiding the Light. – Good deeds avoid the light just as anxiously as evil deeds; the latter fear that pain will result from publicity (as punishment), the former fear that pleasure will vanish with publicity (the pure pleasure *per se*, which ceases as soon as satisfaction of vanity is added to it).

529.

The Length of the Day. – When one has much to put into them, a day has a hundred pockets.

530.

The Genius of Tyranny. – When an invincible desire to obtain tyrannical power has been awakened in the soul, and constantly keeps up its fervour, even a very mediocre talent (in politicians, artists, etc.) gradually becomes an almost irresistible natural force.

531.

The Enemy's Life. – He who lives by fighting with an enemy has an interest in the preservation of the enemy's life.[18]

---

18 This is why Nietzsche pointed out later on that he had an interest in the preservation of Christianity, and that he was sure his teaching would not undermine this faith – just as little as anarchists have undermined kings; but have left them seated all the more firmly on their thrones. – J. M. K.

532.

More Important. – Unexplained, obscure matters are regarded as more important than explained, clear ones.

533.

Valuation of Services Rendered. – We estimate services rendered to us according to the value set on them by those who render them, not according to the value they have for us.

534.

Unhappiness. – The distinction associated with unhappiness (as if it were a sign of stupidity, unambitiousness, or commonplaceness to feel happy) is so great that when any one says to us, 'How happy you are' we usually protest.

535.

Imagination in Anguish. – When one is afraid of anything, one's imagination plays the part of that evil spirit which springs on one's back just when one has the heaviest load to bear.

536.

The Value of Insipid Opponents. – We sometimes remain faithful to a cause merely because its opponents never cease to be insipid.

537.

The Value of a Profession. – A profession makes us thoughtless; that is its greatest blessing. For it is a bulwark behind which we are permitted to withdraw when commonplace doubts and cares assail us.

538.

Talent. – Many a man's talent appears less than it is, because he has always set himself too heavy tasks.

539.

Youth. – Youth is an unpleasant period; for then it is not possible or not prudent to be productive in any sense whatsoever.

540.

Too Great Aims. – Whoever aims publicly at great things and at length perceives secretly that he is too weak to achieve them, has usually also insufficient strength to renounce his aims publicly, and then inevitably becomes a hypocrite.

541.

In the Current. – Mighty waters sweep many stones and shrubs away with them; mighty spirits many foolish and confused minds.

542.

The Dangers of Intellectual Emancipation. – In a seriously intended intellectual emancipation a person's mute passions and cravings also hope to find their advantage.

543.

The Incarnation of the Mind. – When any one thinks much and to good purpose, not only his face but also his body acquires a sage look.

544.

Seeing Badly and Hearing Badly. – The man who sees little always sees less than there is to see; the man who hears badly always hears something more than there is to hear.

545.

Self-Enjoyment in Vanity. – The vain man does not wish so much to be prominent as to feel himself prominent; he therefore disdains none of the expedients for self-deception and self-outwitting. It is not the opinion of others that he sets his heart on, but his opinion of their opinion.

546.

Exceptionally Vain. – He who is usually self-sufficient becomes exceptionally vain, and keenly alive to fame and praise when he is physically ill. The more he loses himself the more he has to endeavour to regain his position by means of the opinion of others.

547.

The 'Witty'. – Those who seek wit do not possess it.

548.

A Hint to the Heads of Parties. – When one can make people publicly support a cause they have also generally been brought to the point of inwardly declaring themselves in its favour, because they wish to be regarded as consistent.

549.

Contempt. – Man is more sensitive to the contempt of others than to self-contempt.

550.

The Tie of Gratitude. – There are servile souls who carry so far their sense of obligation for benefits received that they strangle themselves with the tie of gratitude.

551.

The Prophet's Knack. – In predicting beforehand the procedure of ordinary individuals, it must be taken for granted that they always make use of the smallest intellectual expenditure in freeing themselves from disagreeable situations.

552.

Man's Sole Right. – He who swerves from the traditional is a victim of the unusual; he who keeps to the traditional is its slave. The man is ruined in either case.

553.

Below the Beast. – When a man roars with laughter he surpasses all the animals by his vulgarity.

554.

Partial Knowledge. – He who speaks a foreign language imperfectly has more enjoyment therein than he who speaks it well. The enjoyment is with the partially initiated.

555.

Dangerous Helpfulness. – There are people who wish to make human life harder for no other reason than to be able afterwards to offer men their life-alleviating recipes – their Christianity, for example.

556.

Industriousness and Conscientiousness. – Industriousness and conscientiousness are often antagonists, owing to the fact that industriousness wants to pluck the fruit sour from the tree while conscientiousness wants to let it hang too long, until it falls and is bruised.

557.

Casting Suspicion. – We endeavour to cast suspicion on persons whom we cannot endure.

558.

The Conditions are Lacking. – Many people wait all their lives for the opportunity to be good in *their own way*.

559.

Lack of Friends. – Lack of friends leads to the inference that a person is envious or presumptuous. Many a man owes his friends merely to the fortunate circumstance that he has no occasion for envy.

560.

Danger in Manifoldness. – With one talent more we often stand less firmly than with one less; just as a table stands better on three feet than on four.

561.

An Exemplar for Others. – Whoever wants to set a good example must add a grain of folly to his virtue; people then imitate their exemplar and at the same time raise themselves above him, a thing they love to do.

562.

Being a Target. – The bad things others say about us are often not really aimed at us, but are the manifestations of spite or ill-humour occasioned by quite different causes.

563.

Easily Resigned. – We suffer but little on account of ungratified wishes if we have exercised our imagination in distorting the past.

564.

In Danger. – One is in greatest danger of being run over when one has just got out of the way of a carriage.

565.

The Role According to the Voice. – Whoever is obliged to speak louder than he naturally does (say, to a partially deaf person or before a large audience), usually exaggerates what he has to communicate. Many a one becomes a conspirator, malevolent gossip, or intriguer, merely because his voice is best suited for whispering.

566.

Love and Hatred. – Love and hatred are not blind, but are dazzled by the fire which they carry about with them.

567.

Advantageously Persecuted. – People who cannot make their merits perfectly obvious to the world endeavour to awaken a strong hostility against themselves. They have then the consolation of thinking that this hostility stands between their merits and the acknowledgment thereof – and that many others think the same thing, which is very advantageous for their recognition.

568.

Confession. – We forget our fault when we have confessed it to another person, but he does not generally forget it.

569.

Self-Sufficiency. – The Golden Fleece of self-sufficiency is a protection against blows, but not against needle-pricks.

570.

Shadows in the Flame. – The flame is not so bright to itself as to those whom it illuminates – so also the wise man.

571.

Our Own Opinions. – The first opinion that occurs to us when we are suddenly asked about anything is not usually our own, but only the current opinion belonging to our caste, position, or family; our own opinions seldom float on the surface.

572.

The Origin of Courage. – The ordinary man is as courageous and invulnerable as a hero when he does not see the danger, when he has no eyes for it. Reversely, the hero has his one vulnerable spot upon the back, where he has no eyes.

573.

The Danger in the Physician. – One must be born for one's physician, otherwise one comes to grief through him.

574.

Marvellous Vanity. – Whoever has courageously prophesied the weather three times and has been successful in his hits, acquires a certain amount of inward confidence in his prophetic gift. We give credence to the marvellous and irrational when it flatters our self-esteem.

575.

A Profession. – A profession is the backbone of life.

576.

The Danger of Personal Influence. – Whoever feels that he exercises a great inward influence over another person must give him a perfectly free rein, must, in fact, welcome and even induce occasional opposition, otherwise he will inevitably make an enemy.

577.

Recognition of the Heir. – Whoever has founded something great in an unselfish spirit is careful to rear heirs for his work. It is the sign of a tyrannical and ignoble nature to see opponents in all possible heirs, and to live in a state of self-defence against them.

578.

Partial Knowledge. – Partial knowledge is more triumphant than complete knowledge; it takes things to be simpler than they are, and so makes its theory more popular and convincing.

579.

Unsuitable for a Party-Man. – Whoever thinks much is unsuitable for a party-man; his thinking leads him too quickly beyond the party.

580.

A Bad Memory. – The advantage of a bad memory is that one enjoys several times the same good things for the *first* time.

581.

Self-Affliction. – Want of consideration is often the sign of a discordant inner nature, which craves for stupefaction.

582.

Martyrs. – The disciples of a martyr suffer more than the martyr.

583.

Arrears of Vanity. – The vanity of many people who have no occasion to be vain is the inveterate habit, still surviving from the time when people had no right to the belief in themselves and only begged it in small sums from others.

584.

Punctum Saliens of Passion. – A person falling into a rage or into a violent passion of love reaches a point when the soul is full like a hogshead, but nevertheless a drop of water has still to be added, the good will for the passion (which is also generally called the evil will). This item only is necessary, and then the hogshead overflows.

585.

A Gloomy Thought. – It is with men as with the charcoal fires in the forest. It is only when young men have cooled down and have got charred, like these piles, that they become *useful*. As long as they fume and smoke they are perhaps more interesting, but they are useless and too often uncomfortable. Humanity ruthlessly uses every individual as material for the heating of its great machines; but what then is the purpose of the machines, when all individuals (that is, the human race) are useful only to maintain them? Machines that are ends in themselves: is that the *umana commedia*?

586.

The Hour-hand of Life. – Life consists of rare single moments of the greatest importance, and of countless intervals during which, at best, the phantoms of those moments hover around us. Love, the Spring, every fine melody, the mountains, the moon, the sea – all speak but once fully to the heart, if, indeed, they ever do quite attain to speech. For many people have not those moments at all, and are themselves intervals and pauses in the symphony of actual life.

587.

Attack or Compromise. – We often make the mistake of showing violent enmity towards a tendency, party, or period, because we happen only to get a sight of its most exposed side, its stuntedness, or the inevitable 'faults of its virtues' – perhaps because we ourselves have taken a prominent part in them. We then turn our backs on them and seek a diametrically opposite course; but the better way would be to seek out their strong good sides, or to develop them in ourselves. To be sure, a keener glance and a better will are needed to improve the becoming and the imperfect than are required to see through it in its imperfection and to deny it.

588.

Modesty. – There is true modesty (that is the knowledge that we are not the works we create); and it is especially becoming in a great mind, because such a mind can well grasp the thought of absolute irresponsibility (even for the good it creates). People do not hate a great man's presumptuousness in so far as he feels his strength, but because he wishes to prove it by injuring others, by dominating them, and seeing how long they will stand it. This, as a rule, is even a proof of the absence of a secure sense of power, and makes people doubt his greatness. We must therefore beware of presumption from the standpoint of wisdom.

589.

The Day's First Thought. – The best way to begin a day well is to think, on awakening, whether we cannot give pleasure during the day to at least one person. If this could become a substitute for the religious habit of prayer our fellow-men would benefit by the change.

590.

Presumption as the Last Consolation. – When we so interpret a misfortune, an intellectual defect, or a disease that we see therein our predestined fate, our trial, or the mysterious punishment of our former misdeeds, we thereby make our nature interesting and exalt ourselves in imagination above our fellows. The proud sinner is a well-known figure in all religious sects.

591.

The Vegetation of Happiness. – Close beside the world's woe, and often upon its volcanic soil, man has laid out his little garden of happiness. Whether one regard life with the eyes of him who only seeks knowledge therefrom, or of him who submits and is resigned, or of him who rejoices over surmounted difficulties – everywhere one will find some happiness springing up beside the evil – and in fact always the more happiness the more volcanic the soil has been – only it would be absurd to say that suffering itself is justified by this happiness.

592.

The Path of our Ancestors. – It is sensible when a person develops still further in himself the *talent* upon which his father or grandfather spent much trouble, and does not shift to something entirely new; otherwise he deprives himself of the possibility of attaining perfection in any one craft. That is why the proverb says, 'Which road shouldst thou ride? – That of thine ancestors.'

593.

Vanity and Ambition as Educators. – As long as a person has not become an instrument of general utility, ambition may torment him; if, however, that point has been reached, if he necessarily works like a machine for the good of all, then vanity may result; it will humanise him in small matters and make him more sociable, endurable, and considerate, when ambition has completed the coarser work of making him useful.

594.

Philosophical Novices. – Immediately we have comprehended the wisdom of a philosopher, we go through the streets with a feeling as if we had been re-created and had become great men; for we encounter only those who are ignorant of this wisdom, and have therefore to deliver new and unknown verdicts concerning everything. Because we now recognise a law-book we think we must also comport ourselves as judges.

595.

Pleasing by Displeasing. – People who prefer to attract attention, and thereby to displease, desire the same thing as those who neither wish to please nor to attract attention, only they seek it more ardently and indirectly by means of a step by which they apparently move away from their goal. They desire influence and power, and therefore show their superiority, even to such an extent that it becomes disagreeable; for they know that he who has finally attained power pleases in almost all he says and does, and that even when he displeases he still seems to please. The free spirit also, and in like manner the believer, desire power, in order some day to please thereby; when, on account of their doctrine, evil fate, persecution, dungeon, or execution threaten them, they rejoice in the thought that their teaching will thus be engraved and branded on the heart of mankind; though its effect is remote they accept their fate as a painful but powerful means of still attaining to power.

596.

Casus Belli and the Like. – The prince who, for his determination to make war against his neighbour, invents a *casus belli*, is like a father who foists on his child a mother who is henceforth to be regarded as such. And are not almost all publicly avowed motives of action just such spurious mothers?

597.

Passion and Right. – Nobody talks more passionately of his rights than he who, in the depths of his soul, is doubtful about them. By getting passion on his side he seeks to confound his understanding and its doubts – he thus obtains a good conscience, and along with it success with his fellow-men.

598.

The Trick of the Resigning One. – He who protests against marriage, after the manner of Catholic priests, will conceive of it in its lowest and vulgarest form. In the same way he who disavows the honour of his contemporaries will have a mean opinion of it; he can thus dispense with it and struggle against it more easily. Moreover, he who denies himself much in great matters will readily indulge himself in small things. It might be possible that he who is superior to the approbation of his contemporaries would nevertheless not deny himself the gratification of small vanities.

599.

The Years of Presumption. – The proper period of presumption in gifted people is between their twenty-sixth and thirtieth years; it is the time of early ripeness, with a large residue of sourness. On the ground of what we feel within ourselves we demand honour and humility from men who see little or nothing of it, and because this tribute is not immediately forthcoming we revenge ourselves by the look, the gesture of arrogance, and the tone of voice, which a keen ear and eye recognise in every product of those years, whether it be poetry, philosophy, or pictures and music. Older men of experience smile thereat, and think with emotion of those beautiful years in which one resents the fate of *being* so much and *seeming* so little. Later on one really *seems* more – but one has lost the good belief in *being* much – unless one remain for life an incorrigible fool of vanity.

600.

Deceptive and yet Defensible. – Just as in order to pass by an abyss or to cross a deep stream on a plank we require a railing, not to hold fast by – for it would instantly break down with us – but to give the notion of security to the eye, so in youth we require persons who unconsciously render us the service of that railing. It is true they would not help us if we really wished to lean upon them in great danger, but they afford the tranquillising sensation of protection close to one (for instance, fathers, teachers, friends, as all three usually are).

601.

Learning to Love. – One must learn to love, one must learn to be kind, and this from childhood onwards; when education and chance give us no opportunity for the exercise of these feelings our soul becomes dried up, and even incapable of understanding the fine devices of loving men. In the same way hatred must be learnt and fostered, when one wants to become a proficient hater – otherwise the germ of it will gradually die out.

602.

Ruin as Ornament. – Persons who pass through numerous mental phases retain certain sentiments and habits of their earlier states, which then project like a piece of inexplicable antiquity and grey stonework into their new thought and action, often to the embellishment of the whole surroundings.

603.

Love and Honour. – Love desires, fear avoids. That is why one cannot be both loved and honoured by the same person, at least not at the same time.[19] For he who honours recognises power – that is to say, he fears it, he is in a state of reverential fear (*Ehr-furcht*). But love recognises no power, nothing that divides, detaches, superordinates, or subordinates. Because it does not honour them, ambitious people secretly or openly resent being loved.

604.

A Prejudice in Favour of Cold Natures. – People who quickly take fire grow cold quickly, and therefore are, on the whole, unreliable. For those, therefore, who are always cold, or pretend to be so, there is the favourable prejudice that they are particularly trustworthy, reliable persons; they are confounded with those who take fire slowly and retain it long.

605.

The Danger in Free Opinions. – Frivolous occupation with free opinions has a charm, like a kind of itching; if one yields to it further, one begins to chafe the places; until at last an open, painful wound results; that is to say, until the free opinion begins to disturb and torment us in our position in life and in our human relations.

606.

Desire for Sore Affliction. – When passion is over it leaves behind an obscure longing for it, and even in disappearing it casts a seductive glance at us. It must have afforded a kind of pleasure to have been beaten with this scourge. Compared with it, the more moderate sensations appear insipid; we still prefer, apparently, the more violent displeasure to languid delight.

607.

Dissatisfaction with Others and with the World. – When, as so frequently happens, we vent our dissatisfaction on others when we are really dissatisfied with ourselves, we are in fact attempting to

19 Women never understand this. – J. M. K.

mystify and deceive our judgement; we desire to find a motive *a posteriori* for this dissatisfaction, in the mistakes or deficiencies of others, and so lose sight of ourselves. Strictly religious people, who have been relentless judges of themselves, have at the same time spoken most ill of humanity generally; there has never been a saint who reserved sin for himself and virture for others, any more than a man who, according to Buddha's rule, hides his good qualities from people and only shows his bad ones.

608.

Confusion of Cause and Effect. – Unconsciously we seek the principles and opinions which are suited to our temperament, so that at last it seems as if these principles and opinions had formed our character and given it support and stability, whereas exactly the contrary has taken place. Our thoughts and judgements are, apparently, to be taken subsequently as the causes of our nature, but as a matter of fact *our* nature is the cause of our so thinking and judging. And what induces us to play this almost unconscious comedy? Inertness and convenience, and to a large extent also the vain desire to be regarded as thoroughly consistent and homogeneous in nature and thought; for this wins respect and gives confidence and power.

609.

Age in Relation to Truth. – Young people love what is interesting and exceptional, indifferent whether it is truth or falsehood. Riper minds love what is interesting and extraordinary when it is truth. Matured minds, finally, love truth even in those in whom it appears plain and simple and is found tiresome by ordinary people, because they have observed that truth is in the habit of giving utterance to its highest intellectual verities with all the appearance of simplicity.

610.

Men as Bad Poets. – Just as bad poets seek a thought to fit the rhyme in the second half of the verse, so men in the second half of life, having become more scrupulous, are in the habit of seeking pursuits, positions, and conditions which suit those of their earlier life, so that outwardly all sounds well, but their life is no longer ruled and continuously determined anew by a powerful thought: in place thereof there is merely the intention of finding a rhyme.

611.

Ennui and Play. – Necessity compels us to work, with the product of which the necessity is appeased; the ever new awakening of necessity, however, accustoms us to work. But in the intervals in which necessity is appeased and asleep, as it were, we are attacked by ennui. What is this? In a word it is the habituation to work, which now makes itself felt as a new and additional necessity; it will be all the stronger the more a person has been accustomed to work, perhaps, even, the more a person has suffered from necessities. In order to escape ennui, a man either works beyond the extent of his former necessities, or he invents play, that is to say, work that is only intended to appease the general necessity for work. He who has become satiated with play, and has no new necessities impelling him to work, is sometimes attacked by the longing for a third state, which is related to play as gliding is to dancing, as dancing is to walking, a blessed, tranquil movement; it is the artists' and philosophers' vision of happiness.

612.

Lessons from Pictures. – If we look at a series of pictures of ourselves, from the time of later childhood to the time of mature manhood, we discover with pleased surprise that the man bears more resemblance to the child than to the youth: that probably, therefore, in accordance with this fact, there has been in the interval a temporary alienation of the fundamental character, over which the collected, concentrated force of the man has again become master. With this observation this other is also in accordance, namely, that all strong influences of passions, teachers, and political events, which in our youthful years draw us hither and thither, seem later on to be referred back again to a fixed standard; of course they still continue to exist and operate within us, but our fundamental sentiments and opinions have now the upper hand, and use their influence perhaps as a source of strength, but are no longer merely regulative, as was perhaps the case in our twenties. Thus even the thoughts and sentiments of the man appear more in accordance with those of his childish years – and this objective fact expresses itself in the afore-mentioned subjective fact.

613.

The Tone of Voice of Different Ages. – The tone in which youths speak, praise, blame, and versify, displeases an older person because it is too loud, and yet at the same time dull and confused like a sound in a vault, which acquires such a loud ring owing to the emptiness; for most of the thought of youths does not gush forth out of the fulness of their own nature, but is the accord and the echo of what has been thought, said, praised or blamed around them. As their sentiments, however (their inclinations and aversions), resound much more forcibly than the reasons thereof, there is heard, whenever they divulge these sentiments, the dull, clanging tone which is a sign of the absence or scarcity of reasons. The tone of riper age is rigorous, abruptly concise, moderately loud, but, like everything distinctly articulated, is heard very far off. Old age, finally, often brings a certain mildness and consideration into the tone of the voice, and as it were, sweetens it; in many cases, to be sure it also sours it.

614.

The Atavist and the Forerunner. – The man of unpleasant character, full of distrust, envious of the success of fellow-competitors and neighbours, violent and enraged at divergent opinions, shows that he belongs to an earlier grade of culture, and is, therefore, an atavism; for the way in which he behaves to people was right and suitable only for an age of club-law; he is an *atavist.* The man of a different character, rich in sympathy, winning friends everywhere, finding all that is growing and becoming amiable, rejoicing at the honours and successes of others and claiming no privilege of solely knowing the truth, but full of a modest distrust – he is a forerunner who presses upward towards a higher human culture. The man of unpleasant character dates from the times when the rude basis of human intercourse had yet to be laid, the other lives on the upper floor of the edifice of culture, removed as far as possible from the howling and raging wild beast imprisoned in the cellars.

615.

Consolation for Hypochondriacs. – When a great thinker is temporarily subjected to hypochondriacal self-torture he can say to himself, by way of consolation: 'It is thine own great strength on which this parasite feeds and grows; if thy strength were smaller thou wouldst have less to suffer.' The statesman may say just the same thing when jealousy and vengeful feeling, or, in a word, the tone of the *bellum omnium contra omnes*, for which, as the representative of a nation, he must necessarily have a great capacity, occasionally intrudes into his personal relations and makes his life hard.

616.

Estranged from the Present. – There are great advantages in estranging one's self for once to a large extent from one's age, and being as it were driven back from its shores into the ocean of past views of things. Looking thence towards the coast one commands a view, perhaps for the first time, of its aggregate formation, and when one again approaches the land one has the advantage of understanding it better, on the whole, than those who have never left it.

617.

Sowing and Reaping on the field of Personal Defects. – Men like Rousseau understand how to use their weaknesses, defects, and vices as manure for their talent. When Rousseau bewails the corruption and degeneration of society as the evil results of culture, there is a personal experience at the bottom of it, the bitterness which gives sharpness to his general condemnation and poisons the arrows with which he shoots; he unburdens himself first as an individual, and thinks of getting a remedy which, while benefiting society directly, will also benefit himself indirectly by means of society.

618.

Philosophically Minded. – We usually endeavour to acquire *one* attitude of mind, *one* set of opinions for all situations and events of life – it is mostly called being philosophically minded. But for the acquisition of knowledge it may be of greater importance not to make ourselves thus uniform, but to hearken to the low voice of the different situations in life; these bring their own opinions with them. We thus take an intelligent interest in the life and nature of many persons by not treating ourselves as rigid, persistent single individuals.

619.

In the Fire of Contempt. – It is a fresh step towards independence when one first dares to give utterance to opinions which it is considered as disgraceful for a person to entertain; even friends and acquaintances are then accustomed to grow anxious. The gifted nature must also pass through this fire; it afterwards belongs far more to itself.

620.

Self-sacrifice. – In the event of choice, a great sacrifice is preferred to a small one, because we compensate ourselves for the great sacrifice by self-admiration, which is not possible in the case of a small one.

621.

Love as an Artifice. – Whoever really wishes to *become acquainted with* something new (whether it be a person, an event, or a book), does well to take up the matter with all possible love, and to avert his eye quickly from all that seems hostile, objectionable, and false therein – in fact to forget such things; so that, for instance, he gives the author of a book the best start possible, and straightway, just as in a race, longs with beating heart that he may reach the goal. In this manner one penetrates to the heart of the new thing, to its moving point, and this is called becoming acquainted with it. This stage having been arrived at, the understanding afterwards makes its restrictions; the over-estimation and the temporary suspension of the critical pendulum were only artifices to lure forth the soul of the matter.

622.

Thinking Too Well and Too Ill of the World. – Whether we think too well or too ill of things, we always have the advantage of deriving therefrom a greater pleasure, for with a too good preconception we usually put more sweetness into things (experiences) than they actually contain. A too bad preconception causes a pleasant disappointment, the pleasantness that lay in the things themselves is increased by the pleasantness of the surprise. A gloomy temperament, however, will have the reverse experience in both cases.

623.

Profound People. – Those whose strength lies in the deepening of impressions – they are usually called profound people – are relatively self-possessed and decided in all sudden emergencies, for in the first moment the impression is still shallow, it only then *becomes* deep. Long foreseen, long expected events or persons, however, excite such natures most, and make them almost incapable of eventually having presence of mind on the arrival thereof.

624.

Intercourse with the Higher Self. – Every one has his good day, when he finds his higher self; and true humanity demands that a person shall be estimated according to this state and not according to his work-days of constraint and bondage. A painter, for instance, should be appraised and honoured according to the most exalted vision he could see and represent. But men themselves commune very differently with this their higher self, and are frequently their own playactors, in so far as they repeatedly imitate what they are in those moments. Some stand in awe and humility before their ideal, and would fain deny it; they are afraid of their higher self because, when it speaks, it speaks pretentiously. Besides, it has a ghostlike freedom of coming and staying away just as it pleases; on that account it is often called a gift of the gods, while in fact everything else is a gift of the gods (of chance); this, however, is the man himself.

625.

Lonely People. – Some people are so much accustomed to being alone in self-communion that they do not at all compare themselves with others, but spin out their soliloquising life in a quiet, happy mood, conversing pleasantly, and even hilariously, with themselves. If, however, they are brought to the point of comparing themselves with others, they are inclined to a brooding under-estimation of their own worth, so that they have first to be compelled by others *to form* once more a good and just opinion of themselves, and even from this acquired opinion they will always want to subtract and abate something. We must not, therefore, grudge certain persons their loneliness or foolishly commiserate them on that account, as is so often done.

626.

Without Melody. – There are persons to whom a constant repose in themselves and the harmonious ordering of all their capacities is so natural that every definite activity is repugnant to them. They resemble music which consists of nothing but prolonged, harmonious accords, without even the tendency to an organised and animated melody showing itself. All external movement serves only to restore to the boat its equilibrium on the sea of harmonious euphony. Modern men usually become excessively impatient when they meet such natures, who *will never be anything* in the world, only it is not allowable to say of them that they *are nothing*. But in certain moods the sight of them raises the unusual question: 'Why should there be melody at all? Why should it not suffice us when life mirrors itself peacefully in a deep lake?' The Middle Ages were richer in such natures than our times. How seldom one now meets with any one who can live on so peacefully and happily with himself even in the midst of the crowd, saying to himself, like Goethe, 'The best thing of all is the deep calm in which I live and grow in opposition to the world, and gain what it cannot take away from me with fire and sword.'

627.

To Live and Experience. – If we observe how some people can deal with their experiences – their unimportant, everyday experiences – so that these become soil which yields fruit thrice a year; whilst others – and how many! – are driven through the surf of the most exciting adventures, the most diversified movements of times and peoples, and yet always remain light, always remain on the surface, like cork; we are finally tempted to divide mankind into a minority (minimality) of those who know how to make much out of little, and a majority of those who know how to make little out of much; indeed, we even meet with the counter-sorcerers who, instead of making the world out of nothing, make a nothing out of the world.

628.

Seriousness in Play. – In Genoa one evening, in the twilight, I heard from a tower a long chiming of bells; it was never like to end, and sounded as if insatiable above the noise of the streets, out into the evening sky and sea-air, so thrilling, and at the same time so childish and so sad. I then remembered the words of Plato, and suddenly felt the force of them in my heart: '*Human matters, one and all, are not worthy of great seriousness; nevertheless ...*'

629.

Conviction and Justice. – The requirement that a person must afterwards, when cool and sober, stand by what he says, promises, and resolves during passion, is one of the heaviest burdens that weigh upon mankind. To have to acknowledge for all future time the consequences of anger, of fiery revenge, of enthusiastic devotion, may lead to a bitterness against these feelings proportionate to the idolatry with which they are idolised, especially by artists. These cultivate to its full extent the *esteem of the passions*, and have always done so; to be sure, they also glorify the terrible satisfaction of the passions which a person affords himself, the outbreaks of vengeance, with death, mutilation, or voluntary banishment in their train, and the resignation of the broken heart. In any case they keep alive curiosity about the passions; it is as if they said: 'Without passions you have no experience whatever.' Because we have sworn fidelity (perhaps even to a purely fictitious being, such as a god), because we have surrendered our heart to a prince, a party, a woman, a priestly order, an artist, or a thinker, in a state of infatuated delusion that threw a charm over us and made those beings appear worthy of all veneration, and every sacrifice – are we, therefore, firmly and inevitably bound? Or did we not, after all, deceive ourselves then? Was there not a hypothetical promise, under the tacit presupposition that those beings to whom we consecrated ourselves were really the beings they seemed to be in our imagination? Are we under obligation to be faithful to our errors, even with the knowledge that by this fidelity we shall cause injury to our higher selves? No, there is no law, no obligation of that sort; we *must* become traitors, we must act unfaithfully and abandon our ideals again and again. We cannot advance from one period of life into another without causing these pains of treachery and also suffering from them. Might it be necessary to guard against the ebullitions of our feelings in order to escape these pains? Would not the world then become too arid, too ghost-like for us? Rather will we ask ourselves whether these pains are *necessary* on a change of convictions, or whether they do not depend on a *mistaken* opinion and estimate. Why do we admire a person who remains true to his convictions and despise him who changes them? I fear the answer must be, 'Because every one takes for granted that such a change is caused only by motives of more general utility or of personal trouble.' That is to say, we believe at bottom that nobody alters his opinions as long as they are advantageous to him, or at least as long as they do not cause him any harm. If it is so, however, it furnishes a bad proof of the *intellectual* significance of all convictions. Let us once examine how convictions arise, and let us see whether their importance is not greatly over-estimated; it will thereby be seen that the *change* of convictions also is in all circumstances judged according to a false standard, that we have hitherto been accustomed to suffer *too much* from this change.

630.

Conviction is belief in the possession of absolute truth on any matter of knowledge. This belief takes it for granted, therefore, that there are absolute truths; also, that perfect methods have been found for attaining to them; and finally, that every one who has convictions makes use of these perfect methods. All three notions show at once that the man of convictions is not the man of scientific thought; he seems to us still in the age of theoretical innocence, and is practically a child, however grown-up he may be. Whole centuries, however, have been lived under the influence of those childlike presuppositions, and out of them have flowed the mightiest sources of human strength. The countless numbers who sacrificed themselves for their convictions believed they were doing it for the sake of absolute truth. They were all wrong, however; probably no one has ever sacrificed himself for Truth; at least, the dogmatic expression of the faith of any such person has been unscientific or only partly scientific. But really, people wanted to carry their point because they believed that they *must be* in the right. To allow their belief to be wrested from them probably meant calling in question their eternal salvation. In an affair of such extreme importance the 'will' was too audibly the prompter of the intellect. The presupposition of every believer of every shade of belief has been that he *could not* be confuted; if the counter-arguments happened to be very strong, it always remained for him to decry intellect generally, and, perhaps, even to set up the '*credo quia absurdum est*' as the standard of extreme fanaticism. It is not the struggle of opinions that has made history so turbulent; but the struggle of belief in opinions – that is to say, of convictions. If all those who thought so highly of their convictions, who made sacrifices of all kinds for them, and spared neither honour, body, nor life in their service, had only devoted half of their energy to examining their right to adhere to this or that conviction and by what road they arrived at it, how peaceable would the history of mankind now appear! How much more knowledge would there be! All the cruel scenes in connection with the persecution of heretics of all kinds would have been avoided, for two reasons: firstly, because the inquisitors would above all have inquired of themselves, and would have recognised the presumption of defending absolute truth; and secondly, because the heretics themselves would, after examination, have taken no more interest in such badly established doctrines as those of all religious sectarians and 'orthodox' believers.

631.

From the ages in which it was customary to believe in the possession of absolute truth, people have inherited a profound *dislike* of all sceptical and relative attitudes with regard to questions of knowledge; they mostly prefer to acquiesce, for good or evil, in the convictions of those in authority (fathers, friends, teachers, princes), and they have a kind of remorse of conscience when they do not do so. This tendency is quite comprehensible, and its results furnish no ground for condemnation of the course of the development of human reason. The scientific spirit in man, however, has gradually to bring to maturity the virtue of *cautious forbearance*, the wise moderation, which is better known in practical than in theoretical life, and which, for instance, Goethe has represented in 'Antonio', as an object of provocation for all Tassos – that is to say, for unscientific and at the same time inactive natures. The man of convictions has in himself the right not to comprehend the man of cautious thought, the theoretical Antonio; the scientific man, on the other hand, has no right to blame the former on that account, he takes no notice thereof, and knows, moreover, that in certain cases the former will yet cling to him, as Tasso finally clung to Antonio.

632.

He who has not passed through different phases of conviction, but sticks to the faith in whose net he was first caught, is, under all circumstances, just on account of this unchangeableness, a representative of *atavistic* culture; in accordance with this lack of culture (which always presupposes plasticity for culture), he is severe, unintelligent, unteachable, without liberality, an ever suspicious person, an unscrupulous person who has recourse to all expedients for enforcing his opinions because he cannot conceive that there must be other opinions; he is, in such respects, perhaps a source of strength, and even wholesome in cultures that have become too emancipated and languid, but only because he strongly incites to opposition: for thereby the delicate organisation of the new culture, which is forced to struggle with him, becomes strong itself.

633.

In essential respects we are still the same men as those of the time of the Reformation; how could it be otherwise? But the fact that we *no longer* allow ourselves certain means for promoting the triumph of our opinions distinguishes us from that age, and proves that we belong to a higher culture. He who still combats and overthrows opinions with calumnies and outbursts of rage, after the manner of the Reformation men, obviously betrays the fact that he would have burnt his adversaries had he lived in other times, and that he would have resorted to all the methods of the Inquisition if he had been an opponent of the Reformation. The Inquisition was rational at that time; for it represented nothing else than the universal application of martial law, which had to be proclaimed throughout the entire domain of the Church, and which, like all martial law, gave a right to the extremest methods, under the presupposition, of course, (which we now no longer share with those people), that the Church *possessed* truth and had to preserve it at all costs, and at any sacrifice, for the salvation of mankind. Now, however, one does not so readily concede to any one that he possesses the truth; strict methods of investigation have diffused enough of distrust and precaution, so that every one who violently advocates opinions in word and deed is looked upon as an enemy of our modern culture, or, at least, as an atavist. As a matter of fact the pathos that man possesses truth is now of very little consequence in comparison with the certainly milder and less noisy pathos of the search for truth, which is never weary of learning afresh and examining anew.

634.

Moreover, the methodical search for truth is itself the outcome of those ages in which convictions were at war with each other. If the individual had not cared about *his* 'truth', that is to say, about carrying his point, there would have been no method of investigation; thus, however, by the eternal struggle of the claims of different individuals to absolute truth, people went on step by step to find irrefragable principles according to which the rights of the claims could be tested and the dispute settled. At first people decided according to authorities; later on they criticised one another's ways and means of finding the presumed truth; in the interval there was a period when people deduced the consequences of the adverse theory, and perhaps found them to be productive of injury and unhappiness; from which it was then to be inferred by every one that the conviction of the adversary involved an error. The *personal struggle* of the thinker at last so sharpened his methods that real truths could be discovered, and the mistakes of former methods exposed before the eyes of all.

635.

On the whole, scientific methods are at least as important results of investigation as any other results, for the scientific spirit is based upon a knowledge of method, and if the methods were lost, all the results of science could not prevent the renewed prevalence of superstition and absurdity. Clever people may *learn* as much as they like of the results of science, but one still notices in their conversation, and especially in the hypotheses they make, that they lack the scientific spirit; they have not the instinctive distrust of the devious courses of thinking which, in consequence of long training, has taken root in the soul of every scientific man. It is enough for them to find any kind of hypothesis on a subject, they are then all on fire for it, and imagine the matter is thereby settled. To have an opinion is with them equivalent to immediately becoming fanatical for it, and finally taking it to heart as a conviction. In the case of an unexplained matter they become heated for the first idea that comes into their head which has any resemblance to an explanation – a course from which the worst results constantly follow, especially in the field of politics. On that account everybody should nowadays have become thoroughly acquainted with at least *one* science, for then surely he knows what is meant by method, and how necessary is the extremest carefulness. To women in particular this advice is to be given at present; as to those who are irretrievably the victims of all hypotheses, especially when these have the appearance of being witty, attractive, enlivening, and invigorating. Indeed, on close inspection one sees that by far the greater number of educated people still desire convictions from a thinker and nothing but *convictions*, and that only a small minority want *certainty*. The former want to be forcibly carried away in order thereby to obtain an increase of strength; the latter few have the real interest which disregards personal advantages and the increase of strength also. The former class, who greatly predominate, are always reckoned upon when the thinker comports himself and labels himself as a *genius*, and thus views himself as a higher being to whom authority belongs. In so far as genius of this kind upholds the ardour of convictions, and arouses distrust of the cautious and modest spirit of science, it is an enemy of truth, however much it may think itself the wooer thereof.

636.

There is, certainly, also an entirely different species of genius, that of justice; and I cannot make up my mind to estimate it lower than any kind of philosophical, political, or artistic genius. Its peculiarity is to go, with heartfelt aversion, out of the way of everything that blinds and confuses people's judgement of things; it is consequently an *adversary of convictions*, for it wants to give their own to all, whether they be living or dead, real or imaginary – and for that purpose it must know thoroughly; it therefore places everything in the best light and goes around it with careful eyes. Finally, it will even give to its adversary the blind or short-sighted 'conviction' (as men call it – among women it is called 'faith'), what is due to conviction – for the sake of truth.

637.

Opinions evolve out of *passions*; *indolence of intellect* allows those to congeal into *convictions*. He, however, who is conscious of himself as a *free*, restless, lively spirit can prevent this congelation by constant change; and if he is altogether a thinking snowball, he will not have opinions in his head at all, but only certainties and properly estimated probabilities. But we, who are of a mixed nature, alternately inspired with ardour and chilled through and through by the intellect, want to kneel before justice, as the only goddess we acknowledge. The *fire* in us generally makes us unjust, and impure in the eyes of our goddess; in this condition we are not permitted to take her hand, and the serious smile of her approval never rests upon us. We reverence her as the veiled Isis of our life; with shame we offer her our pain as penance and sacrifice when the fire threatens to burn and consume us. It is the *intellect* that saves us from being utterly burnt and reduced to ashes; it occasionally drags us away from the sacrificial altar of justice or enwraps us in a garment of asbestos. Liberated from the fire, and impelled by the intellect, we then pass from opinion to opinion, through the change of parties, as noble *betrayers* of all things that can in any way be betrayed – and nevertheless without a feeling of guilt.

638.

The Wanderer. – He who has attained intellectual emancipation to any extent cannot, for a long time, regard himself otherwise than as a wanderer on the face of the earth – and not even as a traveller *towards* a final goal, for there is no such thing. But he certainly wants to observe and keep his eyes open to whatever actually happens in the world; therefore he cannot attach his heart too firmly to anything individual; he must have in himself something wandering that takes pleasure in change and transitoriness. To be sure such a man will have bad nights, when he is weary and finds the gates of the town that should offer him rest closed; perhaps he may also find that, as in the East, the desert reaches to the gates, that wild beasts howl far and near, that a strong wind arises, and that robbers take away his beasts of burden. Then the dreadful night closes over him like a second desert upon the desert, and his heart grows weary of wandering. Then when the morning sun rises upon him, glowing like a Deity of anger, when the town is opened, he sees perhaps in the faces of the dwellers therein still more desert, uncleanliness, deceit, and insecurity than outside the gates – and the day is almost worse than the night. Thus it may occasionally happen to the wanderer; but then there come as compensation the delightful mornings of other lands and days, when already in the grey of the dawn he sees the throng of muses dancing by, close to him, in the mist of the mountain; when afterwards, in the symmetry of his ante-meridian soul, he strolls silently under the trees, out of whose crests and leafy hiding-places all manner of good and bright things are flung to him, the gifts of all the free spirits who are at home in mountains, forests, and solitudes, and who, like himself, alternately merry and thoughtful, are wanderers and philosophers. Born of the secrets of the early dawn, they ponder the question how the day, between the hours of ten and twelve, can have such a pure, transparent, and gloriously cheerful countenance: they seek the *ante-meridian* philosophy.

AN EPODE.
AMONG FRIENDS.

(Translated by T. Common.)

I.

Nice, when mute we lie a-dreaming,
Nicer still when we are laughing,
'Neath the sky heaven's chariot speeding,
On the moss the book a-reading,
Sweetly loud with friends all laughing
Joyous, with white teeth a-gleaming.
Do I well, we're mute and humble;
Do I ill – we'll laugh exceeding;
Make it worse and worse, unheeding,
Worse proceeding, more laughs needing.
Till into the grave we stumble.
Friends! Yea! so shall it obtain?
Amen I Till we meet again.

II.

No excuses need be started!
Give, ye glad ones, open hearted,
To this foolish book before you
Ear and heart and lodging meet;
Trust me, 'twas not meant to bore you,
Though of folly I may treat!
What I find, seek, and am needing,
Was it e'er in book for reading?
Honour now fools in my name,
Learn from out this book by reading
How 'our sense' from reason came.
Thus, my friends, shall it obtain?
Amen! Till we meet again.